Eat Cake

5 SIMPLE INGREDIENTS
to a Meaningful & Joyous Life

ERIN FURNER

Copyright © 2018 by Erin Furner
Cover design by Teresa Bonaddio
Published by Divine Life Alchemy
Edited by Debbie Brunettin and Erin Furner

All rights reserved. No part of this book may be reproduced by any mechanical, photographic, or electronic process, or in the form of a phonographic recording; nor may it be stored in a retrieval system, transmitted, or otherwise be copied for public or private use, without written permission of the publisher.

The intent of the author is only to offer information of a general nature to help you in your quest for well-being. In the event you use any of the information in this book for yourself, which is your constitutional right, the author and the publisher assume no responsibility for your actions. The author or publisher shall in no event be held liable for any loss or other damages, including but not limited to special, incidental, consequential, or other damages.

ISBN: 978-0-9941649-1-9
First Edition: November 2018
10 9 8 7 6 5 4 3 2 1

Dedication

To my family—my world.

Miracles and magic are all around us. I know this because you're in my life. I love you beyond words.

••

To you—the reader.
Make the rest of your life, the best of your life.

If you expect to fail, you will. If you expect to succeed, you will. Because what you expect is what you will manifest…always.

Contents

Introduction..10
    Chapter 1 – The Power of You...16
    Chapter 2 – Your New Best Friend..26

Flexibility..29
    Chapter 3 – Become Bendy..30
    Activity #1: *Healing Your Connection to the Universe*...............38

Expectation..43
    Chapter 4 – It Will Happen..44
    Activity #2: *Releasing the Old Memories (Part 1)*....................62

Passion..69
    Chapter 5 – Love Conquers All...70
    Activity #3: *Discovering Your True Desires*............................76
    Chapter 6 – Plan For Success...91
    Activity #4: *Your Desires Are Your Goals*..............................93
    Activity #5: *Your Goals From Easiest and Fastest, to Hardest and Longest*..98
    Chapter 7 – Building Momentum..100
    Activity #6: *Creating Your Own Vision Board*.......................105
    Activity #7: *The Mental Rehearsal Technique*........................115
    Chapter 8 – A Little Step is All it Takes..................................118
    Activity #8: *Your Action Plan to Manifest Your Goal*.............120

Mindset......128

  Chapter 9 – Grab the Bull by the Horns......129

  Chapter 10 – Who Do You Think You Are?......140

    Activity #9: *Why it Has Not Happened Yet?*......143

    Activity #10: *Painting a Picture of the Real You*......146

  Chapter 11 – Imagination is Your Limitation......150

    Activity #11: *Discovering Whether You Truly Believe Your Desire Will Manifest*......154

    Activity #12: *Journey to the Fourth Dimension*......164

  Chapter 12 – The Mother's of All Old Memories......181

    Activity #13: *Revealing the Mother's of All Old Memories*......183

    Activity #14: *Isolate Old Memories*......187

  Chapter 13 – Changing a Core Memory......202

    Activity #15: *Making Peace with the Core Memory*......204

    Activity #16: *Healing Old Memories with Divine Energy (Part 2)*......215

  Chapter 14 – Working with the Light......227

    Activity #17: *Working with the Light (Part 3)*......232

  Chapter 15 – What if Your Desires Do Not Manifest?......236

  Chapter 16 – Thank You, Thank You, Thank You......245

    Activity #18: *The Gratitude Meditation*......248

    Activity #19: *How to Create a Gratitude Jar*......250

Intuitive Action......252

  Chapter 17 – Tune the Radio......253

Activity #20: *Intuition – Are You Intuitive?*...................................263

Chapter 18 – Come Back Into the Body............................270

Activity #21: *Discovering Your Primary Intuitive Sense*...............272

Chapter 19 – Expect Guidance...282

Activity #22: *Connecting to Your Intuition for Divine Answers*........287

Chapter 20 – Live an Intuitively Guided Life.......................291

Additional Manifestation Tools..298

Chapter 21 – Manifesting with the Energy of the Moon..........299

Activity #23: *Moon Ritual – Manifesting with the Moon*..............303

Chapter 22 – In Case of an Emergency.............................315

Activity #24: *Emergency Letter to the Universe*......................317

Chapter 23 – Declutter Your Life....................................322

Activity #25: *Declutter Your Life*.....................................325

Chapter 24 – You Are a Work in Progress........................333

Activity #26: *Overcoming the Funk*...................................335

Chapter 25 – Putting it all into Action...............................341

Activity #27: *Keeping a Manifestation Journal*........................342

Chapter 26 – Where to From Here?................................354

Acknowledgements..360

About the Author..361

Introduction

There is was in all its glory. The most beautiful, iced up, brightly coloured, chocolate button, liquorice laced, princess castle cake I had ever seen. At ten years old I considered this to be not just *any* cake but a stroke of genius. When it was time to blow out the candles and make a wish, I was stumped. What more could I wish for when what I already wanted was sitting right there on a plate in front of me?

That is the beauty of cake. You can design and create *anything* you want out of it; a rabbit with coconut frosting, a ladybird with chocolate freckles, a giant pool with jelly for water, or a steam train with popcorn for smoke. And even when it is fully decorated and ready to eat, it still promises magic by giving you the chance to make a wish before blowing the candles out.

So it begs the question, is getting what you want as simple as eating cake and blowing out candles? If you believe it is, then yes it is. If you believe it is not, then no it is not. Your belief defines what you attract into your life (good and bad) along with three other factors which will be revealed to you throughout the pages of this book.

What I have found very unsettling is that it seems as we get older the complexity and detail of a birthday cake can dwindle; suddenly we are faced with a stale 22 centimetre rounded vanilla cake with no butter frosted icing nor any candles to blow out. It is a recipe of nightmares. But of course it is not the end of the world; it is *just* cake after all. Or is it?

Engaged in a deep and meaningful conversation with my husband in the car, I expressed to him how much I wanted it both ways. I wanted the freedom to create a successful business that can

Introduction

empower, motivate, and inspire thousands of people in this world to live the best life they can. But I also wanted the time to be with my family, particularly my children, and be the kind of mother I was (and still am) inspired to be. I just could not see (or more to the point; believe) that it was possible to have both; there were just so many obstacles stacked before me. If I create a new business and dedicate my time helping others then I will miss out on time with family. But if I spend time with family then I will be unable to create in business. I felt that if I wanted one thing, then another thing would suffer, so it became one giant ball of hopelessness. I wanted it both ways. I wanted to be able to have everything I desired without sacrifice or feeling the pangs of selfishness. As we drove down Victoria Pass, the steepest road in New South Wales Australia, I revealed to my husband exactly what I wanted;

'I just want to have my cake and eat it too!'

And then a quiet inner voice spoke, 'Why can't you?'

Of course! Why can't I? Why can't we? Why settle or compromise for an average life? Why put ourselves through the rigmarole of *trying* to make our lives work the way we want it to when clearly it is working against us. For us as powerful spiritual beings, all it takes is a single seed of belief that magic happens for magic to *actually* happen. But *truly* believing in such a thing is easier said than done!

Determined to never have stale vanilla cake *ever* and most importantly never miss out on time with my family yet still have the freedom to create in business, I decided my primary mission in that moment was to decode what it *really* takes to get what you want (hint: positive thinking is not enough). This book is a result of my findings.

Eat Cake

A major lesson I have learned from committing to this journey is the realisation that we do not create a life we want on our own. No, there are larger forces at work. Call it the Universe, God, Creator, Source, All That Is (throughout this book, the loving and giving energy will be referred to as the 'Universe')—it is constantly tuning into our vibrations to reflect back to us what we are 'giving off'. So if you are 'giving off' for instance, a pungent odour of anger, jealousy, blame, guilt, or resentment, then you will continue to receive that until you *actively* change or raise your vibration (that is the Law of Attraction). And that is the key to the secret manifestation lock, to *actively* change. You cannot simply sit and wait for something to happen. That would just be lazy. You are gifted with free will. So if you truly want to improve your life, you must take inspired action to raise your vibration so it matches the very same thing you desire. This book will show you exactly how to do it.

Raising your vibration to match your desires is not a new concept. In fact it was Thomas Troward, a 19th century author who influenced the new thought movement that said

> *'(…) thought precedes physical form and the action of Mind plants that nucleus which, if allowed to grow undisturbed, will eventually attract to itself all the conditions necessary for its manifestation in outward visible form'*

From the dawn of Homo sapiens time, we have all been striving to get what we want because we know deep down that that is part of why we are here; to create a physical representation of our dreams. So in light of Thomas Troward's insights, we must ask the question, *how?* How do you use your mind to get what you want? How do you bypass all the negative and limiting thoughts so you are only

Introduction

emitting the good ones? And when you are all done and dusted from releasing the self limiting thoughts that were sabotaging your ability to manifest your desires in the first place, how do you know which path to take that will actually lead you to where you want to be?

My inner Virgo, the analytical and organised side to me, wanted answers to these big questions in a succinct and structured way; no fluff, no beating around the bush, just a simple 'how to' approach. While the other side of my spirit, the one that thrives and adores connection to her Spiritual Support Team, wanted a 'let's go with the flow and see where the Universe takes us' approach. Is it possible to incorporate both analytical and intuitive methods as a way to get what we want? Yes it is! In fact, it is absolutely necessary and soon you will find out why.

I believe we have a number of lifetimes under our belt that were full of suffering, pain and loneliness. All you have to do is brush up on your history to understand how difficult and painful the past was. However it is all necessary; we all need to experience such painful things to appreciate the opposite of that. But the trouble is we often find ourselves stuck in a vicious cycle of repeating the same painful experiences. Why? Because we do not know how to get ourselves out of it. After a while the suffering and pain become so familiar to us that we simply accept that this is the way life is. But let me just write this with absolute conviction and certainty; it does not have to remain this way. It is in this lifetime that we can shed all those limiting barriers from our past and open our heart and mind to our limitless potential. Sure suffering and pain is an experience but have you not had enough of that? Why not let that go and tap into the alternative; happiness, passion and abundance?

Eat Cake

'Umm no thanks! I prefer to suffer and experience disconnection and upheaval for the rest of my life' said no one ever.

So this is your chance right now to recognise that you are deserving of all the goodness in this world. And if you do not believe me now then you soon will by reading this book. In this moment you have a wonderful opportunity to break the cycle of endless negativity and it is not as hard as you may think, in fact, with the guidance in this book, it is actually very easy. Now more than ever this world needs you to create love, happiness and fulfilment in your life because what you do with your life affects us all. Like the butterfly effect, even the smallest of changes can result in dramatic outcomes.

So are you ready to create magic?

Over the next twenty-six chapters, this book will be your ultimate manifestation companion. As you turn each page and travel further down the self-discovery rabbit hole, you will experience revelations about manifesting that you may not have ever been aware of. This book will reveal to you more about yourself than you thought you knew. It will help you demolish the suffering, lies, and hurt you have been holding onto from your past so you can become liberated and free to express yourself in any way you choose. It will open the doors to endless possibilities because you will no longer fear what lies ahead. It will have you shedding all that is not in alignment with who you genuinely are so you *can* manifest what your heart wants with ease. Because that is the secret to successfully manifesting what you want;

Introduction

If you work on yourself first, then everything else will follow. It truly all comes down to you and your relationship with the Universe.

Understand however that if you are driven by wanting millions of dollars for the sake of flaunting your wealth, or you want a red convertible sports car because you like the idea of other people feeling jealous of your success, then this book is *not* for you. For the love of the Universe, please put it down now! But if you are looking to manifest your heart's desires and you want to do it in a way that speaks to your authentic love-filled spirit instead of your ego, *and* you are ready to immerse yourself in all twenty-seven activities found in this book because you know they will lead you to where you want to be, then this is the book for you.

Devour this book like you would if it were a chocolate mud cake. Embrace each page as if you were picking up every tasty crumb off the plate. Open yourself up to the endless possibilities that your spirit and the Universe want you to experience. Because life is not about what you can and cannot have; it is not about who deserves it more than another. Life is about eating cake. So by all means, have your cake and eat it too.

Chapter 1 – The Power of You

At the core of your heart where your spirit lives, you are perfection. No one and nothing can change that.

I am going to ask you to expand your mind for a moment because what I am about to share with you may come as a complete surprise or you may deny it altogether. Are you ready? Here goes;

You are perfect.

Once you move past all the negative experiences and trauma in your life, you as love and light is all that is left; complete perfection. You are an exact re-creation of the divine Universe. You are complete, whole, and pure love. That is your true state and when you come from this true state, you are perfect. No intentions. No problems. No fears. A blank slate ready for inspiration. So you chose to come to the Earth plane to experience an Earthly existence and receive inspiration from the Universe. Your presence here is therefore no accident. You have come here for a purpose and your spirit (and your head honcho Spirit Guide) knows what that specific purpose is for you.

But as a collective of spiritual beings, we have all come to the Earth plane to replicate our inner divine into everything we do as a human. We are yearning to go home; the place where we came from without our hardened shell of limiting beliefs and fear we have created over thousands upon thousands of years holding us hostage. Because every experience we create, whether it is good or bad, becomes a memory. These memories, just like data in a computer, run in our subconscious mind governing how we respond to ourselves and the world around us (more about the subconscious mind and how it impacts your ability to manifest in Chapter 5—*Love Conquers All*, page 70). What is important to realise is that *all* memories of each experience are never forgotten no matter if the memory was from this lifetime or from hundreds of lifetimes ago. It becomes stored in our DNA and replicates into the DNA of our children, and their children, and so on. Therefore our own DNA within our body contains all the memories created from our parents, their ancestors, and all the way back to the time when we were animals or plants, on another planet, in another galaxy, and back to the very time of creation (I told you to expand your mind!).

Our DNA is the gate keeper of billions of negative memories (also known as, 'limiting beliefs') that continue to cause us to, for example, be fearful, doubt ourselves, shy away from love, disrespect ourselves and others, or abuse our body. Anything that does not come from a state of love is a memory. So how does this translate into our everyday existence? Have you ever had a thought of gifting yourself with something that you and your spirit (which is your authentic self) would love but you find yourself quickly thinking of all the reasons why now is not a good time? Your reasoning may be that you believe you do not deserve to buy new things or that it is better to give than it is to receive.

For months I drove past a local flower shop on the side of the road that was selling the most beautiful home grown flower bouquets. Each time I thought to myself, 'I would love to buy myself some flowers. I'll stop there next time'. But each time I would come up with a reason why I should not stop; 'I don't have the time', 'There are more important things to buy than a bunch of flowers for myself', or 'It's so selfish to buy myself something when I should be spending the money on other people'. Despite the constant negative memories circulating in my mind, I finally decided to pull over and buy a bouquet of flowers. Beautiful white, pink and yellow flowers. Some flowers I was familiar with while others I have never seen before. It was such a wonderful moment; gifting myself these flowers and enjoying their beauty. I felt a new energy of love toward myself. Just that small experience allowed me to create a new and more joyous memory; a new memory being that it is perfectly okay to gift myself of something my spirit loves. In fact, I deserve it. When I honour the importance of myself (but not going to the extreme of becoming incredibly self-centered) I become more closely aligned with my true essence and closer to the divine that is within all of us.

Do you believe you deserve a life of your dreams?

Your subconscious mind *loves* drama. It cannot get enough of it. It will bring to the surface all the memories it can to remind you of how undeserving you are of your dreams. It will bring up memories of how you cannot get something unless you work extremely hard to get it or how you need to continue to punish yourself for all your wrong doings in all your past lives before you are worthy enough to receive anything that brings you joy. Sure we might not be able to rewire those negative memories / limiting beliefs right away (we can in time), but we can certainly consciously choose whether we listen and act upon those beliefs in any given moment. Had I chosen to continue listening to my subconscious mind that was giving me all the reasons to *not* pull over and purchase a bunch of flowers, then I would still be sitting here today wondering what it might feel like to do something kind for myself and show my spirit that I do in fact love and appreciate it. So it is not so much the act of *what* you do (buying myself flowers may not seem to be the biggest life changing event ever) but it is the *feeling* you get from taking inspired action. And you are being called in this moment to replicate *only* the feelings that contribute to love and joy because that is who you are. You are not your anger, frustration, anxiety or hopelessness. You are love. And you are appreciated more than you can imagine.

So let me ask you a very simple question. When was the last time you did something for *yourself* that made you feel loved and appreciated? If you are struggling to remember a time then perhaps now is the perfect time to start actively doing something to remind yourself of just how special and loved you really are. Because it is impossible to receive love from others if we do not love and appreciate ourselves.

How does this relate to manifesting your dreams, desires and wishes? *Everything*. If you do not believe you are deserving of love and joy, if you do not appreciate yourself and show gratitude toward everything that makes you able to live on this planet, if you cannot see how wanted and needed you are in this world, or if you refuse to forgive yourself for any wrong doings you have done now or in the past (we have ALL done some terrible things in the past) then manifesting your true desires will become next to impossible.

The power to change anything in your life all starts within you.

Take a look at the state of your finances, relationships, health, and career for instance. Are all those elements of your life bringing you fulfillment and joy right now? Are you completely and utterly in love with every aspect of your life? Since you are reading this book I will hazard a guess and say it is likely that you are not the happiest person you know and want to be.

Eat Cake

So where did your lack of finances come from? Where did your unfulfilling love life come from? Where did your lower back pain come from? Where did your struggles finding the right career come from? Simple. They came from the past; Earthbound memories that we are not even consciously aware of. We may guess why we have lower back pain or why we get headaches every second day, but beyond our hypothesis there are millions of unconscious memories attached to each of our experiences. This is our karma; what goes around comes around. Even if we have not been the cause of abuse or trauma in this lifetime, at some point in our past lives we were. I know this may be a hard pill to swallow; to even consider that you or I are still paying a debt we created a few hundred years ago, but instead of seeing this as punishment, I invite you to see it as an enlightening opportunity. Your soul wants to go home and the only way it can do that is to realign your life to the love that you are. Then you can start manifesting the very things that inspire, motivate and ignite the passion within you.

You have all the power within to turn your life around. You have already mastered the art of manifestation just by your existence here on Earth. Now you must learn how to reprogram your very way of thinking, feeling and believing so that you can cease to manifest the less empowering things that make you feel stressed, anxious and defeated, and start to manifest the very things that inspire, motivate, and excite you. It is time for you to interrupt the troublesome cycle you may find yourself in and create a new paradigm that will awaken your limitless potential. Manifestation is the very thing that can help you do this.

Think of manifestation as a beautifully baked and decorated cake; completely delicious in every single way. All the individual ingredients that make up the cake are the elements needed to create your desired reality—elements being your thoughts, feelings, values, beliefs, how you visualise the outcome to look, and the action taken to move you toward manifesting a desire. The way we are able to do any of this is by the use of our mind. Without our mind observing, the physical world does not exist. Professor Werner K. Heisenberg's Principle of Uncertainty states that by simply observing something (thinking about it), you affect the outcome—*'What we observe is not nature itself, but nature exposed to our mental of questioning'*. What we observe in the most basic form is energy. Take your body as an example. It is composed of eleven systems: endocrine, digestive, circulatory, muscular, nervous, skeletal, respiratory, reproductive, immune, lymphatic and urinary. Think about what these systems are made up of—tissues and organs. These tissues and organs are essentially made up of cells. And if we look a little closer we can see that the cells are in actual fact, molecules. Zooming in, we discover that the molecules are atoms which are made up of sub-atomic particles (protons, neutrons and electrons). And if we look ever closer we will discover that these particles are in fact energy. Your entire body and everything you see, feel, hear, taste, smell, think and believe is *energy*.

Everything is energy—you and everything around you. It is constantly moving and interacting with other forms of energy; hence it never stays still (this is why manifestation needs momentum). Take a bouncing ball as an example. If energy is always moving, why would a bouncing ball stop bouncing? The fact is that with each bounce of the ball, the energy is transferred to the surrounding environment, eventually detaching itself from the bouncing cycle. Say you were bouncing a ball on a table. With each bounce, some of the energy would be transferred to the table causing it to vibrate. This vibration moves the air, creating sound. The mechanical vibration of the table also transfers energy to the floor of the room through the table legs and heat is produced and escapes to the room as the table distorts slightly at the point of impact. Even the ball itself undergoes a shift in its energy whereby heat is produced within the ball itself as it stretches and distorts at the table surface. All these transformations allow the energy to escape the bouncing system, resulting in a loss of bounce, but a gain in other elements of the environment. Hence energy is never lost; it simply moves and interacts with other energetic systems.

This analogy is very similar to the way you interact with the Universe. Since you are composed of energy on the deepest level, you are constantly interacting with the flow of other energy systems—sending out frequencies of your thoughts, feelings, values and beliefs which allow energy of the same frequencies to interact with you. It is this interaction that becomes a physical representation of the very things you have been thinking, feeling, valuing, and believing. So you can see that just by your own actions, you can govern practically everything in your life.

But there are limitations to this power. Aside from Universal laws that determine the extent of our power such as the law of gravity (what goes up must come down), one of the most influential power-determining factors is our imagination. Albert Einstein once said, *'Imagination is everything. It is the preview of life's coming attractions.'* In other words, your imagination is the only limit to what you can achieve. Luckily for us, the physical world has all the resources we will ever need to create anything we can think of. We just need to put the right energetic signal out to the Universe to manifest what we truly desire.

So where do you start? The first thing to realise, in terms of ensuring you are sending out the right energetic signal, is that today is all that matters—the past is no longer your concern. You cannot change the past no matter how hurtful it may have been for you. The one thing you *can* do is reflect back on the experience and ask yourself, 'How have I grown as a result of it?' This alternative way of questioning may take some getting used to because essentially you are looking at the experience from the perspective of your Higher Self. You are recognising that sometimes in order to experience love, passion and fulfilment, you must first experience hatred, hurt and pain—how else would you know what it feels like to love if you had not known what it feels like to be unloved? But holding on to such painful past experiences can only serve to build up resentment and entrapment to a point where you become consumed by negativity. Such negative thoughts, beliefs and feelings will inhibit your ability to manifest love and empowerment. In fact, the only things you will manifest are more experiences that further bring resentment and entrapment—and thus the negative cycle continues.

So today is all that matters. Whatever you do today will affect the outcome of tomorrow, next week, next month, next year and so on. You may as well enjoy every moment of today and start reaching for bigger things—no more playing small. Why? Why *not?* It is time we all redirect our energy (thoughts, beliefs, values and feelings) to see how large we can *really* live our life. And when the time comes and we are ready to move on from the Earth plane, we can look back and say, 'I finally moved out of that terrible negative cycle and made every moment count—I am completely grateful and in love with how I lived that lifetime; I kicked butt!'

To kick some serious manifestation butt in this lifetime, you will need to focus on your ultimate desires, get clear on what you really want, and take some important steps that will have you sending out the right signals to the Universe. It is then that you can expect your desires to materialise.

One of the most important elements needed in anything you wish to manifest is momentum. As energy is constantly moving, your desires will need momentum to build more and more energy. Momentum is created by the speed and direction of our thoughts, feelings, values and beliefs. If, for example, you continue to feed a thought of lack, you worry about how terrible your financial situation is, and you are constantly focusing on how little you have in your bank account, then the signal you send out to the Universe is, 'Bring me more opportunities that result in lack.' The Universe does not distinguish between good and bad. It only listens to your thoughts, feelings, values and beliefs. Hence, the more momentum you place on something—that is, the more thoughts you think about, the more feelings you feel, the more you live by your values, and the more beliefs you believe—the stronger the signal sent to the Universe.

Momentum is the key.

That is one of the intentions of this book—to help you build the essential momentum in as little as thirty days. Why thirty days? It takes just thirty days to form a habit. Manifesting your desires is a lifelong process and a truly exciting one at that, so you may as well make it a habit rather than it be something you do every so often with very little positive results. With the help of the practical activities found in this book, including one activity dedicated to helping you create a 30-day manifestation journal (page 342), you will have built the momentum needed to consistently manifest your desires. Think of momentum like riding a bicycle—it takes a lot more effort to get the bicycle moving than it does to keep it going, but as you keep moving forward, much less effort is required. After a while, manifesting what you truly want will not feel difficult. In fact, it will feel like the most natural thing on Earth.

Who said you cannot have your cake and eat it too?

Chapter 2 – Your New Best Friend

The Universe is conspiring to give you everything you want. – Abraham Hicks

Think of something you would love right now. Maybe it is a holiday on a tropical island. Maybe you own a house on that tropical island. Or maybe you own the island itself. Maybe the island that you own has its own private airport where you can fly your own private jet and treat other people to an exclusive and luxurious holiday at no charge (see how we started small with a holiday then managed to grow bigger with the idea of owning our own island with our own private jet? Remember that your imagination is your only limitation). How easy would it be in this very moment for you to own an island with a private airport and jet? Like most people on this planet, you are likely saying, 'Yeah, and pigs might fly!'

It is hard to imagine anything is possible when we truly do not *believe* it is possible. The kind of signal we would send out to the Universe about this would be, 'Even though I really want this desire to turn into reality, I highly doubt it will happen. So please Universe, send me things that will reinforce the doubt I already have.' With that kind of negative energetic signal, the only things you will receive are more experiences that lead to more doubt and desperation.

It is also hard to manifest anything when we think that all it takes is positive thinking with no other action needed. Imagine sitting on the couch and thinking to yourself, 'Gosh I could really go for a snack right now.' But instead of getting off the couch and going to the refrigerator to see what is on offer, you stay on the couch waiting for a snack to appear. Oddly enough, the snack never materialises. Why? Because you need to act on the opportunities that are presented to you.

This is a major reason why many people who have tried to manifest their desires have given up. They surmised that it is not possible to get what they want. A crucial reason such people failed was they did not implement some key strategies. Introducing a new word to your vocabulary that will help you implement these key strategies to achieve manifestation magic;

FEPMIA

Even though this word could be something that describes a kind of contagious skin infection, thankfully it is not. Each letter actually stands for a key step in the manifestation process as well as the order for which you can build the momentum. Like a double whipped cream sponge cake with chocolate frosting, we will devour each component of FEPMIA and understand just how simple manifestation can be and just how powerful you really are to live the most genuine love-filled life imaginable. But for now let us focus on what each letter of FEPMIA means;

> F = Flexibility (letting go of the preconceived ideas about when and how your desires will manifest)
>
> E = Expectation (trusting that whatever you truly want is already on its way to you)
>
> P = Passion (getting clear of what you truly want since your true desires are born from your passion toward life)
>
> M = Mindset (generating self-empowered thoughts and feelings to release resistance to creating a life of your own design)

Eat Cake

> IA = Intuitive Action (connecting to your inner wisdom and universal energies so you become divinely guided in life which will make the manifestation journey easy and fun)

Now it is a matter of sitting in your most comfortable chair with a warm beverage to snuggle into as you move through this book with courage, purpose and excitement. Courage to realise what is holding you back, purpose to move from where you are right now, and excitement in knowing that by actively taking these steps, you are becoming a powerhouse of limitless possibilities.

So before you move forward with this, I just want to let you in on a little secret. You are going to discover that there is so much more to this journey than simply attracting a well deserved holiday or a luxury apartment in Sydney. Oh no! This is bigger than that because it is about restoring your spirit back to its origin of authenticity. It is from this place where you can truly create from the heart because you will finally be in line with what your heart actually wants. It is from this place where you will be free from past burdens and become open to the magic of creating a life that you are genuinely in love with. And it is from this place where you will take control of your life not from a place of fear but from a place of joy and universal trust. When you surrender yourself to all these things, that is when the life your heart wishes to create will come to you easily and naturally. It has to.

So savour each moment because in reality,

There is no such thing as a destination, only a journey.

Flexibility

Notice that the stiffest tree is most easily cracked, while the bamboo or willow survives by bending with the wind. – *Bruce Lee*

Chapter 3 – Become Bendy

'Trust me, I know what I'm doing' – the Universe

I was recently engaged in a conversation with my head honcho Spirit Guide, Benoit (pronounced, 'Ben-wa'). As a side note, Benoit has a wonderful dry sense of humour and is extremely patient with me even during the times when I am acting like an ego-consumed brat. He continues to give me enlightened insights that speak directly to my spirit instead of my ego. I truly believe my life would be very different without his support which is why I feel that connecting to your own intuition is such a necessary factor to manifesting successfully. You will discover how to tap into your own intuitive powers later in this book. In my quest to understand how to successfully manifest our heart's desires, I decided to ask him a question I had running through my mind many times before, 'Why don't we always get *exactly* what we want?' He replied by saying,

"Sometimes what you believe you want is not always in your best interest at the time. There is a greater plan for you that will lead to a greater outcome if you choose to follow it".

Manifesting therefore requires us to be quite flexible in the way in which our desire will manifest. It can be so tempting to think we know how our lives should be *all* the time. Our logical mind loves weighing up our options and deciding the best path to take yet there are other paths we are not always aware of. I realise it can be quite difficult to let go of control but this is a wonderful chance to practice flexibility and faith in the Universe and its divine plan.

Become Bendy

Realise the Universe has your back. It wants the best for you—period. It is fully aware of the lessons your soul is yearning for and it is more than happy to provide your soul with opportunities to help you learn and grow. The Universe sees the bigger picture yet we do not always have access to that picture. For most of us we can only see a few steps ahead but there may be hundreds of steps we must take before our true desires turn into reality. I believe it is a gift that I do not have access to the entire plan or else I am certain I would become overwhelmed and likely give up on my desires completely. It would be thrown into the 'too hard' basket. So thank goodness we do not always know all the details of how we are actually going to manifest our dream life!

But just imagine for a moment how stressful it would be if you governed every single detail that went into the bigger picture of your materialised desire. If you knew how much work you were going to need to put in to organise every step then you would quite possibly have a nervous breakdown. Take your body as an example. As you are reading this sentence, you are breathing subconsciously. The air is moving into your lungs and gas exchange is occurring through the semi-permeable membrane of the alveolar. Your heart is pumping blood around your body. Your blood is picking up oxygen, carbon dioxide and other gases throughout the body. Your kidneys are filtering your blood to remove toxins. Your digestive system is breaking down food you just ate. Your neurons are communicating information between your brain, spinal cord and other tissues to regulate involuntary and voluntary functions, whilst your glands are secreting hormones into the bloodstream and surrounding tissues. Your eyes are moving over each letter of this sentence and your brain is interpreting the words to mean something to you.

Eat Cake

Can you imagine if you consciously controlled every aspect of those processes? You would have no energy to get out of bed—in fact you would have no time to do anything else with your life! We are lucky that we can simply rely on our bodies to take care of those processes knowing they will do the best job they can.

The same goes for manifestation. If you doubt the process, then all you are doing is generating doubt and distrust, and that is the signal you are sending out to the Universe. So the idea is to zero in on your *true* desires, become clear about what you want and how it will make you feel—and then leave the actual process of the *how* up to the Universe. Trust that an opportunity will present itself when you allow it to.

For years I had longed to study Past Life Regression. It is such a fascinating topic that I was curious to learn as much as I could about it. Once I decided it was something I truly wanted and desired I began to start looking around for past life regression courses. Unfortunately I was not able to find the perfect one that would not break the budget, was offered by distance, and was certified by a professional practitioner body. So I let it go. Instead of attaching to the outcome and ultimately trying to force the Universe to give me what I wanted right there and then, I simply let it go. Funnily enough, had I found the perfect course at that particular time, I would not have been able to finish it anyway because it was not that long after that that I fell pregnant with our first child. Instead of worrying and stressing over completing a course, I could spend my time being the kind of Mother I had hoped to be. The Universe knew what was best for me, always has, and always will. Some years later, I was clicking through some websites and came across the very same Past Life Regression course I had wanted to enrol in, only this time enrolment was at a special discounted price, it was offered by distance education, and it was associated with a professional body of natural therapists that I was already a member of. Winner! So of course I enrolled. By the tenth month of study I realised I was not going to finish it in time. With family and work commitments, it would be a stretch—not an unachievable one but it would mean I would have to sacrifice time with family which did not sit well with me (one of my big values in life is family). I intuitively felt called to contact my teacher and ask for an extension. Upon my asking, I received a wonderful surprise; 'Well actually' replied my teacher, 'We have only just changed the policy so the course you are enrolled in can be completed in your own time. There will no longer be time restrictions'. And with that I did a happy dance. Thank you Universe!

The nature of the Universe is infinite. Our conscious minds are not. When we have a desire, we tend to assume when it is going to manifest. It is almost as though we say, 'Okay, I'm clear on what I want now, so why isn't it here yet?' Whether something appears instantly or takes years to come into your life depends on three main things;

1. Whether you are holding onto old fear-based memories that are sabotaging your ability to move forward (more about that further on in this book).

2. How attached you are to the outcome. For instance, you may have a particular car in mind you would love to own. You know what colour you would like, the kind of interior is has, and how it runs. You also want to enjoy the actual process of purchasing the car. As you can tell there are many elements to this—it is not just a car. Each element must be created which takes time. So no matter how badly you want your car right now and no matter how long it takes for all

the elements to come together, realise that it will be exactly the *right* amount of time needed to manifest your desire.

3. How able you are to let go of your expectation as to when and how your desire will manifest.

Letting go of your expectations as to when and how you desire will manifest can be quite difficult because it asks you to release your perceived control over your life and allow nature to take its course. Essentially you are asked to surrender.

Surrendering is not about inaction and wishing for something to happen but rather, it is about taking action on the things that you can act upon and letting go of the things you cannot control. This would be far easier if control was replaced with trust that the Universe has got your back. Albert Einstein once said, '*The most important decision we make is whether we believe we live in a friendly or hostile Universe.*' The type of relationship you have with the Universe is crucially important in the manifestation process because if there is doubt and distrust, then the Universe will pick up that signal and only bring you things that lead to more doubt and distrust. Remember the Universe loves you unconditionally. You are perfect—a complete replication of the Universe itself. So it is not the Universe that has created the distrust and disbelief. It is you.

In order for you to move forward with the manifestation of your desires, you must first have a full belief that you are supported by the Universe. You need to believe wholeheartedly that it is perfectly okay to let go of perceived control and allow the Universe to do what it does best—make your heart's desires a reality.

My husband and I were renting a beautiful house in a location we adored. We were so happy living in this house that we discussed the possibility of buying it should it ever go on the market. But there were a number of key factors we needed to keep in mind. We both wanted children yet the house was far too small for a family so we knew that if we bought the house we would need to do some pretty significant renovations. I envisaged the house with an added second storey, updated kitchen and bathroom, and a newly landscaped backyard. In my mind it looked pretty darn good! In addition to that, my husband needed space for all the tools and equipment associated with his own business and I wanted some extra space to start up my own natural therapies business so I could work from home. It was a big list of desires to say the least—a fairly large list for such a tiny home!

At last it seemed our dreams were starting to take shape. We received notification from the Real Estate agent that the owners of the house were going to put it on the market to sell. I was so excited. 'This is our chance!' I thought. 'Finally we're going to buy this house, renovate it, raise children, and run two successful businesses. It's going to be fantastic!' But our excitement was short lived after we were told of the value of the house. It was completely out of reach for us financially. My heart sank. I had not realised how much I wanted this dream to become my reality until it became clear it would continue to remain a dream. We both felt as though we had walked two steps forward and three steps back. But here is where the deliciousness of the Universe comes in; it knows *exactly* what you want and it has a magical ability to make it happen but only if you have trust it.

For over a month we searched online for other rental properties. Time was ticking by and we had to find a place to rent soon otherwise we would end up living at my parents house which would not be such a bad thing but certainly not ideal. The challenge was to

Eat Cake

find a property that would accept pets as we had two beautiful cats, Sox and Sooty (our fur family), and there was no way I was going to part with them. As each day ticked by, despite the occasional pangs of nervousness that surrounded the fact that we had not found a place to rent yet, I was still in the mindset that the Universe has got our back. Honestly if it were not for the trust I have in the Universe then I am sure the period of trying to find a house would have been so much more stressful and the outcome far less connected to our heart's desires of finding the perfect place.

On one particular Saturday, we were driving from a rental property we had just inspected feeling pretty disheartened with the state of the house and the price the owners were asking, when my Dad-in-law pulls up next to us in his car, 'Do you have a minute to come round our place?' He says with a, 'I know something you don't know' look on his face.

We drove to my in-laws house to hear their exciting news. They had wanted to move out to the country for years but properties out West were very hard to come by; until now. They had found the most beautiful farm in the perfect location for the perfect price. The problem was that in order for them to purchase the farm they would need to rent out their current home to save on mortgage costs. The same home where my husband had been storing his tools and equipment for his business. The same home that had enough room for a growing family. The same home that had additional space for me to work from home and fulfil my dream to be a natural therapist. 'Would you be interested in renting our house?' my Dad-in-law asks. Heck yes! So that is what we did. A year later we had our son, three years later we had our daughter, and two years after our second son. For seven years (and counting) we have been making beautiful memories in a house that not only means a lot to my husband but a lot to me too.

Never settle for what you do not want. Many of the houses we inspected could have been suitable for us to rent but we were just not 'feeling the love' as I like to say. I knew in my heart that the Universe would provide the perfect house and all we had to do was be patient and trust that our needs and wants would be fulfilled at the perfect moment. What I adore about this particular example is the sheer synchronistic events that happened for all of us. My husband and I got to move into a beautiful forever home which was our heart's desire, and my in-laws got to move to the countryside which was their own true heart's desire. I could not have planned it better myself! Trust and connection to the Universe is the key. So too is watching for the signs and acting upon the ones that feel right.

If you are a fairly laid back kind of person who goes with the flow most days with worrying about the future then it is likely you already have a strong connection to the Universe. If, on the other hand, you feel uncomfortable not knowing what is going to happen to you tomorrow or next week and you find yourself planning the day right down to deciding which socks you are going to wear that matches your outfit, then this may be a sign of resistance towards Universal support. If the idea of letting go of control scares you and makes you feel uncomfortable then I recommend you complete Activity #1: *Healing Your Connection to the Universe* before moving any further with this book. The aim of this activity is to reprogram your subconscious mind's relationship with the Universe and see it as a loving and supportive entity. This is your opportunity to turn fear into faith so you can live a divinely guided and abundant life without doubt biting at your ankles. What a wonderful way to live!

Activity #1: Healing Your Connection to the Universe

We are spirits living a human existence so most of us tend to imagine begins of light as having human-type features even though they generally do not have such features. If they appear to us on the Earth plane and they look human, it is generally for identification purposes only rather than their true form.

I had a drawing done of my head honcho Spirit Guide, Benoit, at the local Mind, Body, and Spirit festival some years ago. Even though I know deep down he is a pure ball of energy, the drawing with his long white beard and long hair tied up in a high bun has helped me connect to him from a human's perspective. Interestingly enough, prior to receiving a drawing of him, I connected to a very similar image to what was drawn when I did a *Meet Your Spirit Guide* meditation. I was only twelve years old at the time. Who would have thought that nineteen years later I would receive the same image?! It is moments like these that remind me of the magic of this world and the magic of the Universe!

So visualising your spirit guide with human features can help you connect to them on a deep level. The same goes for the Universe. When you create a visual representation of the Universe, you will feel much more connected to it. Activity #1: *Healing Your Connection to the Universe* will not only help you tune into your visual sense, but it will also help you tap into your other senses to create a real depiction of the Universe. How you feel about the Universe and how you relate to the Universe will make a big difference in how well you manifest considering we are not the sole creators of our lives, we are co-creators. We create alongside the Universe.

Become Bendy

You may wish to invite a friend to read through the activity for you as you complete it or you might like to read through the activity first and then carry out the exercise afterward.

1. Sit comfortably and somewhere you will not be distracted.

2. Take a deep breath in, feeling your stomach expand as you do so. Hold your breath for a moment and slowly breathe out. Repeat this process until you feel pleasantly relaxed before returning to normal breathing.

3. Close your eyes.

4. Now imagine a standard-sized photo placed in front of you. The photo is of a person whom you have never seen before. This person is the Universe. Closely look at the photo and notice how the Universe appears. When there is resistance in letting go of control, it can be due to having no trust in the Universe. It might be due to feeling as though you are alone and unsupported. So you may see the Universe as a person who does not appear friendly and loving; in fact you may see the Universe as angry and arrogant. Simply allow your own thoughts and feelings to manifest the appearance of the Universe as you focus on the photo before you. Try answering these questions as you continue to create the image:

    - Is the Universe male or female?

    - How are they clothed—do they look presentable or messy?

    - What is their facial expression?

Although this is a photo, you are able to pick up other things about the Universe such as sounds, feelings, and smells.

- When the Universe speaks, what do they sound like? What are they saying to you? Is the conversation empowering or is the Universe putting you down? What music is playing in the background? Is it relaxing music or 'nails against a blackboard' kind of music?

- How does the Universe make you feel? Do you feel supported and loved? Do you feel you can trust the Universe? What kind of energy can you feel from the Universe?

- What does the Universe smell like?

5. Continue to focus on the photo of the Universe and take in everything about it—how they look, how they sound, how they act and how they make you feel.

6. As you focus on the photo, you can see a larger photo behind it—this photo is much bigger than the photo at the front except you cannot quite make out the full image because it is being blocked by the smaller photo. You notice a tiny black dot appearing in the centre of the smaller photo at the front, and as you gaze at this black dot it begins to expand, allowing the image of the larger photo in the back to come through. It is like a shutter of a camera, revealing a larger and more beautiful photo.

7. Focus on the larger photo that seems to have engulfed the smaller photo. The larger photo is still the Universe in the

form of a person; however, they look different. The Universe looks vibrant. There is an aura around them that feels warm and loving. You can feel the warmth and loving energy radiate into your very being. The Universe is smiling at you, and when it speaks it sounds powerful and gentle at the same time. Notice the clothing the Universe is wearing and the posture of the Universe. Notice the music being played in the background. Notice the tone of the Universe's voice and the message the Universe is giving you. Notice how the Universe makes you feel—safe, relaxed, loved and supported. Notice any smells you may pick up—smells that remind you of how loved and safe you are.

8. Continue to focus on the photo of the beautiful Universe.

9. Now you notice the photo of the beautiful Universe shrinking—the shutter of the camera is closing and now the smaller photo of the Universe appears once more. You can still make out the larger picture of the beautiful Universe in the background however the full appearance of it is blocked by the smaller picture. You begin to pick up the same sensations you had earlier when viewing the smaller picture—the photo of the Universe that you do not trust. Take notice of how it makes you feel, what you are hearing, what you are seeing, and what you can smell.

10. The shutter opens again gradually and you see the beautiful Universe once more. Take notice of the same sensations you had when you first saw the beautiful Universe's photo.

11. The shutter begins to close again, only this time a little faster. Now you can see the smaller photo once more. Take notice of what you can see, feel, hear, and smell.

12. The shutter opens again faster, and you see the beautiful Universe again. Take notice of what you can see, feel, hear and smell. The shutter does this action 5-10 more times, getting faster and faster as it opens and closes. Opening, closing, opening, closing, opening, closing, opening, closing, opening, closing, opening, closing, opening, closing, opening, closing, opening, closing, opening, closing.

13. Finally, the shutter opens once more with the beautiful photo of the Universe beaming towards you. Sit with this photo of the Universe for a moment and soak all the senses in. All the powerfully loving, protective and supportive energy completely engulfs your entire being.

14. Now open your eyes. Take a few deep breaths in and out before carrying out your normal daily tasks.

This exercise has helped to reprogram your subconscious mind into creating a new and more beautiful perception of the Universe—one that supports and loves you. Such a connection to a loving and supportive energy will help you to let go of control and resistance over the manifestation process.

Expectation

Your job is to show me your new vibration. My job is to show you miracles. – *The Universe*

Chapter 4 – It Will Happen

She realises that want she wants will not manifest until she consciously aligns with it.

There is very little point deciding on what you truly want if you do not believe it will happen, or more to the point, that you do not *expect* it to happen. In fact, your expectation plays a huge role in your ability to design your dream life because if you do not expect it will manifest, then you will unlikely tap into your true desires (more about your true desires in Chapter 5—*Love Conquers All*, page 70). To put it simply,

What you expect is what you manifest

Your expectation is the best way to reveal the future outcome of your life. Think about it; if you expect bad things to happen, bad things *will* happen. If you expect the traffic will be terrible so you are late dropping the kids off at school, or the work meeting will go for too long causing you to lose precious time completing other things, then it is likely it will happen. You are so powerful that you can become your own self fulfilled prophecy. And the minute you expect something bad to happen, then there will be a flow on effect to the rest of your day. I am completely guilty of this.

Prior to reconnecting with my spirit and working with the divine energies, I would expect to have bad days, particularly at my corporate job. There was a time I remember quite vividly where I got out of bed in the morning (I was already feeling fairly negative about going to work) and stubbed my toe on the end of the bed. Ouch! 'This', I thought, 'Is definitely an omen. My day is going to be so damn painful!' And sure enough, it was. I got dressed, brushed my teeth and spilt tooth paste down my front which forced me to change my outfit. I was already running late so this was extremely inconvenient. Then I found the traffic especially bad that day—lots of terrible drivers who decided to tailgate my car which irritates me to no end. I finally got to work feeling fairly on edge and cranky. For the rest of the day I felt I was putting out small fires for other people yet my own work was getting nowhere. Because of that, I had to stay back late to catch up. Then, in the darkness of the night, I discovered the headlight switch that turns my car lights on would only work if I jiggled the switch. This was extremely bizarre as it was working perfectly a few nights ago. So I drove home (in hindsight I probably should not have) with my hand on the headlight switch jiggling it around and trying not to blind the drivers coming the opposite direction with my high beam lights that turned on sporadically—this truly was a recipe for disaster and certainly not something I would do again. But of course it will not happen again because I expect it will not. It was such a fabulous lesson though. It was in that moment that I knew I was not where I was meant to be.

If you are miserable with your life then it is time to change

If you want to turn your life around and consciously create a life of your dreams, then you must expect that good things will happen. However the confusing part of life is that sometimes bad things still happen despite our positive expectations. This is an entirely different topic that relates to our higher divine purpose (even bad things can teach us something wonderful about ourselves and this world) so I will not go into detail about it otherwise I will be digressing from the manifestation topic. But for the purpose of this book realise that it is *always* better to expect goodness in your life.

Eat Cake

After all, that is what you deserve, and it is what you will attract for the most part.

So how do you shift expecting lack and misery to expecting prosperity and happiness? The secret is to *act* as if you expect your true desires to manifest, which is to say, start to make changes in your life that signify that what you want has already come into your life.

The Universe can only bring you what you desire when you are truly ready for it (which means your vibration is a match to your desire), so start making the necessary changes in your life now to make room for what you want. For instance, if you want a new car, then start cleaning the garage out so there is room for your new car. If you want a new house, start exploring locations and houses or attend an open house. Consider what furniture you will have and the paint colours you would like on the walls. If you want to enter a new relationship, start planning what you will wear on your first date—perhaps go window shopping for inspiration. The idea of this is to place your mindset into a state of positive expectation. By actively doing something that relates to your desire, you are telling the Universe, 'I'm ready for this! Send it my way!'

I recommend that as you go about your day simply track your expectation attitude. Consider,

- What do I expect to happen today? Is my expectation for the day a positive one, and if not, how can I turn that around?
- Am I expecting the worst to come?
- Am I expecting things will get better?

It Will Happen

Your expectation of what may be is your choice. So if you do not genuinely expect miracles to enter your life then you will live out your life preventing any kind of miracle from enlightening your path. I realise however that in some cases simply choosing to expect to get what you want may be easier said than done particularly if you are deeply immersed in difficult life-situations. This is where you must believe in miracles because sometimes that is what it takes for your life to improve. You must have faith that your life can and will get better. But no one can do this for you. Since you are gifted with free will, it is up to you to consciously believe that miracles do in fact happen, *and* that they do in fact happen to you. But what if in this very moment you do not believe in miracles? What if your past is so badly tainted with suffering and struggle that the idea of a miracle happening *for* you would be just as likely as seeing a real purple coloured unicorn with a glittery mane and a rainbow tail? The fact is, even if you do not believe in miracles right now and therefore you cannot expect that what you want in life will actually manifest, then that is completely okay. You can easily turn this belief around by following some simple and practical steps further on in this chapter.

I believe however that knowledge is power and often it can be useful to understand the 'why' behind why we create such limiting beliefs that only serve to hinder our limitless potential. Ultimately it comes down to mindset which is a big topic—so big that a large portion of this book focuses on mindset. It has to because the condition of our thoughts is a large player in determining what we receive in life. I have learned from past experience that it is impossible to laser in on what we actually want from life if we do not believe in miracles nor expect to receive the reality of our wishes. If you wished upon your birthday candle that you wanted to be a multi millionaire yet your inner voice replies with, 'Yeah right!'

then it becomes a wasted wish because it simply will not happen. Your mindset must be in the right frequency to attract what you want.

The Universe does not listen to your words; it listens to your frequency. Your frequency must match the same frequency of your desire to manifest it into reality.

What I am about to share with you may require you to expand your perception of the world and your own immortality. This new way of thinking can help you shift your belief from believing that there is no such thing as miracles to expecting that miracles happen as you journey on this manifestation path. This information may take a while to sink in, so like a herbal tea diffusing its goodness throughout a mug of warm water, it may be best to simply allow the information to percolate until it feels right.

I was once a very much left-sided brain (logic and reasoning) medical scientist. Majority of the decisions I made in life was based on logic. I wanted facts, statistics, and proof. If there were no experiments that had either been done or could be done, then I would basically shut out any ideological assumptions altogether (had I known the future me would write a book about manifesting based on intuition and universal connection then I would fallen on the floor in hysterics from disbelief!). So of course I had difficulty believing in miracles even though just the fact that we have a life on Earth is a miracle! Yet over the past decade, I have been gently (and sometimes not so gently) guided to embrace the right-side of my brain (intuition and creativity) which has led me to become increasingly aware of the miracles and mysteries of life. I have found the more I embrace my intuition, the more open I become to receiving what I want even if it looks a little different to how I envisaged. Expecting what I want to come to fruition has become easier because I have realigned my mindset and become intuitively guided to reach my goals. Instead of relying solely on facts and figures, I rely on Universal signs such as seeing numbers repeatedly, finding feathers in unusual places, and experiencing unexplainable synchronistic events that remind me of just how much the Universe has got my back.

Now before I move any further with this, I feel it is important to point out that anything in this book regarding the Universe, believing in miracles, and living an intuitively guided life is not related to any kind of religion. It is my belief that we have come from somewhere (I call it, 'the Universe'). I do not believe we just appeared from thin air and into a cell. Our spirit has been around the block a number of times—not only on Earth but on other planets in other galaxies. How do I know this? Where is the proof? Unfortunately I do not have concrete evidence and if anyone does then I would love to meet them! This is simply a knowing—a belief I feel very strongly about coupled with the guidance I receive from the Universe and my Spiritual Support Team. Since connecting to such powerful forces, my life has improved in dramatic ways. I went from depression, suicidal thoughts and self-manipulation to embracing my authenticity and loving who I am simply by surrendering to control and connecting to a higher source of energy. That in itself was a miracle and one that I am forever grateful for!

So it begs the question; if we as spirits are constantly on the move, currently living a human existence, then what happens to all those experiences we have? Is there a purpose to any of them or do they just get lost in the ether? I believe there is always a reason for everything no matter how momentous or insignificant the reason may be. With each experience we have we generate a memory that becomes stored in our subconscious mind. Yet what happens to those memories when we move onto another lifetime? Are they simply erased from our spirit or do they follow us through subsequent lifetimes? And if they do follow us, then what do we do about the bad memories—the ones that dim our light and stop us creating a life of our dreams?

Now this is the part where I invite you to expand your mind and open yourself up to enriching possibilities. As you read through this part of the book, I recommend you breathe through any uncertainty this may conjure up and keep an open mind and an open heart because it is your heart that will tell you whether what I am about to say is truth for your spirit as it is truth for me.

Your absolute mission on this planet in this very moment is to replicate universal truth in everything you do. This means to live from the inside out: love yourself and others unconditionally, forgive instead of holding on, show gratitude for everything in your life, surrender to your intuition, embrace your gifts and skills, and manifest your heart's desires (which you are well on your way by reading this book). All these practices merge together to create one giant soul-evolved purpose; to lead your spirit back home; back to zero—the place where your spirit originally came from. And from there, experience and feel non-duality (because we are not separate from one another). You may already be aware of this; an unexplainable need to go home even if you are unsure where 'home' is. Yet home is not so as much a destination as it is a feeling of being purely and authentically 'you'. That is your origin. But most of us have drifted so far off course from our origin that it may *seem* an impossible feat to get back home though in reality it is not. You just need to know what the number one thing is that holds you back from evolving as a spirit and manifesting your heart's desires. This number one thing is negative based memories.

It Will Happen

Realise that no memory is lost.
All is remembered; good and bad.

In this very moment we may be living our lives quite innocently. We say hello to our neighbours, we brake for pedestrians crossing the road, and we apologies if we are late for an appointment. Majority of us are pretty innocent for the most part. Yet in our past lives we are *all* responsible for some really terrible things. And even though when we pass over and we reflect on the things we had done that we are not proud of, we are still not free of the old memories that have been created from doing those terrible things. We are not free of the assumptions we made about ourselves and our circumstances during those particular lifetimes even though some of those assumptions were not the truth. These limiting old memories, also known as limiting beliefs, do just that; they limit us from stepping into our *limitless* power and potential. Ultimately they limit us from manifesting what our heart's desires; what our spirit desires.

While exploring past life regression, I discovered that I had done some terrible things that left me feeling incredibly appalled and ashamed of myself. I was looking at it from my present situation and thinking, 'Surely I wouldn't have treated anyone like that. Surely I wouldn't have abused other people in that way'. But being ashamed and appalled is actually a memory—remember that you and I are perfect. There is nothing to be appalled or ashamed of *if* we live from our universal truth however it is practically impossible to live from this truth if we are still holding onto negative memories.

So all the negative based memories we have collected during each lifetime only serve to keep us off track—to pull us further away from our source. And since we have come from one source, we are therefore not separate. This means we all share the *exact* same memories. All the memories you share, I share. All the memories your parents have are also in you. You also have the memories from your Grandparents, and their parents, and their parents, and back thousands of years, all the way back to when life began.

So how do these memories show up in our lives? Generally these memories surface as fear based thoughts. They can appear as procrastination, doubt, self abuse, jealousy, and revenge to name a few. The easiest way to identify if an old memory is creating havoc in your life is if, for example, you find yourself diming your light, which is to say, putting yourself down or putting others down. If you judge yourself or others, take pleasure in being the victim and complaining about how bad your life is, or find yourself settling for a below average life because you do not believe you deserve anything better. If you catch yourself doing one of these things and more (and we all do it) then you know you are not in exact alignment to your authentic nature and you are further away from home than you would want to be. This will certainly make manifestation of your heart's desires fairly difficult!

The scariest part of all of this (if that were not scary enough) is below these particular old memories are millions upon millions of additional negative memories that run in our subconscious mind. Since they are in our subconscious mind we do not have the power to consciously remember them. I am actually quite happy to be blissfully unaware of the millions of negative-based memories in my subconscious because if I were I am sure my brain would melt! Similar to a thick buttercream frosted cake sitting in the hot Sahara desert sun—it would not be pretty!

How do these old memories relate to manifesting and your ability to expect that what you want is already on its way to you? It has *everything* to do with it.

It Will Happen

*Do not use your past as an indication of
what may be in the future.*

It is likely you are currently holding onto a memory from a past life or a memory from your ancestors that says that miracles do not happen *to you*—everyone else deserves something great to happen in their lives but you are not one of them. You may be holding onto a memory that says miracles are a figment of your imagination—when something seems so impossible, it likely is. For example, if you desire forming a relationship with someone who you are deeply in love with (and they feel the same way toward you) yet you just cannot see it happening, you cannot believe it will happen, or you cannot expect it will happen, then it won't. You may also be holding onto the old memory that you must know *all* the steps for your desires to manifest into reality; that it is not safe to just let the Universe do its thing and shower you with abundance (repeat Activity #1—*Healing Your Connection to the Universe*, page 38, if this is still the case). Another quite common memory is that there is not enough of what you want in the Universe—there is a maximum order and you will likely get your order in too late.

And these memories are just the surface. Imagine the thousands of memories relating to manifestation currently circulating through your subconscious mind! At some point you chose to create these memories. Now you can chose to let them go. And when you let them go you will open yourself up to *expecting* the manifestation of your heart's desires without question.

The method of releasing old memories from the subconscious mind and one that I love due to its simplicity and effectiveness is the Ho'oponopono Prayer. The Ho'oponopono prayer is based on an ancient Hawaiian practice which focuses on forgiveness and reconciliation; however the particular Ho'oponopono practice I will share with you in this book has been modified slightly to be in keeping with the realities of the modern day.

*One loving and positive thought
at a time creates miracles*

The Universe is constantly sending us loving energy and intuitive guidance however it is difficult to receive these higher vibrational energies if our subconscious mind is closed off from the loving energies. This is why the Ho'oponopono prayer is so effective because the prayer is directed to the subconscious mind which is the bridge between our conscious mind and the Universe. Once the subconscious mind is cleaned of negative memories relating to various beliefs from our own past and the past of our ancestors, then the Universe can freely send us intuitive messages to help remind us that life is magical, we are all powerful, and dreams really do come true. When we align with this inner knowing, we become true to ourselves and in integrity with our authentic nature. And when we come from this place of authenticity, we can then understand what we *truly* want; that is, what our heart wants instead of our ego trying to convince us that we need certain things that are not necessary for our evolution. Ultimately we come home which is exactly where our spirit wants to be.

The Ho'oponopono prayer is composed of four statements;

*I love you
I am sorry
Please forgive me
Thank you*

It Will Happen

That is it. Four very simple, powerful and easy to remember statements!

So if you are having trouble believing miracles easily happen to you, or you believe this method is far too simple to be effective, or you feel undeserving of receiving something you *want* in addition to what you *need* (more about this in Chapter 5—*Love Conquers All*, page 70) then I invite you to embrace the Ho'oponopono prayer and add it to your spiritual tool belt; use it every time you uncover more past memories that need to be cleansed from your mind, body and spirit.

> Gentle Note: As you continue to read further in this book you will dive deeper into your subconscious mind and uncover other past memories holding you hostage from creating your dream life. So for now see this chapter as a taste of what is yet to come.

And I guarantee you *will* find more negative memories because there are *millions* to be cleaned! It can be likened to an onion effect—layers upon layers of memories. But even though the idea of opening Pandora's box of memories can be quite overwhelming, I assure you it is; 1) absolutely necessary if you truly want to live an above average life, and 2) a wonderful clearing and cleansing method of old memories because there is no need to analyse every single bit of memory and wonder where it all came from.

When I was guided to take this spiritual pilgrimage it initially brought up *a lot* of limiting beliefs / old memories. I felt that once I focused and cleaned one, another would quickly follow. They appeared as unnerving feelings relating to the belief that I was not good enough, smart enough or ready enough to start my own therapeutic business at that time. They showed up as doubt that made me question if I was on the right path or not. They even showed up in conversations I had with like-minded people already in business who proclaimed they had a wonderful business idea and were going to take action right away, yet ironically I too had a very similar (almost exact) idea yet I did not have the guts to follow through with it. A big issue I have had in the past was the state of my finances. I focused on my relationship with the energy of money and realised that a big reason why I was not attracting money was that my relationship with it was terrible; I believed money was the root of all evil. Once I cleared that belief, a new one arose which stated that I do not deserve to receive above average wages. I cleared that and a new belief of 'No one will want to invest in my products or services' reared its ugly head. Urgh! When will these old memories stop surfacing?

It seemed that releasing myself of the old memories was becoming an impossible task. I often found myself wondering if I had made a mistake to even consider shedding the negative layers. How long was it going to take to clean myself of the spiritual baggage I had been holding onto? After a while, though my intentions to clean were good, I started to feel burdened by the negative memories because I was trying to analyse each one; trying to figure out where each one had come from. This was such a terrible way to approach things because it eventually led me to believe I was ill-equipped to be the kind of spiritual person I wanted to be. I was of the belief that the spiritual path was one that would help me become free of my ego but all it felt like it was doing was reminding me of just how much my ego had a hold on me. My kindred spirit, Connie, warned me that once I open the doors of spiritual growth, there is no turning back. And she was right!

Naturally the methods I was using to release myself of the memories were not for me. I was done trying to analyse the who, what, where, and why behind the memories. It was clear that that was *not* the ideal method for me! The Ho'oponopono prayer on the other hand is entirely different and has literally become my saviour for removing the old memories that do not empower my mind, body or spirit. There is nothing for me to analyse or sort out. Instead the Ho'oponopono method only asks that I become aware of what person, thing or situation is triggering me and how I am interpreting and reacting to it. If I am reacting to it in a way that dims my light (doubt, fear-based thoughts, judgement, jealousy etc) then I know there is some cleaning to be done. And all that is needed is to recite the Ho'oponopono prayer: I love you. I am sorry. Please forgive me. Thank you. When we practice this method, the deep memories hiding in our subconscious mind will surface and so too will the *feelings* of the memories. Then from our heart and soul, we let the old memories go and allow the energy of the divine Universe to take care of negative memories—neutralising them and replacing them with universal and loving truth. Simple!

The entire point of this lifelong exercise is to feel love, compassion and empathy in any given situation. It is to feel connected and not separate from the Universe. It is to harness all our creativity and move from the divided mind to the whole mind. It is to experience non-duality and therefore reconnect ourselves to the pure consciousness that we really are. As you continue on this path of spiritual self discovery and continue to clean the old memories, you will get in touch with the infinite consciousness of the Universe; no more jumping through hoops to get there. It is by travelling on this path that you will find out and experience on a conscious human level your true identity. I cannot think of anything greater than connecting to that experience and tapping into the feelings of joy and equanimity. Each time I make a conscious effort to clean an old memory, I feel within my heart and soul that I am reshaping my identity from ego based lies to divine connected truth. If there were a cake to represent the awesomeness of this, then it would have to be the Norwegian 'World's Best Cake' (yes, that is it's official name) which is a meringue sponge cake with clouds of custard layers. Then when you have bitten into this tasty morsel and allowed time for your taste buds to celebrate, multiply the deliciousness of it by at least googolplexian (the largest number in the world; so far) and that may just touch the surface of the feeling generated when you are connected to your spirit wholeheartedly.

This is such important work because in this very moment as I write this book, there is extreme artificial separateness around the world (politically, ideologically, religiously, and racially divided to name a few), and if we continue this way we are certain to face mass extinction. I do not know about you but I want to carry on living in this playground called 'Earth' and experience the infinite possibilities of creativity. So to say this work is important is an understatement; I like to see this as a duty of care for ourselves as divine beings from the same infinite source. If the Universe is a projection of consciousness, and if all consciousness is one, then consciousness cannot be divided. Therefore we cannot be divided. So naturally, if you remove these old memories, you are not only doing it for yourself on a human level, but you are doing it for all of us as one divine consciousness of energy.

A word of warning; once you start doing this work, you will find more old memories will come to the surface. My recommendation when this happens is to practice self care, do not judge what is happening, and above all persevere with the Ho'oponopono prayer. It may feel that nothing is happening or it may feel that your situation gets worse before it gets better, but this is how the memories dissipate. If you remove one memory, more will follow, ready to be cleaned with universal love. And since there are millions of old memories to be cleaned, it is likely you and I will be cleaning for the rest of our human lives. In fact I believe this is one of the bigger reasons why we have come to Earth; to clean the old memories and realign ourselves to our authentic nature. Each old memory therefore is an opportunity for us to eventually come home.

So before you can go ahead and use the Ho'oponopono prayer for manifestation purposes, it is firstly important you understand what the four statements of the prayer actually mean. Then you can fully appreciate the words as you say them either aloud or in your mind.

When you say, 'I love you', you are actually connecting to the Universe; the entire cosmos. This statement alone makes you incredibly powerful because love is your purest form without the memories getting in the way and corrupting your spirit's identity. Once you connect with the energy of love then the rest of the prayer is easy.

When you say, 'I'm sorry' you are saying sorry to yourself for being unconsciously aware of the negative memories playing havoc in your life (remember we are not separate; we all come from the same source so when you say, 'Sorry' to yourself, you are really saying, 'Sorry' to all *including* the Universe). You are apologising for holding onto those memories even though most of the time you are unsure what those memories actually are.

When you say, 'Please forgive me' you are asking your subconscious mind and therefore the Universe to forgive you for acquiring such unhealthy memories for which you do not know where they came from.

Eat Cake

When you say, 'Thank you', you are thanking your subconscious mind and the Universe for removing the memory and replacing it with something far more powerful and in alignment with your spiritual truth. You are basically saying, 'Thank you for taking care of me, supporting me, and making me whole again'.

The order of the statements do not matter just as long as they are all expressed. Even the way in which you practice the Ho'oponopono prayer is up to you. You may wish to light a candle, sit quietly where you will not be disturbed, and breathe deeply as you repeat the prayer a loud or in your mind at least ten times. Or you may wish to go for a walk outside barefoot and repeat the four prayer statements with each step for as long as you feel is necessary. We all have different ways we do things; ultimately it comes down to what you resonate with the most.

The following activity demonstrates the Ho'oponopono method I use. This has been specifically created to help you start believing in and expecting miracles. You simply cannot start manifesting your heart's desires without healthy expectation hence why this activity is so powerful and must be done before reading further into this book. Although Activity #2: *Releasing the Old Memories* is focused on the old memories revolving around the topics of expectation and miracles, you will be asked to refer back to it to clear other old memories that you will likely uncover upon further reading. I recommend that you practice Activity #2 often so it eventually becomes second nature. After all, it is a powerful spiritual tool that will help you manifest miracles.

It Will Happen

*To win the war means to love your opponent.
Direct love toward the old memories and
you will set yourself free.*

Activity #2: Releasing the Old Memories (*Part 1*)

For the sake of this chapter, let us assume you are holding onto the old memory that you do not believe in miracles. If this is the case, you are also likely holding onto the old memory that it is impossible to expect miracles to happen to you. This activity will help you remove these old memories and replace them with divine truth. It is only then that you can continue on your manifestation path.

> Gentle Note: You can easily come back to this activity later on and use it for other old memories you may uncover. As you move through this book, you will uncover two additional methods (titled part 2 and part 3) to release old memories from your energetic system. Once you have explored these alternative methods, you can then decide which method you resonate with the most.

1. Sit quietly where you will not be disturbed and say to yourself, whether it be in your mind or out loud, 'I do not believe in miracles'. As you say this focus on how your body responds. Your body is the best tool to gauge how old memories affect you. It is likely that as you say the statement you will not feel elated but rather saddened; I certainly did.

   What feeling/s do you get when you say the statement, 'I do not believe in miracles' (or try the statements found at the end of this chapter)?

   _____
   _____
   _____
   _____
   _____

2. Give the negative-based feeling a number of strength. Zero means you do not feel negatively toward the statement of, 'I do not believe in miracles' to ten meaning you feel a strong negative-based feeling toward the statement.

   What number on a scale of 0—10 do you sense the negative-based feeling?

   _____

   _____

3. Focus on whatever feeling arises within you and try to pin point where in your body you feel this particular feeling.

   > **Example:** When I wanted to clear my disbelief about miracles happening, I felt great sadness and heaviness in my chest that radiated down to my naval.

   Where in the body do you sense this feeling?

   _____

   _____

   _____

   _____

   _____

4. Now that you have connected to the location of the feeling, it is time to imagine what the feeling looks, moves and sounds like.

   > **Example:** As I focused on the sensation of sadness around the disbelief in miracles, I instantly pictured thick murky dark green and black sticky slime that oozed throughout my

> chest and abdominal area. It was quite disgusting to imagine and because it was so foul, I instantly wanted it removed!

Describe in as much detail as possible what the feeling around the disbelief in miracles looks, moves, sounds and even tastes like.

_____
_____
_____
_____
_____
_____
_____
_____
_____

5. Direct the Ho'oponopono prayer to the feeling you can now easily sense in your body. You may wish to close your eyes as you do this. Breathe slowly and deeply; directing your breath to the area of the body where the feeling resides. As you breathe in deeply say:

I love you
I am sorry
Please forgive me

6. Breathe out and say:

Thank you

7. Repeat. Moving your breath to the area of your body where the feeling of, 'miracles do not happen' and as you breathe in deeply and slowly, say:

> I love you
> I am sorry
> Please forgive me

8. Breathe out slowly and say:

> Thank you

9. Repeat the Ho'oponopono prayer at least ten times. As you continue repeating the prayer, you may find it becomes difficult to sense the original feeling to a point where you no longer feel connected to it; the feeling becomes neutral. You may even sense the feeling changing shape, colour, and texture to one that you can be in love with, or you may not sense any change. Trust in the process. What is meant to happen will happen—do not force it. Simply be in the moment. Continue to repeat the Ho'oponopono prayer and trust the Universe is working through you to clean away the old memories as needed.

10. At the end of this practice, as the old memory fades, you may sense a feeling of regeneration and vitality. This is the perfect time, if you feel called, to invite a new memory to take place of the old— one that is far more empowering and supportive to your highest good. Use this time now to allow the wisdom of your soul to decide on what the new memory will be for you. Do not judge it or question it; simply allow your soul to speak its truth. When you feel the time is right,

imagine the new memory as a healing light entering the area of your body that was once the site of fear and pain. Imagine the light filling any empty spaces to leave you feeling whole and complete. Breathe deeply to infuse this new memory into your very essence before opening your eyes.

11. Refer back to the number you gave to the original feeling behind the statement, 'I do not believe in miracles' after you have repeated the Ho'oponopono prayer at least ten times.

    How strong is the original feeling behind the statement, 'I do not believe in miracles' in your body now from a scale of 0 – 10? (Remember 0 being you do not feel it at all in the body to 10 being it is extremely present and strong in your body.)

    _____

    _____

12. If the number is greater than 2, repeat the Ho'oponopono prayer until you reach 2 or less.

Chances are the number on the scale will fall gradually as you continue to clean the old memories. This also means the original negative feeling behind the 'I do not believe in miracles' statement will diminish too. Eventually you will be able to say the statement, 'I do not believe in miracles' and feel absolutely no attachment toward it. That is when you know you are clean of any associated memories to that statement. It also means that you *do* believe in miracles and when you believe in miracles, miracles will happen.

The beauty of the Ho'oponopono prayer is that it can be used in any given negative situation. As I had written earlier, the prayer is a lifelong practice. So do not practice it sporadically. Practice it as often as you can. The more you do, the more the prayer will become ingrained into your subconscious mind which means you can continue cleaning the old memories in the background as you go about enjoying your human existence.

I love you
I am sorry
Please forgive me
Thank you

Additional Old Memories to Explore

Here are additional old memories that may be hindering your ability to easily expect your true desires to manifest. As you read over each, notice how you feel. If you feel a sense of discomfort or you believe in the statement to be true for you then it is likely the particular memory is affecting you. Simply use the Ho'oponopono prayer to clean, cleanse and release before moving onto the next chapter.

- I don't believe the Ho'oponopono prayer can actually reprogram my subconscious mind; it's too easy
- Miracles do happen but they do not happen to me
- I can't imagine my desire turning to reality; it's too far fetched
- Nothing is easy to obtain; I have to work really hard to get what I want
- It is better to give than it is to receive

- If I get what I want, other people will suffer
- I can't justify getting what I want when there are so many people in need—there isn't enough for everyone
- What I want isn't essential for me to live so it's best I just focus on the essential things and give up on what I want
- I need to suffer and experience lack so others will be happy
- I need things to happen in a *particular* way
- I have to be who I'm expected to be which means I need to continue to struggle and experience lack

These are just some of the more common memories stored in our subconscious mind. We will explore these and more further in the book however it does not hurt to practice the Ho'oponopono prayer for these memories before reading further because:

There is no such thing as too much cleaning, cleansing, and releasing!

Passion

Do more of what lights your soul on fire and fills your well with love. When you do you will find your purpose.

Chapter 5 – Love Conquers All

You will find as you look back upon your life that the moments when you have truly lived are the moments when you have done things in the spirit of love. – Henry Drummond

Dr Felice Leonardo Buscaglia once said, 'The easiest thing to be in the world is you. The most difficult thing to be is what other people want you to be. Do not let them put you in that position.' Often society influences our perception of what is considered to be a great life, such as owning a fancy car, mansion or private yacht. We convince ourselves we want certain things mostly because that is what other people may want, or we believe we may receive more respect for owning a particular thing. Sometimes the choices we make are not made for our own divine self but rather to make other people accept us.

So what if deep down you really did not want all those things? What if you did not want the mansion and the garage the size of a stadium full of mint-condition exotic cars? More to the point—what will people think of you if you do *not* want those things? Will they laugh at you? Will they make fun of you? Will they say hurtful things such as, 'Why wouldn't you want to own your own private jet? Are you crazy? What's wrong with you?'

The fact is the best thing you can do in this lifetime is be true to who you *really* are. Some people will love you for it; while others may disagree with you—but as long as you know you have lived your life true to yourself then that is all that matters. The minute you become happy and accepting of who you are then the minute you will be surrounded by people who mirror the same acceptance and happiness you feel—that is the difference. You can desire something for the sake of making other people happy even though deep down you do not really want it, or you can truly desire something that is personal and empowering to you.

> *True desires are the things that ignite you on the inside. They are your passion.*

They are so pleasurable and exciting that you will just want to continue to create and manifest more. After all, that is a big part of the meaning of life—creating, experiencing, and expanding.

So if you do not become clear on what you *truly* want, rather than wanting something for the sake of 'fitting in', then no amount of trying to attract what you *think* you want will work effectively. Say for instance you *think* you want a holiday house. You think about how wonderful it would be to have a place readily available to you whenever you felt like taking a break from everyday life. Yet if you were really honest with yourself you would say that you do not want to visit your holiday house and use all the time you dedicated for your holiday on the maintenance of the house itself. You might also not want to feel restricted to 'one' particular holiday location, in fact, you would prefer to have the ability to go to different holiday locations. Deep down you might also fear that you would become bored with the same holiday location and feel obligated to visit your holiday home during you spare time to escape from everyday life. Suffice to say that with such doubts and fears about owning a holiday house, it is highly unlikely it will manifest because it is not something you *truly* want. The Universe is very clever in distinguishing what it is you want as opposed to what you do not want but how does it know?

Eat Cake

The Universe does not listen to *just* your thoughts no matter how positive they may seem. The Universe picks up on the vibration of your feelings, values and beliefs. Your feelings, values and beliefs are felt in your subconscious mind. We have already touched on this in Chapter 4—*It Will Happen* (page 44) but let us go a little deeper with this. Think of the subconscious mind as the instigator—it puts everything into operation behind the scenes. It is like the mechanics of a watch. When we check our watch to tell the time, we simply notice the dials and numbers. What we do not see is the intricate mechanism behind the watch face that is the driving force of moving the clock hands which represent the time of the day. There is no way of interfering with the mechanism simply by 'wishing' that the clock hands would move faster. The subconscious mind is the same. You cannot consciously override it. So if your conscious and subconscious minds are not synchronised, then the signal sent out to the Universe is weak and confusing.

This is why it is so important to become clear on what *exactly* it is you *truly* want; what it is you are so passionate about that makes your heart sing. When you do this you will be sending out clear signals to the Universe of your true desires and the Universe will respond with a mirror image of the very thing/s that you long for. Not only does it help to have clarity on what you truly want so that you are sending out a clear signal to the Universe but it is also your way of telling your brain of your real desires.

We are going to get a little scientific here. Within your brain lies the Reticular Activating System (RAS). The RAS is responsible for regulating your sleep/wake cycles as well as, and this is important, filtering out external information so it is possible to focus on the things that are important to you. Say for example you were walking through a busy airport passenger terminal. Think of all the noise you would hear—hundreds of people talking, music playing, announcements over the speakers and luggage carriers banging and clanking, to name a few. Think of how much attention you would give to all the noise—not much as it would all seem like an overwhelming mixture of sounds. It is only when you hear the announcement over the speakers about your flight number, or your name, that you take notice.

The way you noticed such an announcement was thanks to your RAS. Your RAS has the unique ability of passing on what is deemed as important information based on your passion, interest, needs and beliefs to your conscious mind so that when the important information surfaces it is not treated as 'background noise' that you would normally ignore.

This is important when you are on the manifesting journey as without a clear idea of what it is you actually desire, your RAS has no way of noticing synchronistic opportunities that could potentially help you to fulfil your desire. You will remember that it is your job to be clear of what you want and it is the Universes' job to work on *how* what you want will come to fruition. The Universe will not hand to you what you want without you putting some kind of action into place, however it will give you signs of the *right* action that will eventually lead you to enjoying the reality of your true desire. The signs the Universe send to you is picked up by your RAS. It notices the synchronistic signs and passes on messages to your conscious mind to say, 'Take notice! This is what you've been looking for!'

Sometimes the signs may not make any sense to you and you may wonder how taking action on something would lead to you fulfilling your deepest desires. This is where you need to tap into the trust that you have with the Universe and understand that it only wants what you want—even if the journey to get there may seem unusual to you. Sometimes the most amazing experiences are those you cannot predict.

Say, 'Yes' to the unexpected. It could lead you to your dreams!

But before you can enjoy a life of abundance and prosperity, you must first tell your RAS what it is you are looking for from life. And the only way you can do that is by defining what it is you want; what it is that you are *truly* passionate about that will bring you joy.

Once you have clarity on your passion (your true desires) you will then be sending clear signals to the Universe. Essentially you will be telling the Universe that you are now open to opportunities that will help you to achieve your dreams. Remember your desires may not necessarily manifest without you personally taking some form of action to help the process along. Therefore it is the Universe's job to provide those opportunities for you and it is your job to take action on them to fulfil your dreams. We have all been gifted with the freedom of choice so we are all responsible for *choosing* to take action or not.

Quite possibly one of the hardest things to take action upon when uncovering your true desires is ignoring your ego. Your ego believes it knows best. Your ego believes that everything should be a certain way and if it is not then it will encourage you to ignore the other options altogether. The ego can certainly make it difficult for us to hone in on exactly what it is we truly desire. You may find that as you tap into your heart's desires, your ego will come up with all the reasons why you should not even attempt to attract such things. It may make you question your worth, it may try to make you believe there is a lack of abundance in the world (which is completely false), and it may define *how* the desire will come into existence which could discourage you from even taking inspired action. Using the holiday house as an example—say you desire a beach holiday house yet your ego has defined that the only way you will get a beach holiday house is if you have $2 million dollars which you do not have. Since you do not currently have the money needed to buy a holiday house and you cannot imagine any way of gaining that kind of money, it is likely you will give up before you have even started. But remember, anything that your ego comes up with are only old memories. So anytime doubt or fear enters your mindset about your ability to manifest what you truly want, simply use the Ho'oponopono prayer from Activity #2: *Releasing the Old Memories* (page 62). It is *that* simple!

The last important thing I will write about before you move onto uncovering what it is you truly desire is the realisation that the manifestation journey you are on is a truly unique and individual one. That is to say that it is *your* journey and yours alone. You cannot manifest something for someone else. You may feel that a friend or family member would greatly benefit from better health, more free time, better relationships etc, however it is not your place to implement the manifestation process on their behalf. It is against the Law of Free Will. If it is something they desperately need and want then it is up to them to manifest it for themselves. Everyone is here to learn, change and therefore evolve. The only thing you have power over changing is yourself—and only yourself. As you go about successfully manifesting your true desires and cleaning the old memories from your subconscious mind, you will become an inspiration to your friends and family. This in turn may motivate them to reach for the stars and see that anything is possible when you break away from the chains of limitation.

Activity #3: Discovering Your True Desires

Discovering your true desires is as easy as discovering your passion in life. In this activity you will be asked a series of questions designed to help you connect to the passion within. Then you will know exactly what it is you want in life and will start raising your vibration to attract it. But before you get started, I have included a few key points to consider as you go about doing this activity:

- The key is to write your answer in bullet point as quickly as you can so the ego does not have a chance to interfere.

- If you feel uncomfortable about your answer or it almost seems contradictory to what you perceive your life path should be then that is an indication there are old memories still entrenched in your subconscious mind. Just like Activity 2: *Releasing the Old Memories* (page 62), you can simply breathe into the memory and recite the Ho'oponopono prayer to clean and release.

- If you get stuck on a question and simply do not have an answer just move on to the next one. Sometimes the answer will come to you when you are ready to receive it.

- Some of the questions may seem as though they are doubling up and therefore your answers are too—this has been done on purpose so do not worry if your answers turn out to be the same or very similar for various questions.

- I encourage you to be 100% honest here. Do not judge your answers or shrug them off as a silly idea, just write whatever comes to your heart.

- It is also recommended that as you do this, be as specific as you can. For example, writing, 'I'm on a holiday' is not specific. It does not describe the type of holiday, for how long, when, or where. A more specific way of writing this may be, 'I'm on a holiday in Hawaii for the first 2 weeks of the next Summer with my family'. Bliss!

- Where appropriate, please write answers in present tense. This assumes that what you want is already in your life.

- Most importantly, enjoy this activity! This is the beginning of your *true* manifestation journey!

Are you ready? Let's begin...

1. What activities do you find meaningful, fulfilling, enjoyable and important?

_____
_____
_____
_____
_____
_____
_____
_____
_____
_____
_____

2. If you were financially secure and did not need to work for a living, how would you spend your time?

   _____
   _____
   _____
   _____
   _____
   _____
   _____
   _____

3. If you were not being paid for your career or business ownership, would you still be doing what you are doing? Why? If your answer is, 'No', then what would you be doing differently and why?

   _____
   _____
   _____
   _____
   _____
   _____
   _____
   _____

4. Think back to when you were a child. What activities did you love to do where you lost track of time?

   _____
   _____
   _____

5. What childhood dreams or interests did you have that you were not able to fully explore yet still intrigue you to this day?

6. What do you love to do where you lose track of time or forget to eat because you are so involved in the activity?

7. What specifically is it about that activity that you love? For example, you may love reading fictional stories that relate to adventure. So perhaps it is not necessarily the activity of reading that you love but rather the love for adventure

_____
_____
_____
_____
_____
_____
_____
_____

8. What are five big things you would love to accomplish within a year from now? Why?

_____
_____
_____
_____
_____
_____
_____
_____

9. What resources or tools do you need that may help you reach and achieve those goals?

_____
_____
_____

10. How will you feel when you accomplish those things?

11. How will accomplishing those things benefit you and others?

12. What are your top ten non-negotiable deeply held core values—the things that matter most to you? For example, love, compassion, honesty, courage, peace, creativity, spiritual connection, freedom, intuition, happiness, equanimity…? If you have trouble with this, try to consider what makes you angry and find the core value in that. For example, cruelty to animals or the cutting down of trees may make you angry so some core values may be protection, equality, beauty and conservation. If ignorance and stupidity make you angry then perhaps a core value is education. If poverty in third world countries makes you angry then prosperity may be a core value. Or if life crippling diseases makes you angry then a core value may be health. Tune into your anger and use it to uncover what truly matters to you.

_____

_____

_____

_____

_____

_____

_____

_____

_____

_____

13. How does your life currently support or reflect those values? Pay particular attention to the ones you are ignoring or not noticing enough.

_____

_____

_____

14. How have the old memories (fears and limiting beliefs) held you back from living a life of your dreams so far? Name and shame those old memories!

15. What solid evidence (if any) do you have that the old memories are actual truth for you? (Hint: The old negative memories are lies. But it is important that you realise this for yourself. Once you come to terms with their lies, then you can move onto practicing the Ho'oponopono prayer from Activity #2: *Releasing the Old Memories* page 62.)

16. Are you prepared to take some risk and feel a sense of uncertainty to gain your heart's desires? (I find navigating the most unchartered waters brings about the most dramatic and positive changes to my life. Sometimes you need to embrace uncertainty to thrive.)

17. What type of house do you want to live in (be specific) and how will it make you feel when you get it?

18. What is your ideal health level—what does your body look like? How fit are you? How does being healthy make you feel?

_____
_____
_____
_____
_____
_____
_____
_____

19. Say you had $500,000 to give to someone. Who would you give it to and why? How would donating it make you feel?

_____
_____
_____
_____
_____
_____
_____
_____

20. Who are you inspired by the most (famous or non famous) and why do they inspire you?

_____
_____
_____

21. What holiday destination would you love to visit within the next 12 months? How would you feel planning the holiday and visiting this place?

22. What would your ideal day look like if you had no other responsibilities? Describe in great detail from morning until bedtime.

23. What has been the downside of not reaching your heart's desires up until now? (This is your motivation).

_____
_____
_____
_____
_____
_____
_____
_____

24. What is the upside of not reaching your heart's desires, that is, what do you gladly avoid? For example you may avoid finding out whether you succeed or fail (there is no such thing as failure; only feedback), or you may avoid finding out just how truly powerful you can be. Whatever you potentially avoid is an old memory because your mind is trying to predict the outcome from past experiences. Once you have written the upside of not reaching your heart's desires then practice the Ho'oponopono prayer to remove the old memories attached to each limiting belief (Activity #2: *Releasing the Old Memories,* page 62.)

_____
_____
_____
_____
_____
_____

25. What pulls at your heart strings that cause the stirring of deep emotions including compassion, empathy and affection? For example, if I see a child or animal suffering, it instantly pulls at my heart strings. I can literally feel my heart ache with sorrow before I feel a deep urgency to do something about it. Watching someone demonstrate their passion is also another thing that pulls at my heart strings. Simply witnessing their joy and passion ignites such pleasure in my own spirit.

___

26. What do you love to create? And how does it benefit others?

___

> **Reminder to Clean:** Reflect on what you have just written and if any of your answers stir up negative old memories (limiting beliefs) then I recommend that you practice the Ho'oponopono prayer before moving forward with the rest of this activity.

27. **Summarise:** To piece this activity together I invite you to summaries your answers so you end up with a clear list of your heart's desires. You may even notice a reoccurring theme in your answers which are definite desires of the heart. As you go about summarising your answers, keep in mind your core values you have also listed from question 12. Your core values are a part of your unique blueprint. They represent what you stand for and act as motivation and inspiration. So as you summarise your heart's desires, ensure that each desire is in alignment with at least one of your core values. This will make certain that your intention of manifesting your heart's desires to the Universe is a clear and positive one.

    SUMMARY OF MY HEART'S DESIRES

    _____
    _____
    _____
    _____
    _____
    _____
    _____
    _____
    _____
    _____

Eat Cake

Chapter 6 – Plan For Success

A goal without a plan is just a wish

Time management experts will say that it is important to have goals in life because they are what motivate us to take action. I truly believe this, particularly when it comes to manifesting. What I have found is that setting goals aligns your energy (the frequency you send out to the Universe) *with* your desires so that you are dedicating a type of focus that will have you actively creating a life of your dreams. And this is so important because when the Universe provides you with opportunities that act as stepping stones to getting what you truly want, then you will gladly embrace those opportunities because of the focus and intention you have.

Now that you are blissfully aware of what it is you *truly* want in life, you can fine tune those desires and turn them into goals. Interestingly enough, I often find that when I write down my goals most of them can be used as positive affirmations (when you repeat positive phrases that describe how you want to be, it can eventually become a self fulfilling prophecy). As you read through the summary of your desires from question 27 of Activity #3: *Discovering Your True Desires* (page 89) you will be building a deeper and more vivid picture of your goal. This will ignite the necessary *feelings* and *emotions* that are the driving force behind your desires developing into reality (you will soon learn that feelings and emotions play a huge role in manifestation).

The beauty of this activity is that you will become more specific on what you want. So often I have found people give up on their manifestation dreams because they have lacked clarity in their vision. The Universe loves specificity because it makes it easier to provide the necessary opportunities to help you get what you want. If you are too vague on what it is you want, the Universe will still provide opportunities however they may not be the appropriate ones that lead you to where you truly want to be. So it is in your best interest to take the time with this and get really specific with your goals.

> Gentle Note: This is not about telling the Universe *how* you want your dreams to appear. That is not your job. You are co-creating with the Universe so it is your job to tell it what you want and it is the Universes' job to deliver opportunities for you to take action on so you can experience the reality of it.

Now it is time to turn your desires into actionable goals.

Activity #4: Your Desires Are Your Goals

1. Refer to question 27 from Activity #3: *Discovering Your True Desires* (page 89) and choose one heart's desire you have listed. Then tune into how it would make you feel when it manifests into reality.

   For example, if you desire to own a hobby farm then you may feel excited and grateful if this particular desire came to being. Of course this asks you to use your imagination as to how you believe you will feel, but tapping into the feeling *behind* the desire will have you connecting to it in a way that raises your frequency to match the very same frequency of the reality of your desire. The more you *feel* the same feelings that will come as a result of your desire manifesting, the easier your desire will come to fruition.

   Once you have zeroed in on what it is you will feel you can begin writing your goal. Start by writing,

   'I am feeling...'

   And then insert the feeling/s you imagine you will have when a particular desire manifests. Using the hobby farm example, you may write; *'I am feeling excited and grateful....'*

   > Gentle Note: It is important to use your *own* words because they are a reflection of your own spirit. Do not use words that are *not* used in your everyday vocabulary because you will not be able to connect to the goal as well as you would when it is written *just* for you.

2. Next, review the way you have written your heart's desire from question 27 of the previous activity (page 89) and ask yourself if this is the *best* way you can write it. Does it need to be more specific to ensure it is making your heart sing with joy and positivity? Is the language used *your* language? Once you are happy with the specificity of your heart's desire, you can simply add it to the sentence you created from step 1.

   For example, regarding the hobby farm desire: *'I am feeling excited and grateful* (this was from step 1)......*that I own and run a hobby farm that is between 100 – 200 acres in size and is within two hours' drive from Sydney'* (this is your specific desire).

3. Now that you are clear on the feeling you will experience when your desire grows into reality and you are specific on what it is you actually want, you can start to tune into *why* you want this desire to manifest; that is, what is its purpose that ignites your passion? How does it benefit you aside from making you feel absolutely wonderful?

   For example; perhaps your passion is rescuing animals so the reason behind wanting a hobby farm is so you can provide a home for animals that would otherwise be homeless. Perhaps you want a hobby farm to connect with nature and live off the grid because your passion is in environmental conservation. Or maybe you want a hobby farm to create a simpler life away from the hustle and bustle of city life because your spirit is passionate about quiet time and self-reflection. Whatever the reason may be, be sure to write it down as the last part of your goal.

Plan For Success

Once again, using the hobby farm as an example: '*I am excited and grateful* (this was from step 1)....*that I own and run a hobby farm that is between 100 – 200 acres in size and is within two hours drive from Sydney* (this was from step 2)...*because it gives me an opportunity to provide a new life to the animals that need a loving home* (this is the main reason why you would want a hobby farm)'.

4. In summary, you will be focusing on the feelings first. Then the specific desires. Then the purpose behind the desire which should be connected to your passion. And that is your heart's desire turned into a goal that you can work toward with passion and purpose!

> 'I am feeling [insert feeling]....that [insert desire]....because [insert purpose]'

The reason for writing the feeling/s and purpose around a particular goal (heart's desire) is to show the Universe that although you may want this goal, what you *really* want is to experience the feelings and experience the purpose. Your goal is just *one* way you can achieve the same feelings and the same purpose, however the Universe knows that that is not the only way. What we sometimes have difficulty understanding is that there are limitless ways we can get what we want. So although it is extremely helpful to have specific goals because it gives the Universe an idea of what our heart wants, we must realise that our goals do not have to be exactly the way we want them to be. Having a goal is simply a way for us to measure our journey so we can see just how far we have come. Because when we reach a goal, even though it may not look the way we had originally envisaged, it will still be pretty darn good!

Eat Cake

Now it is your turn to create goals from your desires. As mentioned, focus on one desire first and then repeat the steps in this activity for every other desire so that you end up with a goal for each desire you had listed from question 27 of Activity #3: *Discovering Your True Desires* (page 89). Disregard the last column of the table below (Scale of Ease and Time to Achieve) for now. You will be coming back to that column in the next activity.

Goal Number Simply assign a number to each goal	Goal 'I am feeling [insert feeling]....that [insert desire]....because [insert purpose]'	Scale of Ease and Time to Achieve (0 = easiest and fastest, 10 = hardest and longest)

Plan For Success

Activity #5: Your Goals from Easiest and Fastest, to Hardest and Longest

Now that you have all your goals listed, you may be looking at each one (particularly if you have listed more than ten goals) and wonder how exactly you are going to manifest them without feeling overwhelmed. Because the fact is, every intention (goal) that you want to manifest requires you to put energy into it. The energy required for manifestation is both mental and physical. So it stands to reason that the more goals you want to manifest, the more energy you will need to use to make it happen. Suffice to say that the more goals you have, the less energy you can channel for each of them. The idiom of 'having too much on your plate' is very appropriate here! The result will be that you will have too many things to think about and act upon that it will all become one giant ball of overwhelm. Eventually it may well lead you to throwing your hands up in the air and saying, 'I'm done with this!' Therefore, if you want to be more successful with your manifestations, you must chunk your goals down—choose one goal to focus on and complete before moving on to the next goal.

The first goal you choose to achieve should be the easiest and fastest goal to achieve. Do not focus on trying to achieve the hardest one first because it may take longer to manifest than you originally expect. This can lead you to feeling disheartened by the period of time your desire is taking to come to fruition. This is not to say that it will not manifest at all, but it truly helps to be open to the fact that everything will happen at the right time and for the right reasons. So it is for this reason that I recommend you focus on the easiest and fastest goal first because this will build momentum. Once the momentum starts, it is very hard to stop—and that is exactly what you want.

Choosing the easiest and fastest goal to achieve also stands as proof that turning your desires into reality is in fact achievable. Everybody likes to have proof—'The proof of the pudding is in the eating' as they say (or perhaps I should change 'pudding' for cake!). Once you have the momentum going, it will be easier to accomplish the next goal, then the next, and so on.

Go back to Activity #4: *Your Desires Are Your Goals* (page 93) and rate each goal on a scale of ease and time to achieve (0 = the easiest and fastest to achieve, 10 (or more if you have more than 10 goals) = the hardest and longest to achieve), to work out which goal you should focus on first. Record your results in the 'Scale of Ease and Time to Achieve' column before moving forward with this activity.

Now that each of your goals have been assigned a number of ease and time to achieve, which goal will you focus on first? (Select the goal you gave a zero to.)

I have chosen the goal:
_____ to
focus on first until completion.

The beauty of this method is that once you have completed the first goal, you can move on to completing the next goal (number 2 of ease and time to achieve), and then the next (number 3), and so on without experiencing the feelings of overwhelm and confusion.

Chapter 7 – Building Momentum

Once you get going in that direction, it is more likely you'll continue in that direction.

Now you are clear on your true desires and which one you are going to focus on first, the next step is to build momentum. Momentum, in terms of manifesting, is a form of consistent movement. Before we create something, we typically think of it first (mental plane), then give it energy (astral plane) before witnessing it (physical plane). It is through the process of giving the goal energy that we create the momentum needed to witness it in the physical plane. So how do we give our goals energy? By using our thoughts (ideas, plans, and reasoning), feelings (what we sense in our body), values (ideas we hold to be very important to us and are intimately related to our needs) and beliefs (convictions that we generally hold to be true even if we do not have actual proof or evidence).

Every thought, feeling, value, and belief you have about *anything* projects a signal to the Universe. If you continue to feed that thought, feeling, value or belief with the same (or very similar) thoughts, feelings, values or beliefs, then you are essentially generating a type of force that lights up like a beacon. This beacon of light acts like a moth to a flame—the brighter it becomes, the greater the attraction of similar experiences. For example, if you place your focus on how much you dislike your job or your broken relationship, and you continue to feed the thought, feeling, value or belief about your unfulfilling job or your broken relationship, then you will only attract the same frequency that comes with job dissatisfaction and a failed relationship. Subsequently you will get more of what you put out. This is momentum;

The thoughts, feelings, values and beliefs you hold toward your desires and toward yourself will be magnetised by the Universe by way of providing people, circumstances and events.

So the idea is to create movement behind the thoughts, feelings, values and beliefs. I have two very effective methods that will help you do this.

The first method is using a vision board. A vision board is a board (cardboard, cork board, etc.) that includes various images, photos and affirmations (one word or sentences of a positive nature) that complement the very same desire you want to accomplish. The purpose behind a vision board is that it will stimulate the RAS within your brain, as explained earlier in this book (page 72). Essentially, the more focused you are on your desires, the more thoughts and feelings you generate around that desire, and therefore the better the signal to the Universe.

So why is this so powerful? Our subconscious mind is unable to tell the difference between reality and imagination. At the time this book went to press, it was known that the subconscious mind is responsible for 95% of our brain capacity. 95% is huge considering that everything your subconscious mind thinks is taken as factual! So in other words, if you use a vision board that illustrates images of your true desires, your subconscious mind will believe that those things are already in existence. Your subconscious mind will then emit a certain frequency based on the images it sees and the feelings you generate as a result of looking at each image and reading each affirmation, so that after a while you will start to attract the very same thing you are thinking, believing, valuing, and feeling.

Eat Cake

The vision board will also help you to stay focused even in the early hours of the morning. When you awaken the first thought in your mind can determine the proceedings of the rest of the day. And if it is a thought that you continually feed, no matter how positive or negative it may be, then you must be prepared for the kind of reality it can create.

Leanne opened her eyes slowly as her 6:30 AM alarm beeped loudly, abruptly filling the quiet space of her bedroom. She felt more exhausted than she had before she went to bed. Her mind was still ticking over; thinking about her finances, worrying how she would pay the bills on time, and whether she would ever get out of the ground-hog day existence that was ruling her life. She detested her job but chose to stay because she could not see any other option. Leanne could see that the only benefit to her job was that it helped her earn money; not a lot of money but enough to get by. But recently money was becoming more and more difficult to attain. Over the past six months, Leanne had to use up all her sick leave due to various conditions that frequently arose; Bronchitis, the Flu, Migraines, Anxiety, and Irritable Bowel Syndrome to name a few. She felt the year so far consisted of trying to maintain a healthy lifestyle and apologising profusely to her boss each time she could not make it to work. In fact she half expected her boss to fire her since the quality and consistency of her work was suffering. Of course losing her job would be a disaster; where would she live? How would she pay for her bills and groceries? Where would she find work if her old boss gave her a bad reference? With her anxiety levels rising at the sheer thought of losing her job, Leanne decided she was not going to feel any better about her life unless she got out of bed. Throwing the blankets off her body, she swung into action but her lower back had other plans. A sharp and stinging pain suddenly travelled from her lower back region, down her right buttock, to the back of her thigh and down to her foot. It felt like a malevolent being had tied a knot of barbed wire at different intervals between her back and right foot, and were pulling them tighter and tighter. The pain was excruciating! In that moment, Leanne knew she was in trouble—she was stuck; physically and emotionally. She shot an abusive thought to the Universe; 'Why me?!' she thought angrily, 'Why the hell does this keep happening to me?' But she did not receive a response from the Universe. Feeling completed defeated and lost, Leanne cried. She knew her body was reacting to the constant negative thoughts she was feeding herself—she had fallen into the self-pity trap and now she was paying the price. Her greatest fear of potentially losing her job may well have just become her reality.

I wish I could say this was a fictional example, however this kind of situation does in fact happen. When we focus our attention on what we hate about our lives, and we continue to feed that negativity by way of our thoughts, feelings, values and beliefs, then we can eventually create a physical representation of what we *do not* want in our lives. Essentially we become a self-fulfilling prophecy.

You have 17 seconds for a thought to build momentum. In other words, one thought leads to another thought and so on. At 68 seconds, the thought has already started to create new neural pathways in the brain that assist in the thought becoming more prominent. Why is it so important to create new neural pathways and how does this relate to a vision board? The electricity in the brain flows the way water flows through a pipe—finding the path of least resistance. The more you think about the images and affirmations on your vision board whilst also imagining how each goal would feel, sound, taste and smell once achieved, the larger the channel becomes. The larger channel then makes it easier for the electricity to travel through. After a while you will not even need to force yourself to think about your goal and how amazing it will make you feel because the neural pathway will do that for you automatically, thus generating and emitting positive and clear signals to the Universe. The entire thought process will be controlled subconsciously. But in order for the process to be controlled subconsciously, you must first be willing to put conscious effort into creating positive thoughts, feelings, values and beliefs.

Because your first thought in the morning can ultimately govern the state of the rest of your day, it is best to place the vision board somewhere where you will notice it as soon as you wake up. Likewise, keeping the vision board close to your bedside before you go to bed means it is the last thing you see before your body rests yet your neural pathways remain relatively active.

Building Momentum

Activity #6: Creating Your Own Vision Board

You do not need to create a vision board for just one desire that you discovered from Activity #3: *Discovering Your True Desires* (page 89). Instead you may wish to combine the top 3 desires initially and then add more visual items that represent other desires to the board as you progress through the manifestation journey. When I am creating a vision board, I like to avoid overloading the board with too many images and words otherwise I become a little overwhelmed by the number of desires I am trying to manifest. It is best to keep it simple but that does not mean you cannot fill it will inspirational and beautiful things.

Here are some key recommendations and suggestions for getting the most out of your vision board:

1. **Supplies you will need for your vision board:**
   - Poster board, cardboard, cork board, or some other kind of item that will allow you to stick or pin on images and words relating to your desires
   - Different magazines and newspapers (choose ones that have a variety of images and fonts)
   - Scissors
   - Glue, sticky tape, or drawing pins
   - Colourful pens, pencils, marker pens or paint
   - A photo of yourself (optional)
   - Other visual accessories such as glitter stickers and colourful ribbon (optional)

2. **Write your name or use a photo of yourself and place in the middle of the board:** Your name or photo must be in the

105

middle of the board so that all the images, additional photos and affirmations revolve around it. Ever heard of the term, 'The Universe does not revolve around you'? Well, that is entirely wrong. The Universe *does* in fact revolve around you. You are the screenwriter, actor, editor, producer and everything in between of your own Universe—you are always going to be the centre of the Universe from your own viewpoint no matter what. So ensure your name or photo is in the middle of the board so that everything you want can interact with you.

3. **Underneath your name or photo, write, 'This or something better':** An important key to manifesting is keeping an open mind and removing the expectation of how the outcome of your desire will look and feel. Say for instance your desire is to purchase a 2 bedroom cottage that you would like to holiday let. What you may not know is that it is far more cost effective to purchase a 3 bedroom cottage that will house more guests. If however your focus was placed solely on a 2 bedroom cottage than that is what you will receive. Yet if you write on your vision board, 'This or something better' then you are assuming that there are other possibilities you can experience that will bring you the same or better results that you are looking for. This allows you to stay open-minded about the way in which your desire will manifest. The benefit of this is that you will be open-minded to the synchronistic signals the Universe sends to you. These signals can ultimately lead you to experiencing the crème de la crème of your desire, *if* and only if you take action.

4. **Decide on what to include on your board:** This will be easy for you as you have already discovered what your true desires are. If you are an organised freak like me (although in saying

Building Momentum

that I do like the occasional 'place items randomly around the board' exercise) then you may like to separate the vision board into sections for each desire. Select images that relate to your desire and of which you have a strong and positive emotional connection to (emotion is very important!). If you wanted a holiday in Hawaii for example, then you might find an image of the hotel you would like to stay in, the beach you would like to visit, and an image of the people you would like to spend your holiday with such as your family or friends. You can simply cut out images from magazines or newspapers and stick or pin them onto your vision board.

5. **Write affirmations that are related to the theme of the board:** Cast your mind back to the previous activity (Activity #4: *Your Desires Are Your Goals,* page 93) where you wrote your desires as goals. You will remember that those goals have been written in a specific way; 'I am feeling [insert feeling]....that [insert desire]....because [insert purpose]' This can in fact be your affirmations! Affirmations are short and powerful sentences that state the existence of something positive. They condition your subconscious mind to develop a more positive perception about yourself and your life. This means you can easily change harmful behaviours (old memories) that have developed over time into new and positive ones (new memories). Remember you are aiming to generate the most positive thoughts, feelings, values, and beliefs about yourself which in turn sends a signal out to the Universe. This is why affirmations are so powerful. If you can be open to everything that is wonderful about you, if you can truly admit that you are a beautiful person and that you deserve to be loved because you truly and unconditionally love yourself, then that is what you

attract; loving and beautiful life experiences. Is there any better way of living?

Aside from using the goals you have already written which can be used as affirmations, you can also create your own. Here are some important points to keep in mind before writing your own affirmations:

- When writing your own affirmations, think about your own positive attributes then include them in the board. Start by writing 'I' and keep the affirmation in present tense. For example, 'I am generous', 'I am a good friend', 'I am worthy of receiving my heart's desires with ease'.

- Next, focus on the negative self-talk you may have regarding the theme of the board. So imagine reaching your desires, that is, you can see it in your mind, you can feel it, hear the sounds, taste the tastes and smell the smells. Then scan your body to see if there is an area of resistance; for example a gut feeling that is rebelling against this particular desire, or even your inner voice telling you, 'There's no way you'll ever fulfil this dream'. So it is up to you to question the reasons for any resistance—is it because you do not believe you deserve it? Or that you cannot afford it? Or that people will not like you if you have it? Or that you will change as a person? When you write your affirmations, ensure you state positive and empowering things that go against your negative self-talk. Say for instance you want a red sports car and you have the exact one in mind. You love the sound it makes, the overall size, the comfortable interior and the horsepower. Literally every part of the car, right down to the nuts and bolts, you are in love with. You sit quietly and imagine yourself driving the red sports car. You can hear the engine growl, you can smell the leather interior, and you can feel the slight vibration of the seat as you drive down the ocean road. Now you move your focus to your body and the inner self-talk to see what you are *really* sensing. Your ego may be telling you, 'I can't afford it. There's no way someone like me could drive a sports car like that. Besides, what are Mum and Dad going to think of me? They'll probably think I've turned into a snob. And what about my friends?! They'll probably assume I have millions of dollars and abuse our friendship or maybe they'll presume I've become like those self-centred and arrogant people we laugh at'. With all that self-talk, there is no way on Earth you will get that sports car! So when writing your affirmations, make sure you create powerful sentences that set these old memories (limiting beliefs) free. For example, 'I am deserving of owning my own red Ferrari. I am a down-to-earth and easy going person', meaning you are happy with who you are no matter the material things that are in your life. Or 'My close friends love the drives we go on together in my red Ferrari.' Just a word of warning: If you truly want a red sports car, ensure you make it clear that you want a *real* sports car; otherwise you might end up with a toy of the car you envisaged.

- As you reflect on your desire, tune into how it will make you *feel* when it turns to reality. Whatever the feeling is, ensure you write that *before* the rest of the affirmation. For example, if you sense you would feel appreciative and excited to spend your Christmas holidays in Spain then the affirmation may be, 'I am *grateful* and *excited* to spend four weeks during the Christmas holidays with my family in a luxurious hotel in Tenerife, Spain this year'.

- Write affirmations that support the goal you are moving towards. If for example, your ultimate desire is to take a trip overseas for a holiday, then your affirmations could be: 'I love that I am on holidays overseas,' or 'I have taken a year off work and now I am travelling around the world sightseeing.' Ensure you are specific with your affirmations so that you are sending out the clearest signal to the Universe about your true desires. Also remember that even though you have written, 'This or something better' near the middle of your vision board, it is also recommended you write it at the end of the appropriate affirmations to further confirm that you are open to other possibilities, for example, 'I love and adore living in my 4 bedroom farm house that is within walking distance to the beach. This or something better'.

- Never include a negative word in the affirmation such as: *can't, won't, unable, hard, don't, try, attempt,* etc as these words are all limiting in nature. Words such as: *am, have,* and *easily* are excellent words to use for affirmations.

6. **More for all—less for none:** Keep in mind that when you have more, you can help more. Always have the intention that when you receive, it is an opportunity for you to give back where you can.

Examples of Positive Affirmations

Below are examples of positive affirmations you may wish to include on your own vision board.

- I love and adore myself. My body is healthy, my mind is calm, and my soul is peaceful
- I am grateful and excited that wealth comes to me effortlessly. I have more than enough money in my life now and always.
- I feel an abundance of energy in my mind, body, and spirit which allows me to do anything I want with ease
- I love and accept myself for who I am
- I feel joyous because I know everything that is happening now is happening for my ultimate good
- I am surrounded by love and it feels so good
- I love my job and that it nurtures and satisfy's my soul with passion and purpose
- I feel free and limitless because I have the means to travel abroad whenever I want to
- I am radiating joy in everything I do for myself and for others
- I love that abundance and prosperity are always in my life and I am so grateful for it all

Another Way to Build Momentum

The second way to create movement behind the thoughts, feelings, values and beliefs that will help you achieve your dream life, is practicing a different form of visualisation. You have already mastered one of the forms of visualisation by creating your vision board (creatively visualising [imagining] your goal [your heart's desires] as already being in your life) so now it is time to incorporate another method to build a stronger momentum.

Visualisation is quite similar to when we use our imagination as children. For most of us, our childhood years were focused on using our imagination to enter the exciting world of role play. I imagined a pool in the living room with pillows as floaties, an outdoor cherry tree as a shower for my imaginary house, and a secret garden with hidden treasure on the vacant block next door. It was wonderful to have such limitless experiences!

But unfortunately as we get older we tend to believe visualisation is just a waste of time or that we cannot actually do it. This could not be further from the truth! You have used visualisation all your life, even down to choosing what you want to eat at your local takeaway shop. You will often find the takeaway menu is positioned just above the service counter. Interestingly enough, when we move our eyes up to view the menu we are actually tapping into our creative brain—the Occipital lobe (located at the back of our brain). This powerful part of the brain is responsible for processing visual information from the outside world using our eyes, as well as allowing us to freely and creatively visualise within our body with the help of several other regions of the brain (knowing *exactly* which regions of the brain is still an ongoing medical study). With the power of our brain, we can visualise *anything* we want. We have absolute freedom to be as creative as we wish; no one can influence it or touch it. So as we are looking up at the menu, we are in fact visualising what it might be like to eat a chicken burger with chips or a Greek salad with feta cheese. We do this for all the options on the menu until we decide what we want based on the kind of visualisation we received. See? It really is that easy!

In this moment, I would like for you to imagine a cat's body with a head of a fish. You can make it any colour, shape, or texture as you wish. Ultimately, the image in your mind is fairly bizarre! But even though you might not have ever seen a 'cat-fish' you could still piece an image together and quite possibly a pretty funny one at that! Now imagine a purple elephant with rainbow feathered wings and pink flamingo legs? Or on a more 'realistic' level, imagine you are in your room and you realise you need to get something from the kitchen. Imagine walking to the kitchen only to wonder, 'What did I come to the kitchen for?' Imagine your frustration as you return to your room only to find the item you originally needed pop's right back into your mind which causes you to have to go back to the kitchen.

You have just used the power of your mind to visualise (imagine). Your ability to visualise is one of the ultimate superpowers as a human being. Interestingly, our mind is unable to tell the difference between what we see in our physical world as reality to what we visualise internally. For all it knows, what we visualise and imagine is in actual fact reality. This is why visualisation as a method of attracting abundance into our lives is so vital. Our imagination is our only limitation. Whatever you can imagine for yourself is possible if you truly believe it is.

I have written more about the importance of visualisation in Chapter 11—*Imagination is Your Limitation* (page 150) but for now simply realise that by creatively visualising the manifestation of your goals, you are activating the creative subconscious. When this part of your subconscious kicks into action, you will start to generate creative ideas to help you achieve your goals. Visualising your desires coming to fruition also programs your brain to recognise resources that will also help you reach your goals (remember the

Reticular Activating System!). This too raises your frequency so you draw people, resources and circumstances into your life that can pave the way to getting what you desire.

> *Whatever the mind can conceive,*
> *the mind can achieve.*

Suffice it to say that visualisation is an essential tool to manifesting successfully! There are a number of different techniques you can do. You may like to add visualisation to your meditation repertoire if you already meditate. So whilst you are deeply relaxed, simply visualise your goal in your mind as if it is in the present moment. Or take a photo of the very thing you want (e.g. a holiday in Paris) and stick a photo of you somewhere on the original photo so it looks like you are a part of it. Then you can view the photo regularly for a 'visualisation hit'.

There is also another visualisation technique I recommend that incorporates your feelings into the practice because your feelings, as you are already aware, are powerful motivators. They are what have been coined as emotional manifestations which are just as important as physical manifestations. When you go from feeling angry to happy, that is considered an emotional manifestation. From depressed to a little optimistic is an emotional manifestation. Everything is about your energy and vibration, so it stands to reason that by incorporating your feelings into the following visualisation practice, you have yourself a very powerful method of getting what your heart desires.

Activity #7: The Mental Rehearsal Technique

Nothing happens without imagination so this is why the following technique, particularly as it incorporates all your senses including your feelings, is so powerful. For anything to appear in the physical plane of reality we must firstly imagine it, which is to say, rehearse it in our mind. Aim to practice this technique at least once a day for 30 days.

1. Before you begin, decide on which goal (desire) it is that you wish to manifest into your life.

2. Sit somewhere quiet where you will not be disturbed for the next five minutes. Simply relax by taking some deep breaths in and out; calming your body as you breathe in, and releasing any tension and stress as you breathe out.

3. Now imagine that you are sitting comfortably in a movie theatre. The temperature in the room is perfect. The lights are dim but bright enough for you to see clearly. You notice, as you sit relaxing in your chair, that the curtains of the movie screen begin to part and a movie starts to play. It is a movie of you experiencing the reality of your desire. You are watching yourself playing out the manifestation of your goal. Notice as much detail as you can create, including your clothing, the expression on your face, your body movements, the appearance of the environment and any other people may be around. Now add in any sounds you would be hearing with the manifestation of your desire—you may hear laughter, background music, people talking and cheering, birds chirping, or traffic. And finally, as you continue to watch this movie, simply recreate in your body

any feelings you think you would be experiencing if you too were engaged in this activity. As you are watching the movie, be open to any other imagery, sounds and feelings you sense that enhance the experience of this movie. Perhaps there are other elements of your goal that you were unaware of but are welcomed additions to the experience.

4. Now imagine yourself getting out of your comfortable chair, walking down the steps toward the screen. Visualise yourself simply stepping into the movie as it plays. Now you are experiencing the movie again except this time you are the main character—you are embodying the movie through your own eyes. You can look down at your body and see that you are wearing the same clothes you saw when you first watched this movie. You can see everything that you had seen, you can hear all the sounds you had heard, and you can feel the same feelings you would feel. This deepens the impact of the experience within you and it allows you to immerse yourself in the fulfilment of your desire.

5. When you have acted out the experience, you then walk out of the screen and return to your comfortable seat, noticing that the movie of your heart's desire is still playing perfectly. And as you relax in your chair, you reach your arm out and, as if by magic, you grasp the screen easily and effortlessly and shrink it down to the size and appearance of your favourite biscuit. As you hold this biscuit in your hand, you realise that it still contains all the qualities you had felt, heard and witnessed in the movie. Visualise yourself placing the biscuit in your mouth where you happily chew it up, enjoying and savouring every bit of this biscuit before swallowing. Realise, that even though this biscuit is now in

tiny little pieces, each piece still contains the full experience of the reality of your heart's desire. Imagine the tiny pieces of the biscuit which contains the reality of your heart's desire travelling down into your stomach and entering your blood stream where it is delivered to every single cell of your body. Now every cell of your body is infused with the movie of your heart's desire and every wonderful sensation that came with it. Imagine your entire body lighting up with gratitude for having this experience.

6. Take a deep a few deep breaths before opening your eyes and returning to your day.

Chapter 8 – A Little Step is All it Takes

A journey of a thousand miles must begin with a single step.
– Lao Tzu

Not only is visualisation a powerful tool to help you manifest your heart's desires, but it can also give you clues as to what kind of resources you may need to turn your desires into reality. When you are in a relaxed state with the intention of connecting to your desire (particularly during Activity #7: *The Mental Rehearsal Technique*, page 115) the Universe is able to download helpful guidance to you that can act as 'light bulb' moments of inspiration. So if you find you have received inspiration by way of an idea, an image in your mind or a sign on a billboard for example, then what do you do with it? You act on it! And you do it with complete trust that the Universe has got your back because it knows, that in order for you to get what you want, this particular idea you receive is a stepping stone to getting it. The minute you dismiss inspiration is the minute you lose the momentum and then you are back to square one.

To achieve your goals, you must take action.

This is why this chapter is dedicated to creating an action plan. I realise the idea of creating an action plan may sound as though you are moving further away from Universal inspiration and intuitive insights, but it will actually be your manifestation saviour! When you create an action plan, you will uncover and understand the necessary steps you need to take to move you closer to fulfilling your goals. This is where you will be using the Law of Action (not the Law of Attraction) which is the key to accelerated manifestation. This particular law means that you actually need to *do* something that moves you closer to fulfilling your goals. Having written that, for the law of Action to work, you do not need to have an elaborate plan of how you are going to fulfil your dreams, but rather, you can simply take one little step at a time and start doing what you can today. One little step is all that is needed. So this is about taking the vision of your goals that you had realised from the previous chapters, and doing something today with the energy and resources you have with you right now. This is also about realising that you may not have all the resources you need in this very moment so use this opportunity to employ the Universe and lovingly ask it to bring you the resources that it believes will help you fulfil your dreams with ease.

Activity #8: Your Action Plan to Manifest Your Goal

The following action plan will provide you with detailed information on the who, what, where, and how of your goal. This is your opportunity to see the resources that you can use right now and the resources you do not have in this moment. For those that you do not have right now, you can simply request that the Universe help you gain those resources.

Creating your action plan is as simple as answering a few questions relating to the goal you have selected to achieve.

1. Today's Date: _____/_____/_____

2. The goal I intend to complete is *(what is your goal from your list of heart's desires page 96)*:

   _____
   _____
   _____
   _____
   _____

3. The benefits of achieving this goal are *(what will you have accomplished; how will achieving this goal change your life; how will it make you feel; how will it benefit others; what other opportunities will it provide you?)*:

   _____
   _____
   _____
   _____

A Little Step is All it Takes

4. I, and others, will know I have reached my goal when (*what will be different about you or your lifestyle?*):

_____

_____

_____

_____

_____

_____

5. In order to achieve this goal, I will need the following resources: (*Consider the knowledge and skills that are required to enable you to achieve this goal. Do you currently have these knowledge and skills [it is completely okay if you do not have them just yet]? You may also like to reflect back on the visualisations you have practiced from the previous activity and consider if there were any resources that came to mind that the Universe was prompting you on. Sometimes we cannot recognise every single resource that we need but the Universe can help us identify those resources we had not considered before. Remember you are co-creating with the Universe—let it flow through you with trust and acceptance.*)

Resource (knowledge and skills needed to fulfil this goal)	**Is this resource *currently* available?**

Eat Cake

6. For the resources that are **not** available to me right now, I intend to: *What do you intend to do to get those resources?*

> **Gentle Note**: If you are unsure what is needed, simply ask the Universe to provide you with a sign of what the next step may be and then remain open for the rest of the day. If something unusual happens or an idea comes to mind that seems out of the blue, then do not dismiss it. It is likely the Universe is fulfilling your request by providing you with people, situations or ideas to help you move toward fulfilling your goal. If on the other hand you know what you need but you are unsure how you will get it, then you can

also ask the Universe for help. Ask and you shall receive! I find writing my request on a sticky note and keeping it somewhere in full view throughout the day so I am aligning my vibration to my request works wonders. For example, you may realise that the next step to fulfilling your goal of creating a business is to employ a web designer however you are unsure where to source a web designer or whether you will be able to afford their services. So on your sticky note you may wish to write: *'Thank you Universe for sending me a professional website designer who is designing my website for an amount I can easily afford.'* Always write it in the present tense and thank the Universe for sending you the help you need. Then let the Universe do what it does best; create miracles and magic!

7. This goal is important to me because *(Why does this goal mean so much to you; how will it make you feel? What is at stake if you do not complete this goal?)*:

_____
_____
_____
_____
_____
_____
_____
_____
_____
_____
_____
_____
_____
_____
_____
_____
_____
_____
_____

8. Taking into consideration all that I have written, my goal will be completed by: *(insert the **realistic** date on which you will achieve the goal)* _____/_____/_____

9. When I have achieved my goal, I will reward myself by *(ensure you share your success with friends and family)*:

_____
_____
_____

A Little Step is All it Takes

_____
_____
_____
_____
_____
_____
_____
_____

10. The specific steps / tasks I will do that will move me closer to achieving my goal include (*break down your goal into manageable steps—each step, no matter how big or small, will bring you closer to experiencing the reality of your desires*):

Step / Task	Expected Timeframe for Completion (e.g. 2 hours, 4 days, 1 week etc)	Date Completed

Eat Cake

Step / Task	Expected Timeframe for Completion (e.g. 2 hours, 4 days, 1 week etc)	Date Completed

11. **Declaration** (*this will make you accountable*):

I, [Insert Name] _____, am committed to the tasks I have designated, knowing that they are only there to move me closer to my true goal / desire. I will do everything in my power to keep on track, complete each task, co-create with the Universe, and celebrate my successes.

Signed: _____

Congratulations! Now you have a clear action plan that you can tick off as each step is completed. Make sure you review your action plan regularly to ensure you remain on track toward achieving your goal. The more you review the action plan and carry out the steps assigned, the more you will be inadvertently thinking about it, feeling it, and seeing it in your mind's eye. This will ultimately raise your vibration to match the very same thing you desire.

Mindset

The beautiful thing about fear is when you run to it, it runs away. – *Robin Sharma*

Chapter 9 – Grab the Bull by the Horns

When the winds blow, some people build walls and others build windmills. – Chinese Proverb

When I think about manifesting my desires, I like to think of the canoe analogy. If you step into a canoe and decide to paddle upstream against the current then you will likely get tired. The constant battle of pushing the ores against the energy of the water will eventually make your arms and shoulders ache. You may get to where you want to be but it will take you a lot longer and it certainly will not be an enjoyable journey. On the other hand, you may like to step into the canoe and simply allow the energy of the water to take you to where it wants you to go. And as you journey down the peaceful river in the canoe, you may watch the trees and the river bank pass you by naturally and easily. Of course you may need to place your ores into the water occasionally to guide the canoe safely past rocks or fallen tree branches but essentially most of the work is done by the water. All you have needed to do is to trust the water flow, the security of the canoe, and your ability to navigate around the occasional rocks and branches. Soon you find yourself where you wanted to be and the journey you took to get there was peaceful and easy. In life, the river is the Universe. The canoe is the support you have from your Higher Self, spiritual support team and higher beings of love and light, the ores are the choices you make, and the rocks and branches are your old memories.

I believe when you go with the flow and allow the Universe to move you instead of resisting it, life is much more interesting and less of a struggle. I will not go as far to say that life becomes struggle free because where would the fun be in that? If everything were easy then would it really be worthwhile? If we were never faced with a single struggle would we be motivated to refine our desires and talents? Would we feel the passionate fire in our stomach when we have a new idea to do something out of the ordinary? Would we push ahead no matter the cost and fight for our cause? If life were so easy all the time and we were completely free from struggle, would we even bother getting off our butts to do anything? I am not sure we would.

> *Struggle is not a sign of weakness or doom and gloom.*
> *It is a sign of opportunity.*

Inevitably, in order for you to get what you want, there will be an element of struggle. It may not be life shattering but there will still be an aspect of difficulty. For instance you may desire a loving relationship, yet you are holding onto an old memory that you are unlovable. The struggle therefore is to forgive that part of yourself and learn from it before letting it go and replacing it with a far more empowering memory of, 'I am love and I am worthy and deserving to receive love'. Struggle can also show up in the physical realm. For instance, if your heart's desire is to lose weight, then you must be willing to commit to achieving this goal. You must be willing to experience the sweat, the muscular aches and pain, the early mornings, the change in diet, the shift in mindset, and the temptations. If you are not willing to go through the struggle and pain to achieve your desires, then you will likely not succeed.

So as you focus on your heart's desires that you have recently discovered, I invite you to ask the dark questions; what are you willing to struggle for in order for your heart's desires to manifest? What pain are you prepared to experience to get what you want? In a world of duality we simply cannot desire something without experiencing a portion of struggle. That is just the way life is. And the sooner you can embrace the struggle and pain, the easier manifestation will be.

A very synchronistic event happened as I was writing this part of the book. It all started at 7:30 am. I had made myself a cup of tea, sat in my favourite 1970's brown leather chair, and opened up the laptop with excitement. I love writing and I was enjoying writing this particular chapter about struggles. The draft document of the book opened into action as I breathed deeply to connect to spiritual inspiration that would help me write in the flow. I read over a few of the paragraphs of this chapter that I had written the day before and decided that some of the information needed some fine tuning. I placed the cursor next to the paragraph I wanted to delete and hit the 'delete' button. Nothing. I hit it again thinking maybe the laptop was preoccupied browsing through holiday destinations online. Still nothing. I tried the 'backspace' button. No. That did not work either. I scrolled to another chapter of this book and tried to delete a word in case it was the entire draft that was the problem. Luckily it was not the entire document; both delete buttons were working. So it was only this chapter that would not budge. The same chapter that is all about struggles and how you must be prepared to experience an element of pain to get what you want.

Like a woman high on caffeine, I frenetically referred to the Support Manual of the software I was using to write this book in the hope there would be an answer for this very strange occurrence. Frustratingly there was no mention of this problem. I moved onto the online world for guidance; spending well over an hour sourcing through help-forums for advice. Still nothing. 'How is it that it was working fine yesterday but now it decides to do something strange today?!' I thought (technology and I have a love-hate relationship!). Then my poor husband walked into the room and I found myself relaying to him what was happening. Oh yes, I had entered 'verbal diarrhoea' mode. The poor man was standing there listening to my whining through sufferance with a look of, 'I'm trying to understand what you're talking about but you're speaking gibberish'. And through the multitude of words that were flying around the room, I suddenly caught an important part of what I was saying to him, 'I will write about this problem in the book *once* I solve it.' There was my light bulb moment. Through writing about struggles and realising that life is not always ponies, unicorns and rainbows, I too was faced with my own struggle. How much do I want this book to be published? How much pain am I willing to go through to get this book out into the world? Because believe me, writing this book has not been easy. There have been countless hurdles I have needed to overcome; technological problems, fear-based issues, self worth setbacks, running out of herbal tea crises…but I keep going. My desire for my dream to publish this book so I can help you achieve your own dreams is far greater than the struggles and pain I have, and undoubtedly will in the near future, experience. All the pain is worth it. I know it is. And ironically the more hurdles thrown my way, the more determined I feel to get this book published and prove to you that dreams do come true.

So as you consider your heart's desires, simply realise that you may be faced with old memories of the subconscious mind or physical situations that seem to pull you backwards. These struggles are your opportunity to question how far you are willing to go.

*Because if you want the benefits
then you must also want the costs.*

If you want to follow a spiritual path then you must be willing to do the shadow work. If you want to run your own business, then you must be willing to hustle and prioritise your time. If you want to take a career sabbatical and travel the world for a year then you must be willing to accept the probable decrease in income over the year and the challenge of readjusting to normal life when you return. If you are unwilling to go through such pain, then you have two options: either work through the idea of the pain by exploring and clearing any old memories, or give up.

For most of my adolescent life I yearned to be a veterinary doctor. I became completely set on the idea; enrolling in an animal care course whilst still at High School, asking for animal encyclopaedias for my birthday, and sticking animal posters all over my bedroom wall. Before going to bed at night I would play out different scenes in my mind of what it would be like to be a vet—in my dreams I would become super vet; saving one animal at a time. But to make this a reality I would need to study Veterinarian Science at university. Here in Australia, to get into university straight from year 12, you need to reach a certain grade in your Higher School Certificate. To be accepted into veterinary science, aside from needing a score well over 90, you also need to choose science and math based subjects in High School. So that is exactly what I did. I opted for Advanced Mathematics, Chemistry and Biology because I knew they would help me gain entry into university. What I had not anticipated was my total dread in doing all three subjects. I completely hated (yes, hated) Chemistry. The only good thing about it was that my future husband was in that class and I loved sabotaging his experiments so I was not the only one doing a terrible job (I have since apologised to him about that despite the fact that it was extremely funny). Biology was interesting but I never felt completely passionate about it, and math; well let me just say that even with a calculator I still had no hope. So the odds were against me. Despite that, I thought maybe a bit of workplace experience at the local veterinary hospital would help me reignite the passion I once felt. It did not. I remember watching the most beautiful Border Collie dog enter the clinical room (thankfully the Vet did not allow me to enter the same room at that time) only to realise that he was to never come back out. As a child I thought I would be able to help every single animal but I soon realised that being a vet was not all I had thought it to be. Was I willing to go through the heartache of losing an animal? Was I willing to go through that kind of pain when my efforts may not be enough? I tried to convince myself that this is what I wanted; after all, I had done so much work to pave the way for this dream to become a reality. The constant back and forth of whether it was something I wanted or not finally came to an end. My Higher School certificate score made the decision for me having scored less than 90. Not surprisingly I felt relieved that a decision had been made. I loved the idea of saving animals and the joy it would bring to my life, but I was not in love with the amount of work I would need to do to get there or the associated heartache and loss that comes with the job.

Unfortunately in some cultures, this may look like I have given up too early. Some people may say that I could have worked harder to get ahead with the math and science subjects. I could have paid for tutoring. I could have overcome my fear of losing of an animal or the constant questioning of whether I had done enough for them. I could have been more determined and believed in myself. I may be told by some to do more shadow work, write affirmations, or meditate on it. But sometimes the truth is simpler than that: I thought I wanted to be a vet. But it turned out, I did not.

It is completely okay if you discover that the thing you originally wanted is not at all how you expected it to be. If you cannot see past the struggles, it does not mean you have failed. It means that it is time to redefine your desires.

We are not always going to get it right and it is in these instances that help us decide on what is right for us.

So when do you give up? How do you know it is the right time to redefine your desires? I had once joined an online manifestation group. It was full of inspiring stories of people who had manifested some wonderful dreams. But there was one particular post that caught my eye. The post read, 'I give up. Manifestation doesn't work. I now know that it's a waste of time and you should know that you are all wasting your time too'. I believe this is a fairly common reaction when there are constant struggles in life. When the struggles are too hard to bear and it is difficult to remain positive, it becomes very easy to question the magic of the Universe. In fact it can become very easy to blame the Universe for the situation you find yourself in. Even now, despite what I know and believe about manifestation, I still catch myself at times falling into the victimhood mentality (feeling sorry for myself when things do not go as planned, or lashing out at the Universe in anger when things happen that I feel is deeply unfair) before forgiving myself for the outburst and apologising to the Universe. But through this journey I have come to understand a simple truth about struggles:

*You are where you **deserve** to be.*

Eat Cake

If you are experiencing wonderful abundance then you must have done some pretty extraordinary vibrational work to get there. If you are still lacking and surrounded by scarcity, then it is because you have not dared to challenge yourself and embrace and rise beyond adversity. These struggles are not your enemy but rather your greatest teacher, and you can choose to do what you want with them. If you are having trouble knowing whether to continue on the path of your desires, or to give up completely because it all seems too hard, then I recommend you do one of the following:

- *Feel into the situation; are the struggles a result of some old memories that need to be shifted before the reality of your dream can be born?* Firstly I recommend you continue to read this book. As mentioned, there are thousands of old memories lurking in the shadows of your subconscious mind which are likely sabotaging your ability to manifest what you want. Much of what is written in the rest of this book focuses on what those old memories are and how to abolish them completely from your energy field. So do not give up just yet. Keep reading!

- *Have a break from your desire.* If you have been focusing on your desire for some time now but nothing has come to fruition, and all you seem to be doing is taking one step forward and two steps backwards, then perhaps all that is needed is patience. Croft M. Pentz (author) once said, 'The secret of patience is to do something else in the meantime'. Manifestation takes patience and inspired action. Sometimes your dreams can manifest within a day of requesting while other times it takes years. It all depends on how big the desire is (the Universe will wait to see how much you *really* want it by providing you with some hurdles to overcome), how emotionally ready you are (for example, you may want to be a successful singer but you are afraid of success, or you want to be in a loving relationship but you find it hard to commit), and how much of a vibrational match you are to the desire (for example; looking after yourself by eating healthily and exercising, clearing away negativity, thinking positive thoughts, practicing gratitude for the life you already have, and clearing away the clutter in your home). If the process of manifesting your dreams all seems too much, then take a break. Do something else that you love to do and allow the Universe to do what it does best; which is to create miracles. Often times my desires have manifested because I removed myself from the equation. I just asked the Universe with specific detail about what I wanted, waited, and acted when I was inspired to act (you will learn how to receive inspiration from the Universe in the Intuitive Action section of this book, page 252).

You may even find that something better comes your way; something you may have not even realised was an option until it unexpectedly makes itself known to you. The key thing to remember here is that the Universe knows exactly what you want and the exact methods of how you can get it. It is up to you to trust that it has your back and be open and willing to the fact that it is not just *you* that is creating; you are actually co-creating with the Universe. You have to otherwise nothing will materialise. When it comes to turning your desire into reality, the Universe does about 99% of the work. It is as happy as a one year old diving into a smash cake if it has the chance to create—all it needs is a destination. No request on your behalf is too big or too small as long as your request is for your highest good and the highest good of others.

Affirmation: Regardless of what happens, I know I am in the exact place and the exact time that I need to be to manifest my dreams

- *Love and appreciate the struggles:* I know it may be hard to love and accept the struggles, particularly when you are faced with hurdles that create angst and frustration, but once you come to terms with *why* the struggles have arisen then you may come to love and appreciate them instead. Struggles teach us about our infinite power to create. They help us decide between what we want and what we do not want. Struggles fuel our determination and confirm to us that if we are willing to go through the pain then we are on the right track to fulfil our big dreams. Struggles create a sense of accomplishment when they are overcome, that is, they remind us of our inner power. In fact I believe that many of us shy away from our struggles not because we are afraid of failing but because we are afraid of finding out how truly powerful we are. So each time you come across a new hurdle that seems to stop you in your manifestation tracks, greet it with curiosity and love. You might like to ask the question, 'I wonder what you will teach me about myself and others this time around?' and be open to the response. This struggle has come into your life because it knows you are ready to shine your light. See it as your friend since it is an opportunity to let go of resistance. That is what the Universe needs you to do; identify the resistance and dissolve the resistance, *then* your dream will materialise.

- *Give up on your desire and move on.* I realise this may not be the kind of advice you are looking for, but if you find you are experiencing more heartache, frustration and sadness than you are joy, love and passion around a particular desire, then it may be a sign to move on particularly if you have worked at overcoming the struggles but with very little movement forward. When in doubt, apply the Pareto principle.

Also known as the 80/20 rule; 80% of the road to turning your desire into reality must be filled with passion and happiness while 20% of the road will likely be filled with struggle and pain. Sure there may be times when the 80/20 rule spikes and declines whereby you feel you are struggling with the manifestation process more than you are loving it, but majority of the time you should be feeling the 'happy feelings' 80% of the time. If the struggle turns into complete hatred and resentment then I recommend you give it a break or break up with the desire altogether. I believe that once you find yourself in a negative frame of mind whereby you place an unrealistic timeframe as to when your desires are to be born into reality, or you become greatly obsessed with the outcome, then you will be creating a vibration that matches desperation. This energetic resistance is not conducive to getting what you truly want. What you *will* get are more experiences that remind you of your desperation. So let it go. Then you are surrendering to the flow of the Universe and allowing it to work through you instead of against you. See this as an opportunity to learn from what you do not want so you can become specific about what you *do* want.

Chapter 10 – Who Do You Think You Are?

Be yourself; everyone else is already taken. – Oscar Wilde

Manifestation is a tricky process as not only does it take commitment and belief in the commitment, but it also takes belief in oneself about whether we are worthy enough to *receive* the reality of what we want. A low self-esteem can instantly block our ability to receive what we want simply because we may not believe we deserve it. We may believe that good things only happen to the lucky people. We may even believe that we should not want *more* because there are other people worse off—and wanting more turns us into greedy people. Essentially judgement is placed on ourselves as we consider our true desires and whether they will indeed manifest. I have written a little about this already but I feel now is the perfect time to dive deeper and explore this further by doing some much needed shadow work.

Shadow work is a way of bringing to light all the things we are ashamed of, have repressed, and denied and as such, have hidden away over many lifetimes in our subconscious mind (these are old memories). It was not that long ago that I would watch other spiritual people who I was inspired by to try to replicate their appearance and lifestyle. I would dress into my purple and yellow tie-dyed singlet top and navy and white elephant pants, and sit crossed legged chanting, 'Om' for 15 minutes because that is what I thought spiritual people did. I just wanted to be like them so badly because they seemed to have it altogether; so cool, calm and collected. And I wanted a piece of that! Little did I know that it was my shadow self telling me to compare myself to others because it believed that to be spiritual, I must act a certain way, talk a certain way, and look a certain way. My shadow self was convinced that it is unsafe to go out alone; 'Safety in numbers' it would say. It was no wonder I was constantly playing the compare game. The danger of this was that I would lose every time. I could never be like those people no matter how hard I tried because I am *not* those people. To be comfortable with who I am and actually love who I am, did not happen overnight. I did a lot of shadow work. It was uncomfortable to admit the lies I had been feeding myself about myself, but it was necessary to come to a place of peace within. This is still an ongoing process and if I am to be honest, I am unsure if it will ever end in this lifetime. But what else is there to do? Keep the demons in the dark or release them to the light?

The big light bulb moment from doing shadow work has been realising the essentialness of the work. If we all continue to ignore our deeper darker selves and pretend we are spiritually aligned and perfect, then we are only kidding ourselves. Our shadows (the old memories we have collected over so many lifetimes) will continue to govern our lives if we ignore them. We must 100% own them instead of repressing or ignoring them. I know this may all seem a little frightening, but it is so necessary if you want to realign your life to a state of abundance, love and joy.

So let us focus on one of the major shadows that are certain to be playing havoc in your life:

The belief that you are not good enough

It never surprises me when this particular shadow comes up in my client's lives because it seems to be so imbedded in most of our energetic fields; mine included.

Eat Cake

By reading this book, you have learned that the Universe picks up on not *just* your thoughts, feelings and values but also your beliefs. So it stands to reason that if you believe you are not good enough to receive your desires then you are telling the Universe, 'Wait! I'm not ready to get what I want. I'm not perfect enough, smart enough, in control enough, or liked enough by others. Don't send me anything that my heart deeply wants until I'm at that point where I think, feel and believe that I'm good enough and deserving enough!'

But what if your perception of yourself was different? What if you considered yourself to be worthy of abundance and prosperity? What if you knew wholeheartedly that the more you receive, the more opportunity you have to give to others in need? But even words in a book about self-empowerment and increasing your self-esteem level cannot always shift your perception of yourself, simply because your identity of who you are and what you deserve is not present in the conscious mind, but rather your subconscious mind where all the old memories; your shadows, lie. You will remember the subconscious mind plays a large part in how well you are able to manifest your true desires. So before you can expect to receive your heart's desires, you must first address your identity—the real 'you'.

Your perception of yourself creates your reality

Activity #9: Why It Has Not Happened Yet

Consider for a moment the very thing/s you desire and then ask yourself this question:

'Why hasn't it happened yet?'

Now complete an honest list of the <u>personal</u> reasons as to why it has not happened yet. Consider what conclusion you could make about yourself as to why your desires have not manifested into the physical. As you are doing this you may need to reflect on your past as evidence to support your opinion of yourself. For example you may say to yourself, 'It hasn't happened yet because people like me don't make that kind of money. I have never been rich so why should now be any different?' or 'It hasn't happened yet because I'm not worthy of being loved. I've been rejected before so there must be something wrong with me' or 'It hasn't happened yet because all my life I've been faced with struggle so I mustn't deserve what I want'.

It has not happen yet because....

_____
_____
_____
_____
_____
_____
_____
_____
_____

Eat Cake

Who Do You Think You Are?

_____
_____
_____
_____
_____
_____
_____
_____
_____
_____
_____
_____
_____
_____
_____
_____
_____

You should now have a clear picture of your own identity—what you truly believe about yourself. This belief about yourself is consistently projected out into the Universe on a daily basis without you even knowing it. So if we do not change this picture into one that supports your desires, then the Universe will continue to bring evidence into your life that confirms the very things you think, feel, value, and believe about yourself.

Manifestation of a magical life happens easily to people who believe they deserve it

Activity #10: Painting a Picture of the Real You

It is time to reshape your opinion about yourself to one who knows that you are deserving and worthy to receive all the limitless abundance, joy, love and prosperity that life has to offer. After all, that is exactly what the Universe wants for you.

1. Sit comfortably where you will not be distracted.

2. Close your eyes and take a deep breath in through your nose and breathe out slowly through pursed lips. Repeat until you feel completely relaxed, and then return to normal breathing.

3. Imagine the ideal you in the future. The 'future you' embodies the reality of your desire. So in other words, the future you is living the life you have dreamed of. The future you has already gone through the process of overcoming your old memories (limiting beliefs) and opinions about yourself and is now simply living your life from a loving and powerful perspective. No longer does your past influence your present. The future you is happy, excited, confident, grounded, passionate, spiritually abundant and loving every aspect of life.

4. Notice your appearance as the future you. What clothes are you wearing? What facial expression do you have? Who else is with you at this time? Where are you? Try to picture it as a movie, bringing as many sensory experiences (seeing, hearing, feeling, smelling and tasting) as you can into this visualisation. How do you feel? What are people saying to you? What sounds can you hear? Can you smell or taste anything? Spend some time with this image because this image is a reflection of the very best of you.

5. Now remove all the outside elements of the visualisation, and only focus on the 'future you'. Take as much time as you need to visualise an overall picture of the 'future you'. Make it so everything you are feeling, seeing, hearing, tasting, and smelling is intensified.

6. Now see this overall picture of you in the future positioned on a grid about a foot (thirty centimetres) from your face. This grid has lines running vertically and lines running horizontally.

7. With one hand, physically point to the location on the grid where the 'future you' is positioned. Place your hand back in your lap.

8. Open your eyes quickly, and close your eyes once more.

9. Now reflect on the list you had made earlier about the reasons why your desire has not happened yet. Take time to connect with the list which is a representation of your current opinion about who you are in your own eyes.

10. Now visualise the 'current you' appearing before you. This current you is a mirror image of everything you listed about the reasons why your desire has not happened yet. Take notice of what you are wearing, your facial expression, how you are feeling, and if you can smell or taste anything. Try to bring all your senses into this picture to create a truthful vision of you at this current time. Make it so everything you are feeling, seeing, hearing, tasting, and smelling is intensified to a point where it cannot be amplified any further.

Eat Cake

11. Now notice the grid appear before you once more. See that the current you is also placed on the same grid as 'future you'. Using your hand, physically point to the location on the grid where 'current you' is positioned—chances are it is a different location to 'future you'. Place your hand back in your lap.

12. Simply observe for a moment both the 'current you' and 'future you' on the grid.

13. Now with your hand, physically and slowly move 'future you' *toward* 'current you' on the grid. As you slowly move 'future you' toward 'current you', notice the appearance, feelings, sounds, smells and tastes associated with 'current you' start to change. Notice that as you move 'future you' closer to 'current you', the 'current you' is slowly morphing into the same appearance as 'future you'. The closer you move 'future you' toward 'current you', the more the 'current you' appears similar to 'future you'—the clothes are starting to look the same, the feelings are starting to feel the same, the facial expression is starting to look the same, the smells and tastes are starting to smell and taste the same. In fact, everything about 'current you' is starting to become identical to 'future you'.

14. Finally, move 'future you' on top of 'current you' on the grid so that both characters become one. 'Current you' and 'future you' become one and the same. The 'future you' is the *real* you right now.

15. Take a deep breath in and sit with this visualisation for a moment to allow all the senses of the *real* you to expand into every cell of your body.

16. When you are ready, you may open your eyes and take a few more deep breaths to ground yourself before returning to normal activities.

In this activity, your perception of yourself has changed. You have tapped into your own inner power, inner resources, and inner beliefs that were once originally lacking and allowed them to come to the forefront of your life. If you wish to test this, go back to Activity #9: *Why it Hasn't Happened Yet* (page 143) and read over the reasons why your desires have not manifested yet. Chances are you will be able to easily disprove your original thoughts of yourself and instead respond with the enlightened truth of who you *really* are.

You will now project this positive and enlightened new belief about yourself out into the world and the Universe. This means you never need to worry about whether your idea of yourself will affect the manifestation process because you truly believe you are deserving and worthy of everything you want. In fact, since your subconscious mind has been reprogrammed to expect good things, you will start to see a shift in your life that reflects goodness in every aspect of your life and the world around you.

Chapter 11 – Imagination is Your Limitation

Logic will take you from A to B. Imagination will take you everywhere. – Albert Einstein

Of all the challenges that come with manifestation, one of the hardest obstacles is whether or not you believe your desire will actually manifest. This belief does not come from whether you deserve to have what you want (you have already overcome that particular hurdle), but rather whether you believe miracles happen. I covered a little about this in Chapter 1—*The Power of You* (page 16) but you have come such a long way that I feel you are ready to go deeper.

Believe that anything is indeed possible and it is

Our logical mind is very quick to assume *how* things will happen in life by calculating the probability from our so called 'options'. The downside to this way of thinking is that we assume how things will present itself to us whilst ignoring other possible options that could have led us to fulfilling our desires much sooner.

Earlier in the book it was revealed that the RAS (Reticular Activating System) of your brain notices synchronistic signs sent from the Universe and relays the signs to your conscious mind for actioning. This is wonderful if you are open-minded about *how* the Universe will provide you with the resources and opportunities you need to fulfil your desires, but what happens if you only remain

Imagination is Your Limitation

focused on one trajectory? If you have your blinkers on, only seeing a certain route to get to your goals, then you might miss the other signs the Universe is trying to deliver.

Say for instance you desire a penthouse apartment near the beach. You check the estate prices and discover that to be able to afford your penthouse apartment you would need at least $1.5 million dollars. This of course assumes that the way in which you will receive the penthouse is by buying it—but what about the other options? Perhaps someone may gift you with the apartment or perhaps you might win the apartment in a competition. These are other additional possibilities, but they do not include *all* the possibilities. Yet if you do not believe that there are indeed other possibilities then it is likely you have an old memory running in your subconscious mind of,

'What I want isn't possible'

Let us explore what *is* possible. Right now, as you are reading this book, you are experiencing everything from a third-dimensional (3D) plane. Everything around you is in 3D. That means that every object you see before you seems to be physically present because there is an X, Y, and Z axis, for example, width, depth and height. But this is where I invite you to open your mind to other possibilities and go beyond what this 3D world tells you (and the people in it).

You are not *limited* by living in a 3D world. There are other worlds beyond here—the next one of course is the fourth dimension. Most people cannot physically see the fourth dimension with their naked eye (although some can, for example, those who can see ghosts) which is why it might be difficult to believe that such a dimension exists. Yet strangely enough, we are always tapping into this dimension without even knowing it. How? We think, we have ideas, and we imagine. They are all fourth dimensional—consequently, on the fourth dimension, that are *no* limitations of possibilities.

This new information will change your perception of *what* is possible. Take a look around you—the buildings, the furniture, the floors, the windows, the cars; they all originate from the fourth dimension. They were all ideas before they became physical things. Essentially, anything you desire must first come from the fourth dimension and yet, since there are no limitations in this dimension, what you want is already waiting for you. This may seem difficult to believe because for many people, 'believing is seeing', yet there are many things we use in our everyday life that are fourth dimensional besides our imagination.

Time is fourth dimensional. It plays a big role in our lives yet we cannot see time; we simply know what it is by checking our watch or looking at the position of the sun for instance. Numbers are also fourth dimensional. We can put three candles on a birthday cake which represents the number '3'. We can even put a candle that is in the shape of the number '3', yet we have not *actually* seen the number 3 or any other number because it is in the fourth dimension. Weight is also in the fourth dimension. If you were to carry a bag of potatoes weighing 2 kilograms, it is likely you would know how heavy that is, but you cannot know what weight is because you cannot see it. It would seem that *seeing* is not always *believing*—and this relates to the way in which you are able to manifest your desires. You cannot manifest what you want if you do not believe there are other manifestation possibilities beyond what you *know*. Once you believe that anything is possible, then you will expand your awareness and be open to the limitless possibilities waiting for you right now.

For anything to manifest into your life, you must first believe it will, no matter how 'far-fetched' it may seem.

Activity #11: Discovering Whether You Truly Believe Your Desire Will Manifest

Just like your unique fingerprint, you also have your own unique energy system. Your nervous system is a 59.5-kilometre antenna which allows subtle frequencies to move through. While electroencephalograms (EEGs) and magnetic resonance imaging (MRI) can pick up vital information about the body, they cannot target the more subtle frequencies. The subtle frequencies can be targeted in a very different way. Every thought and feeling produces a certain response in your nervous system which in turn affects your motor responses (movement of your body).

This phenomenon is the basis of kinesiology (muscle monitoring). Kinesiology uses muscle testing where a question is asked, or a statement is made, and then a particular muscle in the body is tested for strength or weakness. If a question is asked for which the answer is true, then the muscle will be strong. If a question is asked for which the answer is false, then the muscle will be weak. The same goes for the body's posture. The body is naturally drawn to a positive or truth statement, while repelling itself away from something that reflects a negative or false statement. This is known as the Sway Method and it can be used to tap directly into your energy system and the subconscious mind to discover the *true* thoughts and feelings you have around a particular desire.

In this activity you will be using the Sway Method to determine whether you truly believe your dream will manifest.

1. Before you begin drink a glass of water as a lack of water in the body can affect the results.

Imagination is Your Limitation

2. Stand or sit upright with both feet pointing directly forward.

3. Relax your body and place your hands by your sides. Position your chin to the floor with eyes looking down.

4. Now say out loud a statement that you know is true for you; for example, 'My name is [*say your real name*].' Sense your body's reaction to the statement. For this 'yes' response, you should feel your body being gently pulled forward or pushed backward (or even to the side), as if you were falling forward or backward with your feet remaining static. So take note which direction your body sways. You may also feel peace and calm, knowing the statement is the truth for you.

5. Now realign your body so that you are standing or sitting upright once more.

6. Now say a statement that you know is false for you; for example, 'My name is [*say a name that is not your real name*].' Sense your body's reaction to the statement. For this 'no' response, you should feel your body moving in the opposite direction to the 'yes' response your body gave you, that is, you may feel it being gently pushed backward if the 'yes' response pulled you forward, or your body may feel as though it is being pulled forward if the 'yes' response pushed you backward. You may also feel a sensation of uneasiness and stress, knowing that the statement is untrue for you.

> Gentle note: The direction of your body's movement may be different. For example, your body may push backward

> for a 'yes' response and forward for a 'no' response. Or it may sway to the right for a 'yes' and to the left for a 'no' or vice versa. Everybody is different so try to say some other statements that represent true and false for you to gauge which direction your body will move in its response to 'yes' and 'no'.

7. Realign your body so you are standing or sitting upright once more.

8. Now that you have discovered which direction your body will move to represent a 'yes' response and a 'no' response, say the following statement out loud: 'I do not believe my desire of [*describe your desire*] will actually manifest.' Allow your body to react to the statement and take notice which direction it sways to represent a 'yes' or 'no' response.

9. Now realign your body so you are standing or sitting upright once more.

10. Say the following statement out loud: 'I believe completely and without a doubt that my desire of [*describe your desire*] will manifest.' Allow your body to react to the statement and take notice which direction it sways to represent a 'yes' or 'no' response.

11. Return to your normal posture.

On completing this activity, you should have a clear idea of whether you truly believe your dreams will manifest into reality.

Imagination is Your Limitation

Other Self Muscle Tests You Can Do.

If you had difficulty with the Sway Method, I have included some other ways of self muscle testing. Try each method and see which one you are most comfortable with and of which gives you the most accurate results. The two statements to focus on (after you have ascertained how the body reacts to statements that you know are true and false) are:

i. 'I do not believe my desire of [*describe your desire*] will actually manifest', and

ii. 'I believe completely and without a doubt that my desire of [*describe your desire*] will manifest.'

Ensure you have drunk plenty of water prior to performing each method. During each method keep your chin in line with the floor and eyes looking down.

- **The Finger Loop Method:** Stand with your chin parallel to the floor and eyes looking down. With your non-dominant hand positioned up near your face, create a circle by touching one of your finger tips (e.g. middle finger tip) with the tip of your thumb. Then with your dominant hand, place your index finger into the circle. As you say a statement that is true for you (such as your real name), move your index finger against the circle bond (the point where the thumb and finger joins) to try to break it. Since you are stating something that is true, the bond should not break. As you say a statement that is false for you (such as saying for example, 'My name is Cheese Cake'), move your finger against the circle bond and it should break which means the statement is weak and does not ring true to your subconscious mind.

- **The Raised Finger Method:** Place your hand flat on your leg or a table and lift up one finger. With your other hand you will be pressing down on the raised finger after you have made a 'yes' or 'no' statement. When you say a statement that your subconscious mind believes to be true or a 'yes' then the raised finger will remain raised even if you attempt to press down on it. When you say a statement that your subconscious mind believes to be false or a 'no' then the raised finger will drop as you press down on it; that is, it will become weakened.

- **The Double Circle Method:** Similar to the Finger Loop Method but instead you will be creating a circle on both hands that interlink one another like a chain. Hence, using any finger you want, create a circle on your left hand with one of your left fingers touching the left thumb tip. Next, create a circle with your right hand using one of your right fingers touching the right thumb tip. Join these two circles together so they become interlocked. Then as you make a true or false statement, move one of the hands to try to disengage the lock. If the circles break then the statement is false or weak. If the circles remain joined after making a statement then you will know the statement has revealed a 'yes' or 'true' response.

- **The Sticky Smooth Method:** This is an unusual method but you may resonate with it particularly if you are out in public since you can do it discretely. Using any finger on any hand, rub the fingertip around in circles (it does not matter

Imagination is Your Limitation

which direction) on your thumb and say a positive statement and then a negative one. As you rub by saying a positive statement (e.g. 'My name is [*say your real name*]') then you should feel a smooth sensation between your finger and thumb. There should be no difficultly in rubbing the fingers around in a circular movement. As you rub your fingers around in circles and say a false statement (e.g. 'My name is [*say a name that is not your real one*]') then you should feel a sticky or perspiration-type sensation between your finger and thumb which will make it difficult to move the fingers in a circular motion. Cool huh!

- **The Scissor Method:** Make the shape of scissors with one hand (index finger and middle finger separated so they look like scissors) and with your other hand, try to push the two fingers together as you say a positive statement and a false statement. When you say a positive statement, the scissor fingers should stay relatively locked open / strong. When you say a statement that is false, the scissor fingers should become weakened and collapse.

- **The Pendulum Method:** For this method you will need a pendulum such as a crystal pendulum. If you do not have a crystal pendulum you can also use a necklace. Rest your elbow on a flat surface to keep your arm steady as you hold the pendulum. Initially the pendulum should be fairly still. When you say a positive statement, you will notice the pendulum moves a specific way. It may move forwards and backwards, or it may move clockwise or counter clockwise. It is important to realise that you are not forcing the pendulum to move. All you are doing is keeping your elbow and hands nice and still, however it is your energy that is working through the pendulum and making it move. Make a note of the direction the pendulum moves for the positive response. With your other hand, stop the pendulum moving to start the method again. When you say a false statement you will undoubtedly see the pendulum move in a different direction to the positive statement. Take notice of which direction this is. Once you have noted the way the pendulum moves for a 'yes' and 'no' response, you can ask it just about anything, including whether you believe your desire will manifest.

Gentle Note: If you get a strong response for both a 'yes' and 'no' statement, or a weak response for both a 'yes' and 'no' statement, then it may be because of dehydration. It is so important that you stay hydrated so drink plenty of water. Another reason is the attachment around the statement. Sometimes deep down we do not want to find out the answer. If you have drunk plenty of water and are still getting unusual results, then do some deep breathing exercises to re-centre your mind and body such as the Alternate Nostril Breathing Technique (see below). You may also like to explore other relaxation options such as taking an Epsom Salt bath, using an oil diffuser with your favourite essential oil, or listening to soothing music.

The Alternate Nostril Breathing Technique

1. Sit comfortably with your spine erect and shoulders relaxed. Keep a gentle smile on your face.

2. Place your left hand on the left knee, palms open to the sky or you may wish to gently press the thumb and index finger tips together.

> 3. Close your eyes and remember that during this exercise, you will be taking long, deep and smooth breaths in and out without any effort or force.
>
> 4. With your right hand, place the tip of the index finger and middle finger in between the eyebrows, the ring finger and little finger on the left nostril, and the thumb on the right nostril. You will use the ring finger and little finger to open or close the left nostril and thumb to open and close the right nostril.
>
> 5. Press your thumb down on the right nostril and breathe out gently through the left nostril.
>
> 6. Now breathe in from the left nostril and then press the left nostril gently with the ring finger and little finger. Removing the right thumb from the right nostril, breathe out from the right. Breathe in from the right nostril and exhale from the left. You have now completed one round. Continue to do this for at least nine more rounds.

If by doing the self muscle test resulted in a negative response, that is, your body indicated, 'No' to the statement, 'I believe completely and without a doubt that my desire of [*describe your desire*] will manifest' then continue reading this chapter. If your body indicated that you do in fact believe without a shadow of a doubt that your dream will manifest then continue on to the next chapter of this book.

We do not get what we want,
instead we get what we expect.

Eat Cake

There are two ways you can shift the old memories around your disbelief of your dream manifesting into reality; you can practice the Ho'oponopono prayer from Activity #2: *Releasing the Old Memories* (page 62) or if you prefer to use visualisation you can continue onto the next activity. I would like to add that neither technique is more or less powerful. I believe that we are all on unique spiritual paths so I like to include various mindset techniques to suit your own unique personality and journey. As the Chinese proverb goes, 'There are many different paths to the top of the mountain, but the view is always the same'.

In Chapter 7—*Building Momentum* (page 100) I wrote about the importance of incorporating the visualisation practice into your daily routine. As you will remember, the idea of visualisation is that you simply envisage yourself playing out the part of what it would be like to *have* the very thing you desire. Visualisation is a third dimensional experience where you give your desire more shape, colour, depth, and emotion to make it as realistic as possible. This is still a very powerful technique and if you are finding that it is bringing you some wonderful results, then by all means please continue to do it. However, visualisation can still limit you by what you *think* is possible. How can you leave all limitations, old memories, and a boxed mindset behind and enter a world where you know that *anything* is possible and that you can manifest from a place of limitless possibilities?

Enter the fourth dimension and you will see that *anything* is possible. You will have a unique opportunity to experience it as if you were living it in the physical plane. And when you realise that what you want in life is possible then you will start to attract it on the physical plane. You will bring all the feelings you experienced in the Fourth Dimension back to the physical world. You will *know* what it feels

Imagination is Your Limitation

like to have your desires already present in your life and with that knowing comes believing. You will then expect (yes, expect!) that your desires will manifest. No more doubting and no more worrying. And of course, with no doubt and worry, you will be sending a clear signal (a specific vibration) to the Universe that you expect that what you want in your life will manifest. The Universe has no choice other than to match your specific vibration with something of the same vibration—a physical representation of your original thought / idea / imagination. But this can only be done on the fourth dimension.

Activity #12: Journey to the Fourth Dimension

The following is a meditation script to help you enter the fourth dimension. You may wish to have someone who you feel comfortable with to read it to you as you participate in the activity, or you can simply read through the script a few times to familiarise yourself with it before actively doing it.

Before you begin, choose the desire you wish to manifest into your life; preferably the one that you had chosen in Activity #11: *Discovering Whether You Truly Believe Your Desire Will Manifest* (page 154) that gave you a negative muscle test result. Keep this desire in your mind as you begin this exercise.

Meditation: Journey to the Fourth Dimension

1. Find yourself a quiet place to sit. Turn off your phone and dim the lights. This is your time. A time to reconnect and experience the life you thought could only remain a dream.

2. Take a moment to make sure that you are warm enough and that you are seated comfortably. Rest your hands loosely in your lap and close your eyes.

3. Take a long, slow, deep breath in........hold it for a moment, and then slowly exhale. Just allow any tension to melt away as you gradually relax more and more deeply with each breath.

Imagination is Your Limitation

4. Take another long, slow, deep breath in...hold it, and then exhale. Empty your lungs completely with your out-breath.

5. Take a third deep breath in. Take your time. Hold it for a moment, and then let it go. Already you are beginning to drift into a state of deep relaxation.

6. Return your breathing to a normal rate that is comfortable for you—feeling completely at peace and totally relaxed.

7. As you continue to allow yourself this time of deep relaxation, I would like for you to think about your life, specifically the area of your life you want to change the most. Think of that area of your life, and say out loud, or in your mind...... "I want....." and finish the sentence with what you want in your life. For example you may want more money, more happiness, more freedom to do what you want, or more love. Simply choose what you want more of in your life now.

8. Now that you have defined what you want *more* of in your life, focus now on how having it would change your life. How would your life be different if you had it in your life right now?

9. During this exercise you will be experiencing what your heart really wants. If you chose that you want more money in your life, then you will be experiencing what it is actually like to have more money in your life—what remarkable experiences you will have when you have an

abundance of wealth. This is not a, 'It's too good to be true' exercise—this is your new form of realty and in a moment you will be experiencing this new reality in the fourth dimension. Realise that this dimension is boundless—anything is possible here so you will easily and naturally expect miracles as you move into this new plane of existence.

10. The fourth dimension is where your ideas and imagination come from. And in the physical world, the world you are in right now as you continue to breathe naturally and peacefully, you can turn your ideas and anything you imagine into physical reality. So as you easily enter the fourth dimension during this exercise, you will be setting your intentions and expectations for what you want in your life right now.

11. And you will easily receive what you want because the fourth dimension is a plane of limitless opportunities. Lower level energies that you feel in the physical world such as fear, poor health, lack of abundance and despair, do not exist on the fourth dimension. Only endless peace and love exist.

12. Realise that in a moment, by entering the fourth dimension, you will also experience the same peace and love because that is your true essence. And since you will be moving away from lower level energies and into a higher vibration of love and peace, you will then expand your awareness and see that anything *is* truly possible. Anything you want in your physical world, you can have in the fourth dimension. And when you experience it in

Imagination is Your Limitation

the fourth dimension, you can easily bring the same experience into the physical world because you *command it to* in your own loving way. When you set your intentions and expectations that what you want in your life will soon *be in your life*, then the Universe has no option other than to lovingly give you what you want.

13. And so the fourth dimension is your way of showing the Universe your intentions and expectations. It is your way of experiencing what you want in the fourth dimension, and then soon enough, you will experience it in your physical world as well.

14. So as you continue to breathe naturally and peacefully, I would also like for you to focus on the top of your head, and as you focus on the top of your head, I want you to just begin to imagine, sense, feel or trust that there is going to be a nice deep wave of relaxation that is going to begin to work through your body and your mind. You can imagine this deep wave of relaxation as your favourite healing colour, so you can watch this happening or you can just sense, feel or trust that this does happen—however it works for you is absolutely fine.

15. Focusing now on the top of your head as you sense a deep wave of relaxation begin to move down from the top of your head, moving down through the forehead, feeling it move behind the eyes, through the eyes, and behind the eyelids. Feel it moving down into the hundreds of tiny muscles in the cheeks, face and jaw. Feel it just gently moving over the throat, towards the back of your neck and down to the very base of your spine,

relaxing, releasing and just letting go. This wave moves out into every muscle, cell and fibre of your back as you just continue to relax deeply and effortlessly.

16. Feel the deep wave of relaxation move over your shoulders, chest and stomach and all the way back down your arms and to the very tips of your fingers.

17. Feel the wave move through the hips, legs, knees, calves and all the way down to the tips of the toes, taking you twice as deep, twice as relaxed. Feel the wave move from the toes to the head and right back down to the toes again.

18. Beginning now to feel the support of the very thing you are sitting or lying on. Feel how it is supporting the body effortlessly. And with every breath you can sense your body sinking down and deeper down into that support. Letting your body become heavier and heavier as the higher mind becomes more clear, more alert and more receptive. Feel yourself now begin to just mentally move higher and away from this room. Higher and higher into the distance toward a beautiful meadow with a circle of magical trees growing beyond. Sense yourself now floating down towards this meadow without any resistance to the Earth itself. Feel yourself now in that meadow with those long blades of grass that float around your legs and feet, where the weather is a perfect temperature, and where you feel completely calm, safe and relaxed.

Imagination is Your Limitation

19. You notice that to reach the magical circle of trees there is a single pathway to take. Begin to just feel yourself now take those few steps along the pathway feeling the ground underneath you, feeling the path. As you enter that magical circle of trees there is one tree in particular that stands out to you, and as you take a step over to the tree, you imagine taking a finger and just running it down the bark of that tree. As that happens the most wonderful healing energy comes from that tree and moves into every level of your being.

20. And take a deep breath in and out. Allowing that wonderful healing energy to come through every level of your being, deeper and deeper relaxed. And as you look around the circle of trees that stand so tall above you, supporting you and protecting you, you become aware of a staircase that appears in the centre of the trees. This staircase beckons and calls you with its beauty and love. You instantly feel compelled and excited to explore where these steps lead.

21. You move to the top of the first step and peer down to the bottom, sensing that there are 20 steps. You begin move down each step 20, 19, relaxing deeper, 18, 17, moving effortlessly down, 16, 15, 14, 13, 12, relaxing easier and deeper, 11, 10, 9, 8, deeper and deeper relaxed, 7, 6, breathing deeper still, 5, 4, nearly to the bottom, 3, 2 and 1. Taking a deep breath in and out as you reach the bottom.

22. And in this relaxed state you become aware of a golden door appearing just ahead of you. This is the most

beautiful door you have ever seen. You can feel this door emanating love toward you. You can hear angelic sounds that come with simply looking at this golden door. You can feel the loving energy pulling you toward it and you can hear yourself saying, 'Yes, I am ready to move toward you', knowing that as you do, you are completely safe. In fact this is the safest of energies that you have ever felt. This energy reminds you that you are connected to something much bigger than you could ever imagine in the physical world.

23. You can sense yourself moving towards the golden door. You can see your feet walking towards this loving energy that is calling you. You are experiencing profound peace and joy. It is the most beautiful experience you have ever had.

24. You have reached the golden door and you can see your fingers of your hand wrapping around the doorhandle. As you feel the pleasantly warm door-knob in your hand, you become aware that the loving energy that this door and door-handle are vibrating at is now travelling up through your hand, through your arm, and moving into and throughout your entire body. Any lower level energy of fear and stress that were once stored in your body are no longer there. You look down at your body and you can see it glowing—it is a pure bright white light that is illuminating with love. You can feel the love within you, moving through every cell of your body. You can feel that your heart is bursting with this miracle of love as you smile at this new sensation— this new form of being.

25. And with this new feeling that has filled you up, you realise that the only thing you need to do is surrender and let go. If you are finding resistance with this, simply say, 'I am ready to let go and allow my spirit to lead'.

26. And as you set your intention to surrender, you watch as you begin to turn the doorhandle, hearing a click of the latch as it unlocks. Slowly you open the door, curious and excited to know what is behind it. What wondrous things are waiting for you behind this golden door?

27. The loving energy within you feels electric. It seems to be getting stronger and stronger. You have never felt such powerful love until now. It is the familiar feeling of coming home because it feels like your spiritual home. The angelic sounds you heard when you first noticed the golden door are beautifully louder now, calling you closer as you start to move through the door way. As you place one foot in front of the other, you notice that your foot no is longer bound by your physical body, instead it appears clear and translucent. This does not bother you, in fact you welcome it because it allows you to finally see past your physical skin. As you focus on your translucent foot, you can see the beautiful glow within. This loving energy that is glowing so brightly brings you warmth, a kind of warmth that is comfortable and blissful. The transparency of your foot is now travelling up your leg as you step further into the new dimension. Your leg is no longer bound by the physical body; it too is transparent. You can see through your leg and connect with the beautiful glow within; pure loving energy that is your true essence. Your leg and foot feel liberated; uninhibited by

the physical body. This feeling is so joyous to you that you make the choice to step fully into this new dimension—the fourth dimension. You take a step, and another step, and another, and suddenly you are no longer stepping as you would in the physical world but rather you are floating with complete control of where you want to go and how you want to do it. Everything you have ever wanted to experience, you can here.

28. You can hear yourself squealing with excitement and joy. The beauty of this place is breathtakingly stunning. The vibrant colours and textures before you are awe-inspiring. What you imagine to be the most beautiful scenery you could ever encounter is right before you. Something you thought you would never experience, or did not even think existed, is right in front of you—waiting for you; calling you to embrace it.

29. Allow any kind of beautiful scenery that you want to see and feel to appear in this dimension. And witness how easy it is for it to appear. You did not have to do a thing other than to imagine and believe it would. There was no resistance in the way it simply and easily appeared before you. It just came to you because you wanted it to.

30. And with this scenery that you have just created, you can now feel it. You can sense how the textures feel as you interact with this landscape. You can feel the texture is beautifully smooth or beautifully rough. It feels soft, hard, sticky, slippery, warm, cold, or a combination of sensations. Whatever you feel, simply notice that it is igniting complete pleasure within you. Something you

Imagination is Your Limitation

thought you would never experience is happening right now and you are filled with gratitude for this opportunity.

31. You notice too that your other senses are tuning into this beautiful landscape. You can hear your surroundings; what you want to hear the most, the very thing that makes your heart sing, can be heard right now in this landscape. And as you are interacting with this landscape, doing what you want to do, feeling complete bliss and gratitude for the fourth dimension, you also realise that now is a good time to experience something else you want to experience—something else you would like to take with you to the physical world because that is the reason why you have come here, to joyfully experience what you want to without resistance and fear.

32. So take this time, and focus on what it is you want *most* in your life right now—your true heart's desire. However instead of focusing on a material thing, simply focus on an experience. So if you wanted money in the form of coins and notes which of course are material things of the physical world, then consider what wonderful experiences you want to have as a result of the money in your life. And as you are focusing on what you want right now, your biggest desire that you want in your life right now, you can see it appearing all around you. You are in the centre of this experience, watching it all unfold before you. You can hear yourself announcing to the Universe,

'I'm here in the fourth dimension to experience what I want…this or something better'

33. And as you make this announcement watch what you want in your life continue to effortlessly come into view so now it is your reality. See how easy it has appeared all around you. Realise that this is not an image, it is real life within the fourth dimension—and you are in it. Do not see this from an outsider's perspective as if you are watching a movie. Realise that you are right in the centre of this experience and you are living it just as you would with any experience. So go live it.

34. See how the experience and everything relating to the experience; the scenery, people, sounds, colours and textures, and the smells surrounding you manifest beneath you, above you, and all around you.

35. What are you actively doing in this experience? Are you moving? Staying still? Creating something? Speaking? Holding something? Watching? Driving? Whatever it is, feel yourself actively participating in this experience.

36. If there are people you want in this experience, then invite them in and see them becoming a part of this experience, actively participating as they normally do.

37. Where are you in this experience? What things are around you? What can you see? What can you hear? What can you feel? What can you taste or smell?

38. Bring all your senses into this experience so that you can fully appreciate how it feels, how it looks, how it sounds, how it smells and how it tastes. This experience is something you have wanted and it is finally here. It is

Imagination is Your Limitation

real. You are living this experience in the fourth dimension. It is so naturally easy.

39. Continue to focus on what you desire to experience that is your life on this plane and appreciate that you're participating in it right now.

40. Continue to notice what it looks like.

41. Continue to notice what it feels like both through touch and how it makes you feel emotionally.

42. Continue to notice any sounds.

43. And if appropriate continue to notice what it smells like. Notice what it tastes like. Do this for as long as you wish.

44. Realise that if there is more than one experience that you want to have then you can easily move into the fourth dimension anytime you wish to take part in it. There are no limits here; nothing is impossible. Yet the only condition in this dimension is that what you want comes from a state of love and peace, as does everything in this dimension. So in each experience that you take part in, you realise that you are also experiencing the limitless energy of love and peace. You have surrendered yourself completely in this plane and feel liberated from doing so. You expect what you want in your life to come to you naturally and easily because that is how the fourth dimension works. This is a wonderful world of limitless possibilities and you are here completely engaged and immersed in it right now.

45. As you are actively in this experience right now, realise that this is the same experience you would also have in the physical world—the third dimension of Earth. The difference of course is that you are not bound by fear. And yet fear is only present when we do not believe something is possible. But you have already proven that fear is false by experiencing what you want on the fourth dimension. And since you have expanded your awareness and seen that what you want in life is easily achievable in the fourth dimension, you can return to the physical world and expect that what you want in life will come to you naturally. Remember that *everything* in the third dimension came from the fourth dimension.

46. That is how it has always been. Because every single thought and idea has come from this fourth dimensional plane and then manifested into the physical third dimensional plane in some way. You, and what you want in life, are no exception to this because that is the way energy works, and you are energy at the primary level.

47. So affirm to yourself,

> *'What I want in my life is already in my life right now— and so it is done'*

48. Simply sit with this realisation for a moment and breathe deeply.

49. In a minute you will be returning to the physical third dimensional world but it will be different. You have

experienced your heart's desire in the fourth dimension and you whole heartedly believe it to be possible. You have experienced it, touched it, seen it, heard it, smelt it and tasted it. How wonderful it going to be when you are back in the physical world, experiencing what you want in life on a physical level. Moving all your knowledge and everything you sensed from the fourth dimension and bringing it all into the physical world of Earth. This is such a remarkable opportunity.

50. So as you look around you in the fourth dimension, you can feel a great sense of gratitude for this plane; this expansiveness of limitless possibilities. This is where you will go to carry out what you want in life and then bring the experience into your physical world. And so you imagine the beautiful glowing door you had once stepped through easily appearing before you. You can hear the angelic sound emanating from this door. Feel the endless vibration of love pulsating from its frame. It beckons you toward it and you follow; effortlessly and gently. You mentally ask the door to open and it does with ease. Take a deep breath in as you walk through the door. See your feet, your legs, your hands, arms, and torso transforming from being transparent to taking on a physical form; your physical body. You become aware of your shoulders, your neck, and your head—all a part of your physical body. Yet you do not feel limited by this because you know you can easily enter through the golden door again. You appreciate this opportunity to live your life through a physical reality and Earth allows you to do that. You turn and see that the glowing door that is the gateway to the fourth dimension has closed, but you realise you only

need to come back to this place and easily enter through the door. It has and always will be here for you when you need it.

51. You see the beautiful staircase before you with the 20 steps, and you begin to move up each one effortlessly, counting 1, 2, 3, 4, moving higher, 5, 6, 7, becoming more alert and aware, 8, 9, 10, 11, 12, over half way now, 13, 14, 15, 16, 17, moving closer to the top, 18, 19, and 20. You reach the top of the steps, back to the lush green grassed meadow with the circle of magical trees. It is time now to prepare to come back completely into the third dimension. The place where you will bring all that you have experienced in the fourth dimensional plane and turn it into a physical representation of the experience. Now you believe and know that anything is possible.

52. Take a deep breath as you bring yourself back to this present time, this place, and this day. Remembering all that you have seen, felt and experienced. Prepare yourself now to return. Returning to this time, this place and this day. Bringing with your this new awareness and understanding. Bringing with you inspiration and insights. Coming back and becoming aware of your body. Coming back and becoming aware of this room; grounding and reconnecting. Realising and knowing that what you have just seen, felt and experienced will stay with you in this third dimensional place and it will help you to manifest your heart's desires. Coming all the way back now, 1, 2, 3, coming up, 4, 5, all the way back now, feeling your body fully, 6, 7, moving your body, 8, 9, and 10, moving your body, breathing deeply, awakening fully

Imagination is Your Limitation

and letting your eyes open when you feel ready to. Be here now.

Now it is time to test how the fourth dimension has changed your mindset from disbelieving your heart's desires will manifest to believing they will. Repeat Activity #11: *Discovering Whether You Truly Believe Your Dream Will Manifest* (page 154) and see if your body indicates that it *does* believe. If your body indicates that it is now storing the positive belief that your dreams will manifest, that is, your body gave a 'yes' response, then you can move onto Chapter 14—*Working With the Light* (page 227). However if your body gave a 'no' response then read on.

I live by the techniques in this book. These techniques at the exact ones I have used countless times to clear my lower negative vibrations (old memories) and they truly work for me. I would not write a book about them if they did not work! But even so, there is always a chance that despite your best efforts to manifest your heart's desires, they just do not come to the party. There are two major reasons why this can happen:

1. There is a far greater plan for you that will lead to an even better experience however it takes time for the Universe to set this up, so sit back, relax and let it unfold, or

2. There are still some major heavy duty old memories still lurking in the shadows that are sabotaging your manifestation journey.

I like to encourage focusing on the old memories first because then you know you are clear of the unnecessary 'crap'. I have written a number of times in this book that it is not your words that the

Eat Cake

Universe hears, but rather your frequency. The reason I write about this often is because it is *so* important that you understand this. Your frequency that the Universe listens to is a combination of your thoughts, feelings, values and beliefs. When they are all synchronised to the very thing you desire, that is, there is a vibrational match between your own frequency and the frequency of your desire, then your desire will manifest into reality. If there are still old memories sabotaging this frequency somehow in the way you think, feel, what you believe and value, then no amount of wishful thinking will conjure up your dream life. This is why I recommend releasing the old memories before sitting back and waiting for something to happen. Then you will open yourself up to inviting all the positive goodness that is waiting for you. Because what you want is already in existence, you just have to align your frequency to receive it.

Chapter 12 – The Mother's of All Old Memories

The only thing limiting us in life is our belief that there are limits.
– Unknown

So far I have covered what limiting beliefs are; old memories stored in our subconscious mind that are the primary culprits of why our heart's desires do not manifest. You have already realised by experiencing your heart's desires in the fourth dimension that it is completely possible to experience in the third dimension, since everything initially comes from the fourth dimensional plane. So why does your body continue to say that it does not believe your dreams will manifest? Let me introduce you to the mother's of all old memories. These low-life memories will sabotage your belief about whether you can actually *change* your life. They are old memories *about* old memories, old memories about *creating* reality, old memories about your *ability* to create your reality, and old memories about your *ability to change* your beliefs.

Some years ago I was doing one-on-one consultations as a holistic health therapist. A particular client came to see me for help on quitting smoking. She had tried everything; cold turkey, patches, hypnosis, counselling; but nothing seemed to work. She had come to me because I offered alternative methods outside the norm. I was convinced that after doing a few sessions there would be an improvement but to both our dismay, there was little to no change. I could not understand it. We had great rapport (which I believe is essential for any kind of healing to take place) and we were using techniques I had used countless times before on other clients with great success. Yet for some reason this time was different. Naturally all sorts of old memories surfaced for me during this time; 'I am not good enough, the client will think I am a fraud because their issue does not seem to be improving, what I do does not make a positive difference...blah, blah, blah'. The experience itself was wonderful as it was an opportunity to clear more old memories I was harbouring in the subconscious mind, and funnily enough, once I did that, inspiration came through. I realised that the one thing I had not done was check whether the client actually *believed* in the therapy techniques we were using. The next time she came for a session, I checked her belief about the therapeutic techniques and whether she believed she could in fact quit smoking. Hallelujah! Her body indicated that she did not believe the techniques will work for her and that it is not possible to heal so quickly and easily. Naturally we cleaned those beliefs, replaced them with divine truth, and happily moved forward. You see those old memories can seriously affect the manifestation outcome!

So let us uncover whether you are harbouring any of the mother of old memories in your energetic system so that you can clear them and move forward on your manifestation journey with ease.

Activity #13: Revealing the Mother's of all Old Memories

Before you can move forward on your manifestation journey, you will need to alter the mother's of all old memories from your energetic system because these are the major players stopping your manifestation success.

As you read over each old memory, take notice of your reaction and whether you resonate with one or more. In fact I encourage you to use the selected Self Muscle Test (page 154) that you resonate the most with, and recite each of the statements to test whether your body indicates a 'yes' or 'no' response. Take note of the old memories your body agrees with so you can cleanse them in a moment.

THE MOTHER'S OF ALL OLD MEMORIES

Manifestation works for everyone but me:
- Even if I change my beliefs, my world will not change.
- No matter how hard I try, nothing ever works for me.
- I do not have what it takes to change my beliefs, so how can I expect to change my life?!
- I do not have the ability to create a life that I actually want
- It is hard to create what I want
- I am not powerful enough to change my beliefs

Creating the life I want is not possible or easy:
- We don't really create our own realities so therefore I cannot create my own
- I cannot change my beliefs, it is impossible
- It is difficult to create my reality

Eat Cake

- It is hard to change my beliefs
- I cannot easily discover my subconscious beliefs
- I cannot change my beliefs about _____ (myself, money, love, men, women, health, work, other people, etc)
- The beliefs I have make me who I am, and I cannot change
- Changing my beliefs does not happen quickly and easily. It has to be a long and difficult process for it to work

It is wrong/unspiritual to create a life I want:
- I do not have the right to change my beliefs, it is wrong
- I will be punished by a higher source if I change my beliefs
- Only the Universe can change my beliefs, I am powerless
- It is unspiritual to change my beliefs
- It is unspiritual to want more than what I have
- Only the Universe can create my reality, I cannot have any part in it
- It is blasphemous to believe I can create my own reality, who am I to believe I can?!

I am not ready:
- I am not ready to change my beliefs about _____ (money, love, men, women, health, work, other people, etc)
- I am not ready for the success that will happen when I change my beliefs
- I can only have the realities I desire after I clean *all* my blocks / old memories
- I am not healed enough to create my reality
- If I successfully create my own reality the responsibility of that would be too much for me to handle

The Mother's of All Old Memories

- I am not (old, young, wise, capable, seasoned, experienced, smart, etc.) enough to create my own reality
- I am not good enough just yet to get what I want
- I do not have all the skills I need to get what I want
- I am unsure I am ready for my life to change if I manifest my heart's desires

It is not safe:
- My success that happens as a result of changing my beliefs will make people I care about feel badly about their own life
- If I change my beliefs about _____ (money, love, men, women, health, work, other people, etc) and my world changes, someone I care about (or use an actual name) will be hurt
- Something bad will happen if I change my beliefs
- If I get what I want, people will judge me and ridicule me
- If I change my beliefs, I will change as a person and I am unsure who that person will be
- I will be alone if I get what I want
- It is not safe to create all that I want

Most of the time the old memories written here are surface memories, that is, there is a memory of far greater substance than those written here. I have discovered with most memories that there are lower core memories which must be isolated and cleaned. A helpful way to understand this is to visualise a tower of blocks. Each block represents an old memory. The bottom block is the core memory as it holds the rest of the blocks in place. It is the root of all other old memories. If you remove the root of the memory, then all associated memories are removed too. This is why at times some people can work hard on the memories that are on the surface yet

Eat Cake

they see very little results in their lives because the core memories are still present in their energetic system.

You must heal the core memory—the root of all memories, to completely heal your life

Activity #14: Isolate Old Memories

> **Prerequisite:** You must have completed Activity# 13— *Revealing the Mother's of all Old Memories* (page 183) before moving onto this one.

For each old memory statement from Activity #13—*Revealing the Mother's of all Old Memories* (page 183) that your subconscious mind is holding onto, ask yourself 'digging' questions to isolate the old memories one by one until you reach the core memory. You can do this by simply asking yourself five easy questions:

'Who?' (e.g. 'Who told you that?')

'What?' (.e.g. 'What is the worst thing about that?')

'When?' (e.g. 'When did that first happen?')

'Why?' (e.g. Why did your father tell you that?')

'How?' (e.g. 'How did that make you feel?')

These five simple questions will help you peel away the layers of old memories. The idea of this is to keep asking yourself a, 'Who?', 'What?', 'When?', 'Why', or 'How?' question until you run out of answers—the last answer is generally the core memory / limiting belief. This will require you to be brutally honest with yourself otherwise you will be simply cleaning only the surface memories and none of the deeper ones.

Realise that *you* have the true answer but it might take a bit of digging to get there.

What if you get stuck yet you know you have not reached the core memory? If you find you get stuck (I call these Subconscious Blocks), then ask yourself,

'If I knew the answer, what would it be?'

I love this question! There have been a number of times where my subconscious mind has tried to block the truth from me as a way of protecting me, yet by asking this question it detours around the block and helps me laser in on the real answer. The answer is always there yet you may need to ask a different question to find it.

Another wonderful question to use if you find yourself stuck is,

'What is the worst thing about that?'

With this question you are imagining what the worst possible thing is that could happen as a result of the old memory statement. The 'worst thing' may be sensed as a *feeling* or it may be a *prediction of an experience* as a result of the old memory. If you find that you repeat the predicted outcome or feeling throughout the digging process then it is likely that whatever you have repeated is in actual fact the core memory.

Included here are some examples that may help you understand how to uncover the core old memories. You will likely find that the core memory you uncover is in actual fact a fear. Trust this process. Do not dismiss what comes up for you. Simply go with the flow and see where it takes you.

The Mother's of All Old Memories

Example #1
Surface Memory: 'It is hard to create what I want'

- **Old Surface Memory:** It is hard to create what I want
- **Digging Question:** *Why* is it hard to create what you want?
- **Old Memory:** Because I'm not entitled to get what I want.
- **Digging Question:** *Why* are you not entitled to get what you want?
- **Old Memory:** Because I'm not deserving.
- **Digging Question:** *Who* told you that you're not deserving?
- **Subconscious Block:** I don't know.
- **Digging Question:** If you did know, *what* would the answer be?
- **Old Memory:** I feel it's a past life thing, I feel that there's an element of me not deserving from a past life.
- **Digging Question:** *What* is the worst thing about feeling undeserving?
- **Old Memory:** I don't feel I can have everything I want.
- **Digging Question:** *What* would happen if you don't get what you want?
- **Old Memory:** I would have failed.
- **Digging Question:** *How* would failing affect you?
- **Old Memory:** I would feel I would lose everyone around me.
- **Digging Question:** *What* is the worst thing about losing everyone around you?
- **Old Memory:** Loneliness.
- **Digging Question:** *What* is the worst thing about loneliness?
- **Old Memory:** Then I'm living a pointless life if I don't have anyone to share it with.

- ❖ **Digging Question:** *What* would happen if you're living a pointless life?
- ❖ **Old Memory:** Then I'm not truly existing. There's no point in existing if I don't have any purpose.
- ❖ **Digging Question:** *What* is the worst thing about not existing?
- ❖ **Core memory:** There is nothing worse than not existing. That would literally be the end of me. I fear not existing.

From the example above it was discovered that the core memory from the surface memory of, 'It is hard to create what I want' is actually the fear of not existing. Now that the core memory is brought to light, it is much easier to clean and clear. It is simply a matter of tapping into what it may feel like to be free of that particular fear and embrace the opposite to it. For this particular example, you would be focusing on what it would feel like to be free of having the fear of not existing as well as tuning into the feeling of living infinitely (we will talk about this in more detail as you read further into the book).

You may have also noticed in the above example that there were a combination of predictions of what will happen in the *outer world* and predictions of what *feelings* will be felt as a result of experiencing a certain old memory. You may find you will explore both (how you will affect the outer world and how your inner feelings will be affected) to get to the core memory.

Example #2
Surface Memory: 'I am not good enough to get what I want'

- ❖ **Old Surface Memory:** I am not good enough to get what I want.
- ❖ **Digging Question:** *Why* are you not good enough to get what you want?
- ❖ **Old Memory:** Because only smart successful people get what they want.
- ❖ **Digging Question:** *Why* is it only smart and successful people that get what they want?
- ❖ **Subconscious Block:** I don't know.
- ❖ **Digging Question:** If you did know the answer, *what* would it be?
- ❖ **Old Memory:** Because the richer get richer and the poorer get poorer.
- ❖ **Digging Question:** If that were true, *what* does that make you?
- ❖ **Old Memory:** Poor. I am definitely poorer than the rich people.
- ❖ **Digging Question:** *When* did this happen?
- ❖ **Old Memory:** Well I have never been rich. As a family we didn't experience poverty, but we certainly weren't experiencing richness either.
- ❖ **Digging Question:** *What* was the worst thing about not being rich as a child?
- ❖ **Old Memory:** Hearing my parents talk about how worried they were that they had another bill come through. Seeing the stress in Dad's eyes. He would become extremely moody and irritable.

- ❖ **Digging Question:** When your Dad became irritable and moody, *how* did that make you feel?
- ❖ **Old Memory:** I didn't want to add to his stress. I would avoid him so I didn't upset him more.
- ❖ **Digging Question:** *Why* would you upset him more?
- ❖ **Old Memory:** Because I'm annoying.
- ❖ **Digging Question:** *Who* told you that?
- ❖ **Subconscious Block:** I don't know.
- ❖ **Digging Question:** If you did know who told you that, *who* would it be?
- ❖ **Old Memory:** I had a small group of 'friends' in infants school (I was about 7 years old) who would decide each morning whether they wanted to be my friend that day. Some days they wanted to be my friend while other days they didn't. Sometimes their reason for not being my friend was because I annoyed them somehow.
- ❖ **Digging Question:** *How* did that make you feel?
- ❖ **Old Memory:** I felt extremely lonely and unwanted.
- ❖ **Digging Question:** *What* conclusion can you make about yourself if they made you feel this way?
- ❖ **Old Memory:** That there must be something wrong with me. If they valued me and thought I was someone special then they wouldn't have treated me like that.
- ❖ **Digging Question:** *What* would happen if you were wrong and ordinary as a person?
- ❖ **Old Memory:** Then I'd never feel like I belong. I would always feel like an outsider.
- ❖ **Digging Question:** *What* is the worst thing about not feeling like you belong and being an outsider?
- ❖ **Old Memory:** Being alone

The Mother's of All Old Memories

- ❖ **Digging Question:** What is the worst thing about being alone?
- ❖ **Core memory:** I think that would be the worst of it. Being alone.

So the core memory from the surface memory of, 'I am not good enough to get what I want' is actually the fear of being alone. This means anytime the surface memory of, 'I am not good enough to get what I want' comes to light in a day-to-day situation, there is a deeper and stronger old memory working beneath that which is the fear of being alone. That is the *real* issue. And of course, there are other issues along the way such as being wrong and ordinary (not special), being annoying, and feeling poor. However if you deal with the core memory, then you subsequently deal with all the other ones that the core memory is supporting.

I have been asked the question, 'How do you know you have found the core memory?' and my answer, as disappointing as it may seem is, you will just know (or you can do a Self Muscle Test, page 154) and ask, 'Is this the core memory associated with the surface memory of [describe the surface memory]?') Your body is your intuition. Anything you know is sensed through the body—it has to because we are living as humans right now with our own body that can indicate to us how centered and balanced we are. So I encourage you to trust your body. Listen to your heart. You will know you have reached the core memory because you will feel it in your heart or your body will provide you with some other kind of sensation. Be open to what it says and you cannot go wrong.

Example #3
Surface Memory: 'No matter how hard I try, nothing works for me'

- ❖ **Old Surface Memory:** No matter how hard I try, nothing works for me.
- ❖ **Digging Question:** *Why* doesn't anything work for you when you try?
- ❖ **Old Memory:** Because I'm meant to struggle.
- ❖ **Digging Question:** *Why* are you meant to struggle?
- ❖ **Old Memory:** Because that's the way it's always been; nothing comes easily to me. I have to work really hard to get what I want.
- ❖ **Digging Question:** *Why* do you have to work really hard to get what you want?
- ❖ **Subconscious Block:** I don't know, I just do. Like I said, that's just the way it's always been (Notice how there is a repeat of the old memory, 'That's the way it's always been'. This means the client is stuck in a blocked cycle so different digging questions are required to move past the blockage)
- ❖ **Digging Question:** If that were true, that it's always been like that, then *what* does that make you?
- ❖ **Old Memory:** Wrong. I must have done something wrong in the past. Maybe this is my karma.
- ❖ **Digging Question:** *Who* decides this is your karma?
- ❖ **Old Memory:** The Universe.
- ❖ **Digging Question:** *Why* is the Universe involved in your karma?
- ❖ **Old Memory:** Because that's what the Universe does; it judges. The Universe will punish me if I have done

something wrong so I feel that struggling in life is my punishment in some way. I must deserve it.
- **Digging Question:** *How* does that make you feel?
- **Old Memory:** Like shit. I must have let the Universe down so badly but I don't even know what I've done wrong.
- **Digging Question:** If you have let the Universe down badly, *who* does that make you?
- **Old Memory:** A bad person. I'm a bad person. A criminal.
- **Digging Question:** *What* will happen if you are seen as a bad person or criminal in the eyes of the Universe?
- **Old Memory:** I'll continue to be punished.
- **Digging Question:** *What* is the worst thing about that?
- **Old Memory:** I'll never make amends to what I've done. I'll continue to struggle for the rest of my life.
- **Digging Question:** Then *what* happens?
- **Old Memory:** Then I'll die and come back and repeat this theme of struggling over and over again because that's what I deserve.
- **Digging Question:** If that were true, *how* does that make you feel?
- **Old Memory:** Abandoned and rejected by the Universe.
- **Digging Question:** If the Universe has abandoned and rejected you, *who* or *what* does that make you?
- **Old Memory:** Worthless.
- **Digging Question:** *What* is the worst thing about being worthless?
- **Old Memory:** If I'm worthless then I mean nothing to the Universe. I may as well not exist.
- **Digging Question:** *What* is the worst thing about not existing?

Eat Cake

- ❖ **Core memory:** Nothing. There is nothing worse than not existing

So the core memory from the surface memory of, 'No matter how hard I try, nothing works for me' is the fear of not existing. As you move through the old memories for each of the surface memories, it is likely you will find common fears; the fear of not existing is one of them. This might not necessarily relate to the fear of death, but rather the fear that our light will eventually dim and we will become absolutely nothing. Of course if we live out our lives afraid of death and afraid that we will cease to exist, then we miss out on actually *living*. This seems to be fairly counterintuitive does it not? But most of the time, when it comes to core old memories, we cannot provide logic to what we fear. They are simply memories; old programs running in the background of our subconscious mind that tell us about our reality, even if what it tells us is in actual fact false. How lucky we are to correct the memories this lifetime and subsequently realign ourselves to the truth of who we really are.

Example #4
Surface Memory: 'It is unspiritual to want more than what I have'

- ❖ **Surface Memory:** It is unspiritual to want more than what I have.
- ❖ **Digging Question:** *Why* is it unspiritual to want more than what you have?
- ❖ **Old Memory:** Because wanting more makes me a greedy person.
- ❖ **Digging Question:** *Why* does wanting more make you a greedy person?
- ❖ **Subconscious Block:** I don't know.
- ❖ **Digging Question:** If you did know, *what* would it be?
- ❖ **Old Memory:** Because the more you have, the greedier you are.
- ❖ **Digging Question:** If that were true, *what* is the worst thing about being greedy as a result of having more?
- ❖ **Old Memory:** Forgetting my true self. I would become so self involved that I would lose sight of who I truly am.
- ❖ **Digging Question:** Then *what* happens?
- ❖ **Old Memory:** I would turn into someone I'm not.
- ❖ **Digging Question:** *What* is the worst thing about turning into someone you are not?
- ❖ **Old Memory:** Losing myself; losing my spiritual identity.
- ❖ **Digging Question:** *What* would happen if you lost your spiritual identity?
- ❖ **Old Memory:** Then I'm completely lost. Sure I'd be living but I would have lost my true essence and if I became so self-involved then I'm afraid I wouldn't know how to get my true essence back.

- ❖ **Digging Question:** If that happens, *who* do you become?
- ❖ **Old Memory:** A fake and a fraud.
- ❖ **Digging Question:** *What* is the worst thing about being a fake and a fraud?
- ❖ **Old Memory:** Living a lie and letting everyone down.
- ❖ **Digging Question:** Then *what* would happen?
- ❖ **Old Memory:** I would die with so much regret and shame. It would eat away at me.
- ❖ **Digging Question:** *What* is the worst thing about dying with so much regret and shame?
- ❖ **Old Memory:** The judgement I'd receive from living that kind of life. I would have let so many spiritual beings down.
- ❖ **Digging Question:** *Who* would you have let down the most?
- ❖ **Old Memory:** The Universe. I don't want to let the Universe down.
- ❖ **Digging Question:** *What* would happen if you let the Universe down?
- ❖ **Old Memory:** I wouldn't deserve universal love.
- ❖ **Digging Question:** *What* happens if you don't receive universal love?
- ❖ **Old Memory:** Then I'd come back and live a really unhappy and loveless existence.
- ❖ **Digging Question:** *What* is the worst thing about living an unhappy and loveless existence?
- ❖ **Old Memory:** Being alone. If there's no one to love, and no one to love me, then I'd be alone.
- ❖ **Digging Question:** *What* is the worst thing about being alone?
- ❖ **Core memory:** I truly don't believe there is anything worse than being completely and utterly alone.

The Mother's of All Old Memories

So the core memory from the surface memory of, 'It is unspiritual to want more than what I have' is the fear of being alone.

Notice in the examples provided how the old memories that followed the path to the fear of being alone are *different* for each surface memory. This means that even though we can cleanse and clear the fear of being alone for a particular surface memory, we cannot eradicate the fear completely from every single surface memory. It would be similar to constructing three different block towers. All three towers have the same red square bottom (the same core memory) but differently coloured and shaped blocks that create the rest of the three towers. These differently coloured and shaped blocks are different old memories. Despite knocking the first tower down the other two towers remain standing. Which is to say that despite clearing the core memory of 'I fear being alone' that is attached to the surface memory of, for example, 'It is unspiritual to want more than what I have,' it does not clear the same core memory (the fear of being alone) that is attached to a *different* surface memory of, for example, 'It is hard to create what I want' because they run on different neurological pathways of the brain. I will not go into detail about the physiological side of how a limiting belief or fear affects the brain because neuroscientists are still attempting to understand it—even in this day and age we are still exploring the amazing capabilities and functionality of the human body!

Funnily enough, I believe it is a good thing to clean and clear the core memories for *each* surface memory separately. When we clean and clear a core memory, we are actually consciously evolving and learning as a spirit which is incredibly empowering to say the least! The fact that you can look at a core memory (a type of belief) and say, 'Hang on a second, that core memory isn't the truth for me—I'm not going to believe that anymore!' is very empowering. When you actively make an effort to replace a core memory with something far more empowering (and truthful), you are actually honouring the importance of your spirit. You are telling yourself, 'I love myself enough to no longer carry this lie'. Is there anything more uplifting than that? I am not sure there is! I also believe that some fears we hold onto actually benefit us and keep us from harm such as the fear of heights. If we were to eradicate the fear *completely* from our subconscious mind then we may in fact put ourselves in unnecessary danger. So some core memories are beneficial to us while others are just there to get in the way of our spiritual and manifestation journey.

Now it is your turn to isolate the core memory from the surface memories you connected with from Activity #13: *Revealing the Mother's of all Old Memories* (page 183). Remember to keep digging until you reach the core memory.

> Gentle Note: I recommend that you write the entire process down; similar to how it has been written in this book as it will be useful for the next activity. Also, as you ask yourself digging questions, be sure to answer them quickly so your logical mind does not have a chance to 'think' of an answer. The idea is to tap into your heart instead of your head to express your divine truth.

Once you have done that you can move onto the next chapter where you will be making peace with the core memory and inviting your Spiritual Support Team to help you heal your past memories to change your future in profound and positive ways.

A word of advice before you begin. Of course you can do this activity whenever you feel guided too however, since you will be dealing with a lot of shadow work (revisit page 140 if you are unsure what shadow work is), it may be useful to do it during a full moon.

The Mother's of All Old Memories

Why do I love doing shadow work during a full moon? Because of the powerful and intense energy the full moon brings. During this time the full moon tends to illuminate the old memories my spirit is ready to release despite my ego's protests. As such it is a great time to purge, unburden, and let go of all the old memories that no longer serve my highest good. I also love that the full moon occurs roughly every 29 days so it is a wonderful reminder for me to check in with myself during each lunar cycle and explore more of the darkness of my subconscious. If you resonate with this, then by all means complete this activity during the next full moon (I have included more information about this in Chapter 21—*Manifesting with the Energy of the Moon,* page 299).

As you go about doing shadow work, you may like to create a sacred space; light a candle, burn some incense, make a hot cup of tea, and sit amongst comfortable pillows. And make sure you have a box of tissues handy (or two or three) because at times shadow work can be brutal to your ego and spirit. But it is all so necessary *and* just the simple act of crying will help you release and let go!

Crying is how your heart and soul speak
when your lips cannot explain the
pain and sorrow you feel.

Chapter 13 – Changing a Core Memory

You will break the chains of limitation when you believe and know you are limitless.

To change a core memory, or any belief for that matter, there must be a willingness to do so. Ironically in a very weird and twisted way, we have held onto old memories because they have benefited us in some way. I know this may sound crazy! Why would anyone want to hold onto thousands of old memories when we know full well they are limiting our true potential? Because despite the limitations, the old memories serve to keep us safe in various ways. This is why it can be so difficult to change them because our ego wants to continue to hold onto them tightly; not willing to let them go in fear of what may potentially happen. So it is important to make peace with the core memory and create a sense of willingness to change the memory so it will happily move on from your belief system. Realise that every experience you have had is by no accident. Each experience is an opportunity for you to learn something empowering about yourself. So before you can change the core memory, it is important to explore how holding onto the memory is positively and negatively serving you.

The benefit of holding onto any surface memory (and all the subsequent memories) is that you avoid experiencing the connected core memory.

The core memory can either be what you truly believe about yourself in this moment (e.g. I am alone), or it can be a prediction of what will happen if you do the *opposite* to what the surface memory says (e.g. I will be alone). So with this knowledge it is easier to accept *why* we all have held onto such old memories because it keeps us safe in some way such as avoiding the feeling of, for example, a deep sense of loneliness (fear be alone) or inexistence (fear of not existing). The downside however is that such old memories limit our true potential, which in turn limits our ability to manifest our desires. To put it bluntly, if you do not change the old memories (particularly the core memory) then you will have great difficulty turning your dreams into reality. After all, it is your thoughts, feelings, values and beliefs that create your reality. It is a mixture of those vibrations that the Universe listens to which determines the kind of life you have. If your vibration does not match the very thing you desire, then you will continue to struggle to get it. So let us rework your vibration by making peace with the core memory. Then you will be in a much more harmonious state to change the core memory to one that supports your highest good.

It is easy to have peace and abundance in your life when you are free from the burden of negative memories

Activity #15: Making Peace with The Core Memory

1. From Activity# 14 - *Isolate Old Memories* (page 187) choose one surface memory you wish to work on the most. It might be the one that is impacting your life the most.

> **Example:** The surface memory I am choosing to work with is the memory of, 'I am not good enough to get what I want'.

2. Next read through each of the old memories that were uncovered from the chosen surface memory and write here the ones you feel are impacting your life the most, the ones you are scared of the most, and/or the ones you are saddened by the most (ensure you include the core memory).

_____
_____
_____
_____
_____
_____
_____

> **Example:** The following old memories that affect me the most and of which are connected to the surface memory of, 'I am not good enough to get what I want' include:
> - Only smart successful people get what they want
> - The richer get richer and the poorer get poorer
> - I am annoying
> - I am wrong and ordinary
> - I am an outsider

> - I am alone (*this is the core memory*)

3. **Intention Setting Statement:** Before you can go ahead and change the old memories, it is wise to set an intention to yourself (and to your Spiritual Support Team) about the old memories you are willing to work on.

   I wish to change the old surface memory of [*describe the old surface memory*] _____
   _____

   that is deeply rooted to the core memory of [*describe core memory*] _____
   _____

   > **Example:** I wish to change the old surface memory of '*I am not good enough to get what I want*' that is deeply rooted to the core memory of '*I fear being alone*'

4. How has holding onto this old surface memory benefited you? What is the upside of keeping this old memory? What do you essentially avoid? I find it useful to follow the statement with a 'because' since it will give you the *real* reason behind why you want to avoid a particular experience or feeling. List as many benefits to keeping this old memory in your life as you can. (Consider the core memory and other old memories linked to the core and consider whether you would prefer to have those beliefs in your life as opposed to the opposite. Most of the time you will not but there may be times that stepping into your own power is far scarier than diming your light.)

_____
_____
_____
_____
_____

> **Example:**
> - I avoid finding out if I am in fact a powerful manifestor because power is scary (fear of power).
> - I avoid becoming an arrogant rich person if I were successful because rich people are arrogant [old memory]).
> - If I were good enough than that puts a lot of pressure on me to do everything right. If I make a mistake I could potentially lose everyone I care about because no one will forgive my mistakes (old memory).

5. How does holding onto these old memories (surface memory, subsequent memories and core memory) negatively affect you *right now*? What is it stopping you from experiencing and feeling? How is it impacting other people in your life?

_____
_____
_____
_____
_____
_____
_____

_____
_____
_____
_____
_____

> **Example:**
> - I am missing out on experiencing the joys of life that I know are possible it if weren't for these old memories stopping me from taking a chance on myself.
> - The memories keep me feeling weak and fragile.
> - I am not evolving as a spirit because of these memories.
> - They make me worry and fearful about my future because I'm constantly second-guessing myself.
> - I've become quite serious in nature because of the limitations these old memories have on me.
> - I am missing out on having a close relationship with the Universe because I do not trust that the Universe has my back.
> - The memories are affecting my children. They can only learn from what they see in me and all they see is an unconfident stress-ridden woman who cannot manifest what she wants. I don't want them to hold the same memories that I do. They deserve all the goodness the Universe has for them.

6. Who will you become in 10 years as a result of holding on to the core memory and subsequent memories connected to it?

_____
_____
_____
_____

Eat Cake

_____
_____
_____
_____

> **Example:**
> Unfulfilled, saddened, and regretful that I didn't do something about this sooner. I would have wasted 10 years of repeating the same limitations over and over.

7. What will the cost be in 10 years time if you do not change this core memory and subsequent memories connected to it?

_____
_____
_____
_____
_____
_____

> **Example:**
> If I hold onto the core memory that I fear being alone, or that I am alone, then that is what will happen. I will experience deep loneliness. I will miss out on living my fullest potential (whatever that may be). My life will be like it is today without any evolution. I will just exist but not truly live in the way my heart yearns for. I won't be the role model I want to be for my children.

8. Who would you become and how would you act if you changed the core memory and all other memories connected

Changing a Core Memory

to it? (This is your chance to question and challenge the validity of the old memories since majority of them are completely false.)

_____
_____
_____
_____
_____
_____

> **Example:** If I changed the core memory of fearing loneliness and all other associated memories including the surface memory of 'I'm not good enough to get what I want' then I would be set free. I would become happier and confident within myself. I would feel supported and connected to the Universe and because of that I would know that I'm never alone. I would love myself because I would feel good enough and worthy enough for love. And I would become a powerful manifestor who uses their manifestation abilities to help those who really need it.

9. As a result of your answer from question 8, are you ready to replace the core memory and all associated memories now?

_____
_____
_____

> **Example:** Absolutely!

10. **Create intention cards**: Choose new, healthy and empowering memories that your spirit would like to believe instead of the current core memory and associated memories (hint: you can simply write the opposite to what was written for question 2. Additionally, for each new memory, try to consider how you would like to feel and include that feeling in the new memory. This is very important because our feelings are a primary component of the manifestation puzzle). Completing this particular part of the activity may take some time. It is also perfectly natural to write more than one positive new memory for each old memory. In fact, write as many as you feel inspired to. Once you are done you can transfer the new memories onto pieces of paper or cardboard. Place them where you will see each continually throughout the day so you can remind yourself of your spiritual truth.

But before you dive into this portion of the activity, I want to share with you my experience with this. As I worked through this aspect of the activity, I felt hesitant to consider that there were possible alternatives to my way of thinking. It had been such a long time of holding onto such negative memories that my ego was very much in a state of denial that there could be other more empowering and positive ways of thinking, believing and feeling. Because of the hesitation, it took a little longer to create new memories. Not only did it take a little longer than expected, but it also brought up a lot of disbelief within me about the new memories that I was writing. This is completely natural! Your subconscious mind will not instantly believe in the new memories because it has not been programmed to do so. We will take care of that in the next activity (Activity

#16: *Healing Old Memories with Divine Energy,* page 215). The important thing is to realise that it *is* possible to change if you really want to. After recognising what could potentially happen to my life in 10 years time if I chose to keep the old memories in my subconscious mind, I was then better prepared to let the old memories go. And because I was better prepared and committed to releasing the memories that no longer serve me, my spirit (Higher Self) could easily speak through me instead of my ego. This is vitally important because it is your spirit that knows the actual truth of what *is*.

Here are some examples that may help you with this part of the activity.

Example of Creating Intention Cards:

OLD MEMORY	NEW MEMORY
I fear loneliness (core memory)	I feel elated and grateful that I'm connected to everyone and everything now and always. I love and appreciate my own company.
Only smart successful people get what they want	I feel loved and deserving of all the good in this world no matter my intelligence.

The richer get richer and the poorer get poorer	I feel so grateful and relieved that all my wants and needs are easily and effortlessly taken care of. I feel excited that my life is abundant now and always.
I am annoying	I am free to be me and my presence brings great happiness to others.
I am wrong and ordinary	I feel excited that I am living a life of purpose. I forgive myself for times when I make mistakes because I know they help me grow as a spirit. I am at peace with who I am and who I am becoming.
I am an outsider	I am wanted and needed in this world. I love and approve of myself unconditionally.

Now it is your turn!

OLD MEMORY	NEW MEMORY

By completing this activity you have prepared your conscious mind for the shift that is about to take place. But what about your subconscious mind? For your desires to manifest, the conscious mind and subconscious mind must work in harmony with one another otherwise the signal you send to the Universe will be weak and confusing. So if you are ready to kick the core memories and all associated old memories to the curb, then there are a number of ways you can do this. I believe that when it comes to self healing there is no cookie cutter approach. We are all so unique that even

Eat Cake

the way in which we heal is unique. Because of this I have included a number of ways you can heal your core old memories and associated ones.

1. If you resonate with the Ho'oponopono prayer and would like to continue to use it to release yourself of the core old memories and subsequent ones, then refer to Activity #2: *Releasing the Old Memories* (page 62)

2. If you wish to include your Spiritual Support Team (Higher Self, Spirit Guides, Angels, Higher Beings of Love and Light, and the Universe) into your healing then I recommend moving onto Activity #16: *Healing Old Memories with Divine Energy* (page 215)

3. If you are a little time constrained and would prefer to have a more 'in the body' experience, then I recommend moving onto Chapter 14—*Working with the Light* (page 227) which includes an old memory clearing activity (Activity #17: *Working with the Light,* page 232).

Activity #16: Healing Old Memories with Divine Energy (*Part 2*)

In this activity, you will be replacing the core memory and all associated memories (including the surface memory) with the new memories you had connected to in the previous activity. The point of this activity is to realign your belief system to the actual truth of who you are *and* it will connect you to your Spiritual Support Team which is such a joy (in fact this activity is one of my absolute favourites!). When you do this, you will change the signal that you knowingly (and sometimes unknowingly) send out to the Universe. For instance, say you were holding onto the old memory that you are undeserving of abundance, and you replaced that old memory with a new memory of, 'I feel excited and grateful to receive all the abundance I want and need in my life now and always'. The Universe can only acknowledge that signal and provide you with what you *truly* believe is in your life; limitless abundance. Can it *really* be that simple? Yes it can!

This activity will place you in a deep meditative state. There are a couple of ways you can do this: you may like to ask a close friend to read through the activity while you follow their prompts, or you may like to read through the script (or record your voice as you read through the script) before carrying out the activity by yourself.

Preparation:

1. Have your answers from question 10 of Activity #15: *Making Peace with the Core Memory* (page 204) as you find yourself a quiet space and comfortable position. You may wish to light a candle, surround yourself with crystals, or play soft peaceful

music in the background. Whatever you choose to do please ensure you will not be disturbed. This is your time to release and heal the old memories.

2. Before you enter a meditative state, it is important to call upon your Spiritual Support Team. These are your unseen (and sometimes seen) friends residing outside the Earth plane who have been assigned to help you on your spiritual journey. You may call them Spirit Guides, Guardian Angels, Beings of Light or any other name that resonates with your spirit. With the intention to involve your Spiritual Support Team, you may like to say,

'I call upon my Higher Self, angels, guides, and other beings of love and light who wish to help me successfully change these old memories. Please infuse my entire mind, body and spirit with your love, protect me from harm, and assist me on this journey that is for my greatest good. Thank you.'

Meditation: Healing Old Memories with Divine Energy

1. Close your eyes and focus on your breathing, taking some nice deep breaths in and out. Breathing in comfort, peace and relaxation, and exhaling any tension, tightness and anything that is not needed in your mind and body. Simply let it all go effortlessly and naturally.

2. As you continue to breathe deeply and peacefully, you are making the intention of changing your old memories into new and positive ones. You are ready to remove the psychic baggage

from your energy system, and like a phoenix out of the ashes, become reborn with the truth of who you really are. Just sit with this intention for a moment.

3. Now allow your breathing to return to its normal relaxed rhythm. And as it returns to that normal relaxed rhythm, you notice how easily and naturally it just sits there in the background, cleansing your body with oxygen, and removing anything your body no longer needs. And as your breathing sits rhythmically in the background, you can also invite your busy conscious mind to take a step back. It may like to return now and then during this meditative session but you are in such a relaxed and peaceful state that it is just as easy for you to acknowledge it and return to your intention, which is to change the old memories into new and empowered ones.

4. And so with each breath, you feel yourself, know inside yourself, that you are letting go and becoming more and more relaxed. Becoming aware of the chair, the bed, or the floor that is supporting your physical body. And it is almost now that with every breath, you allow yourself to sink into that support; easily and naturally letting go. Going deeper and deeper now, and more and more relaxed.

5. So bring your mind now to focus just below your heart centre; below the diaphragm but just above the stomach. And as you bring your mind to focus on that area, you find that it is very easy to move your breath into that area now. And as you breathe into that area, you can feel the sensation of relaxation moving out from the heart centre into every muscle, every fibre, and every cell of your body and of your being. Your entire existence radiates pure peace and calm. And as your physical

body becomes heavier with relaxation, it opens up a clear channel for your Higher Self to come forth and provide you with authentic guidance and support as you prepare to go on a magical and healing journey.

6. But before you take this magical journey, simply become aware of the presence of your Higher Self. It may be useful to imagine your Higher Self as a separate entity with a white angelic cord attached to your heart centre and theirs. You may imagine your Higher Self as a person with the same or similar characteristics as you, or someone with their own unique features. Just sense as much detail about your Higher Self as you can. And as you imagine this person appearing before you with the angelic cord connected to you, you may also sense the love, guidance and protection your Higher Self is constantly sending you. You may sense this as a simple knowing or feel it as tingles, heat, or electricity moving through your body. You may even see or sense pure white loving light encasing both you and your Higher Self's body. You may feel or see something completely different or you may not sense anything at all which is completely okay too. But realise in this moment that you are connected to this higher state of loving consciousness whether you sense it or not because this state is *you*. It has always been you yet it can be difficult to truly connect to it when the busy conscious mind is running at the forefront of your life. So welcome your Higher Self into your sacred space. Place trust in this higher being of light because it is this intelligent and loving energy that is eager and ready to hear exactly what you need so it can provide the support and guidance that is vital to getting what you want.

Changing a Core Memory

7. Now it is time to tell your Higher Self what you want; which is that you wish to change the old memories (the core memory and associated memories) to new and empowering memories. Sense yourself having this conversation with your Higher Self and notice how your Higher Self gladly agrees to take you to where you need to go to change the old self-limiting memories—it is for you highest good after all.

8. You see your Higher Self clicking their fingers and a gorgeous big white fluffy cloud suddenly appears floating before you. This cloud will support you perfectly—helping you float away from any cares and worries. It is a very special cloud especially handpicked by your Higher Self just for you. Visualise your Higher Self gesturing you to climb onto the cloud. You follow their guidance and step onto the floating cloud feeling peaceful and relaxed. You can stretch out on this cloud, sit cross legged, or curl up in a tiny ball, whichever is most comfortable for you. Notice that the temperature on this cloud is exactly as you like it. You can sense the bright sun warming your face and body, and a gentle breeze that soothes you as you let yourself float on the cloud up and away from the room your physical body is safely in, and up into the sky. Floating effortlessly and peacefully.

9. And as you drift and float on the fluffy white cloud with your Higher Self beside you, you find yourself talking about how ready and willing you are to be releasing yourself of the old memories. You may hear yourself telling your Higher Self of all the reasons why now is the perfect time to let your old memories go. Simply focus on this moment as you continue to drift and float in the air.

10. You can feel yourself moving higher and higher through other wispy clouds until all the clouds are beneath you and only a golden white light surrounds you, your Higher Self, and the fluffy white cloud that you are travelling on. You can hear soft angelic music playing somewhere in the distance as you easily reach your destination—a long glass pathway spans before you that leads to a large wooden door. It is time to step off the fluffy white cloud, knowing that as you do so you are perfectly safe and supported with your Higher Self by your side.

11. Feel yourself step off the fluffy white cloud onto the glass pathway. And as you peer toward the large wooden door, you feel a sense of excitement and anticipation. The wooden door almost pulls you toward it as you make your way along the glass pathway with your Higher Self by your side.

12. You reach the large wooden door. Just take a moment to appreciate the features of this door. There may be intricate detail on this door. There may be symbols engraved on it. It may be a modern or ancient door. It may be rectangular or circular or any other shape. It could look like anything at all. Whatever it looks like it is perfect for you.

13. You place your hand on the door knob and open the door. You step through the doorway with your Higher Self beside you and you are instantly welcomed by a beautiful healing light that permeates every part of your body. And once your eyes adjust to the loving energy of light, you can see that you have entered a very large etheric room. This large etheric room can look like anything you want. It may contain brightly coloured pillows, rugs, or tapestries. There may be large crystals and candles burning a sweet or citrus fragrance. The room may have large

stone columns or timber beams supporting the ceiling. Or it may look completely different. Just take a few deep breaths in and out now as you immerse yourself in the beauty and sacredness of this space.

14. And as you relax into this etheric space and continue to breathe deeply and calmly, you become aware of three doors. One in the middle that is a golden colour, one to the left that is purple and one to the right that is indigo blue. You notice the middle door opens and more golden light illuminates your sacred space as you watch a number of figures moving toward you from the door. These figures are your Guardian Angels, Spirit Guides, and any other beings of light that wish to help you on this journey. You can feel their love infuse your body; this may remind you of the feeling of coming home.

15. The beings of light thank your Higher Self for bringing you safely to this sacred space. They look to you with excitement and say, 'Welcome. We are so happy to see you. What is it that we can help you with?' You imagine yourself telling them that you wish to change your old memories; be specific of which old memories they are including the core memory and any other associated memories you wish to release and heal. The beings of light ask you, 'Are you sure you wish to change them?' You can hear yourself replying with, "Yes, I am sure". The higher beings of light look to your Higher Self for permission and your Higher Self nods with consent. 'Very well', they say.

16. They beckon you and your Higher Self to follow as they move toward the indigo blue door located to the right. You both follow just in time to see the higher beings of light opening the indigo blue door, stepping through the doorway, and suddenly

moving down what seems like an endless corridor. You can only just keep up as you follow the beings of light along the corridor, and around corners, left and right and left again. Up and down straight and spiral staircases, along more corridors, past differently coloured and shaped doors, through magnificent arches, and down hallways that open up to various purpose built rooms. Up more staircases and twisting down another corridor until finally you stop at a plain looking door. There does not seem to be a door handle or any other detail besides a sign in the middle of the door that says, 'Memories'.

17. You watch your Guardian Angel gesture for the door to open and sure enough it does. You feel yourself moving through the doorway along with the beings of light including your Higher Self into a plainly decorated room. You can see there is a table in the middle of the room with two chairs on one side of the table and one chair on the other side. You may also see other items in the room or you may not. The one thing that catches your eye is a mysterious leather bound book on the table with the words, 'My Memories'. Your Spirit Guides encourage you and your Higher Self to take a seat next to each other.

18. You both take a seat. Your Higher Self reaches for the book and begins to flick through the pages until the old memory you wish to change is reached. There it is; written in such simple black text. You find it hard to believe that something written in a book can affect your life in such a way. But not everything is as it seems. Below the written memory you notice an indigo blue coloured button; the same colour as the door you had originally walked through before travelling to this room. Your Higher Self turns to you and asks, 'Are you ready?' and of which you reply with a tentative, "Yes". Your Higher Self

pushes the button and a miniature tornado begins to form from the old memory text within the book. It gets bigger and bigger, swirling and rotating from the book and moving to the spare chair that is positioned opposite you and your Higher Self. Suddenly out of the tornado appears your old memory in human form. This old memory represents the core memory you wish to change and any other associated old memories including the surface memory.

19. The tornado disappears, leaving your old memory sitting on the chair opposite you looking slightly dazed and confused. You breathe deeply and wait for the old memory to speak. And as you patiently sit and wait, you notice how unhealthy this old memory looks. They may look weathered with eyes sunken and dishevelled hair. They may smell slightly *off*. Their clothing may be in tatters and rags. You get a sense that their energy is low. They may even look exhausted and burnt out. Despite their appearance, smell and low energy, they look excited to see you. The old memory speaks with a touch of desperation in its voice, 'I am so relieved to see you. I have been in your life for such a long time but it is so good to meet you face-to-face'.

20. Your Guardian Angel encourages you to talk with this old memory. 'Perhaps', says your Guardian Angel to this old memory, 'You can explain why you have stayed around for so long and....', your Guardian Angel turns to you, 'Perhaps you can tell this old memory why you are ready to release it from your energy system'. You agree and so you sit with this old memory and talk about how this memory has served you well in the past and why now is the perfect time to let them go. [*Wait a while to allow yourself to have this conversation*]

21. You realise that you have both come to a state of agreement and peace. You can hear the old memory apologising to you and your Higher Self, 'I'm sorry for causing any trouble or harm to you. It was not my intention. I merely thought I was helping you but now I realise that I too can be free if you will release me that is'. You realise that it was not *just* the old memory that had a hold on you, but it was also you that continued to hold onto the old memory. You both agree that now is the time to release each other *from* each other.

22. Your Guardian Angel speaks to the old memory, 'Are you ready to be set free?', "Yes, I am ready" replies the old memory. Your Guardian Angel then turns to you and asks, 'And are you ready to be set free?', "Yes" you reply. And with that your Higher Self hands you a golden pen. You take the pen and smile at your old memory with gratitude. The old memory smiles in return with love as you begin to use the golden pen and draw over the written old memory; making each letter of the old memory disappear as if by magic. And with each stroke of the golden pen, you notice that the old memory sitting opposite you begins to fade amongst a healing and loving light. Lighter and lighter it becomes until it disappears completely. Now the human form of the old memory has been released into love and light and the old memory text that was once written in the book has disappeared as well; completely erased. All that is left is a plain white page in a book.

23. 'We cannot leave this page blank' says your Higher Self. 'It is time to write a new memory—one that will empower you from this day forth'. You agree and begin to write the new memory on the page using the golden pen. You watch as golden ink effortlessly transfers onto the white paper with each letter and

Changing a Core Memory

word of the new memory. And once you are done, you give the page a quick blow with your breath to dry the ink. You then read your new memory out to all the Beings of Light who nod with joy and excitement. You take a deep breath in and peer at the new memory with gratitude and elation. This new memory will change your life in profound ways.

24. You hand the golden pen back to your Guardian Angel and close the book of 'My Memories'. The book begins to fade from the table. It all feels so complete.

25. The Beings of Light gesture you to follow them through another door only this time it is purple. You leave the 'Memories' room and walk through the purple door. A bright purple healing light filters through your energetic body, cleansing and healing, as you find yourself in the large etheric room once more. Your Guardian Angels, Spirit Guides and other Beings of Light surround you. You thank them for their love and support. They reply by reminding you that you can visit this place anytime you wish. You then watch them exit through the golden middle door before your Higher Self takes your hand and leads you to the wooden door you had originally come through, down the glass path, and back onto the fluffy white cloud.

26. You get yourself comfortable on the fluffy white cloud with a whole new outlook to your life. You find yourself excited about the wondrous things that are going to happen. Down, down, down the fluffy white cloud travels until it reaches the room where your physical body exists. Your Higher Self and you disembark the fluffy white cloud and look at each other smiling. 'Shall we do this together?' your Higher Self asks, "Absolutely"

you reply. With hands holding and the angelic cord still attached to your heart centres, you both step back into your physical body becoming one again.

27. When you are ready you can bring your awareness back to this day, this time, and this place. Back to the chair, couch, floor, or bed you are being supported by. All the way back now. Wiggling your toes and fingers. Moving your feet, ankles, and legs. Moving your shoulders, arms and neck. And when you are ready, open your eyes.

Follow Up from the Meditation:

You may wish to practice the self muscle test (page to 154) to check if your subconscious mind is clear of the old memory that was changed during Activity #16: *Healing Old Memories with Divine Energy* (page 215). If the self muscle test indicates the old memory is still in your subconscious mind then repeat the activity again, only this time you may wish to speak to the Beings of Light in the large etheric room and ask them for extra assistance on releasing the old memory. Your Spiritual Support Team will happily support and guide you toward a positive outcome.

Chapter 14 – Working with the Light

The energy of your spirit is the essence of life. Look after it.

During a psychic development workshop, we were all asked as a group to tune into one of the workshop attendees aura and talk about what colours we could sense. The aura is our energy field (or electromagnetic field) that surrounds our physical body and if you look at the area surrounding the physical body you can sometimes pick up on various colours that the aura is emitting. It is believed that the colours represent our emotions, higher-mind beliefs, spirit, intuition and overall connectedness to the Universe. So if you are familiar with the meaning of colours then it can be quite fun to read your own aura to get a sense of the condition of your true essence.

We all starred at the man with the curly brown hair and then various people spoke of seeing yellow, green and red. 'Yes!' said the workshop leader. 'I can see that too'. I blurred my vision a little more and continued to stare at the man hoping I would see something; anything! But all I could see was a man and a white wall behind him. As the majority of the group chimed in on what they could see, I stood there in silence hoping the workshop leader would not notice that I was unable to see this man's aura.

Some people can see auras. Other people cannot. Do not feel bad if you struggle to master the art of physically seeing the energy field. With practice you may but there are other ways to tune into energy fields since colour is not the only way the energy vibration is projected. The easiest way is to simply focus on the person. Notice their posture, the sparkle in their eyes, the position of their head as they talk to you, how quickly they respond to your questions, the radiance of their skin, the way they walk with a bounce in their step. The list goes on! A person's interaction with the environment can give you so many clues as to the condition of their true essence and whether they look after themselves physically, mentally, emotionally and spiritually.

Those who give much of themselves to others but rarely take time out for their own needs will show it in their slouched shoulders, bowed head, dull skin tone and dim eyes. Yet when someone is actively taking the time to look after themselves and are frequently energising their bodies, there is a bounce in their step, they face the world with confidence, their skin glows with vibrancy even if they have naturally pale skin, their eyes radiate happiness, and even if they are not smiling there is still a slight upper curve of the mouth. So a lot can be said for putting your needs first! It is not selfish, in fact it is absolutely necessary.

Had the workshop leader asked me to read the energy of the man with the curly brown hair without tuning into his aura but rather simply 'being' with his energy, then I would have said that he was charismatic. Someone who lights up a room simply by their presence. He seemed spiritually connected to his ideas and because of his high energy, I felt that he could actively act upon those ideas without procrastination. There was a joy around him and a genuine passion for life itself that could be mistaken as over confidence. There was also an element of fear of disapproval so the heightened energy of his presence almost acted as a shield to protect him from criticism. Interestingly, as we spent more time as a group, I came to see that what I had sensed about his energy was very much in keeping with who he was as a person. You see? Seeing an aura is one way to tune into your own energy but it is not the only way.

So I would like for you to stand in front of a mirror and simply look at yourself. Notice the appearance of your eyes and your skin's complexion. Notice your posture and whether your head is tilted a little or if it's facing straight toward the mirror. Then reflect on previous conversations you have had and consider whether your responses are said quickly or slowly. Do you take the time to listen or are you quick to jump in and have your say? Next, go inwards and tune into your stamina levels. Are you feeling refreshed and ready for the day or could you go back to bed and sleep for a few more hours?

The point of this is to understand whether your energy field is at its most optimum or whether you are over-committing to life itself and disregarding your own needs. Of course we as spirits are limitless in energy but it is important to remember that our body's energy is not—the body's energy is more like a battery pack. There is only so much energy we can expel and give to others before we find ourselves straining to do even the most simplest of tasks without feeling fatigue and general unease.

Even doing nothing is still an active exercise and an extremely vital one at that!

In terms of manifestation, if you do not give yourself permission to relax and rest then you can ultimately destroy the momentum. A rested energy field is the greatest attracter of your heart's desires. You simply cannot expect to receive joy, love and happiness in your life if you continually drain your energy by over committing to the needs of others. Your body is not built to go on and on and on. It will wear down eventually. You do not need to be a clairvoyant to see that!

Eat Cake

So if you feel fatigued and withdrawn from the world and your appearance does not match someone who is full of energy, then it is possible you are on the road to burnout. And to make matters worse, if you are trying to manifest your desires by following the activities in this book but you are starting to lose the motivation because you simply do not have the time or energy, then the likelihood of your dream coming to fruition is very slim. Creating your dream life should be exciting and uplifting. It should not be seen as a chore.

It is entirely possible to look after yourself and still have time to create your dream life. You do not have to choose between the two. So my reasoning for writing this particular chapter is that I understand that some of the meditations in this book may be a little too lengthy for you if you are already time constrained. So I have developed an alternative activity that will still provide the same results as the mediations but in less time. This means you can still move forward with the shadow work (removing the old memories), start bringing in what you want in life, and still have time for yourself to do the things that bring you joy right now. Because you will remember that all you have is now, and now is all that the Universe listens to. So if you are fatigued and withdrawn and you do not do anything about it, then you will remain in that state for as long as you choose.

The next activity is focused on working with the light. This is just another way of saying that you will be working with the energy of the Universe. In a visual sense, you will be working with pure white light. Why pure white light? Because it is the colour of universal source energy which encompasses *all* the colours of the rainbow that make up the visual aspects of each dimension; similar to the way in which the Universe encompasses *all* possible scenarios for every desire we have. In addition to working with the light, you will also be working with your body which houses positive and negative energy. It is the negative energy (old stagnant memories) that you will be cleaning, clearing and transmuting with the help of the universal source energy (pure white light).

Eat Cake

Activity #17: Working with the Light (*Part 3*)

In this activity you will be cleaning, clearing, and transmuting the old memories that you had uncovered from Activity #14: *Isolate Old Memories* (page 187) by working with the light and your body. This activity can be done relatively quickly so if you are a little more time constrained then this will be perfect for you.

1. Firstly choose which surface memory and therefore associated core memory you wish to work on during this activity. You would have uncovered the core memory from Activity# 14: *Isolate Old Memories* (page 187).

2. As you consider the surface memory (*not* the core memory because that will come later), ask yourself, 'On a scale of 1 – 10, how connected to that belief/memory am I?' (1 = Not connected at all so it is not affecting you, 10 = severely connected so it is severely affecting you). Make a note of the number you have chosen.

3. Now it is time to work with the light. Close your eyes and take a few deep breaths to centre yourself. Now imagine a beautiful white light beginning to shine from your heart centre. See it expanding from the heart and moving over your entire body, above your head, below your feet, out into your auric field, beyond your aura, out into the room you are in, and forever expanding out into the infinite Universe. Your light is limitless in its expansiveness; connected wholly and completely to the Universe. It is in this connectedness and expansiveness where you cannot feel fear since fear is a restriction.

4. And so in this state of connectedness and expansiveness you can receive an answer to any question you seek. As you reflect on your chosen surface memory, ask yourself, 'What age was I when I first felt that?' and simply wait for the information to come to you.

5. Now ask yourself, 'Who did I get this memory from?' (Was it your Mother, Father, Brother, Sister, other family member? Perhaps it was a teacher, religion, culture, yourself, someone or something else).

6. And with this knowing of who this memory is attached to, now ask yourself, 'What is the most prominent feeling/emotion I have around that particular memory?'

7. As you focus on the memory and the prominent feeling you feel around the memory, ask yourself, 'Where in or around my body do I feel this the most?'

8. Once you have a location, imagine the infinite white light radiating and glowing in that same location of your body. Here, visualise a vortex whereby the core memory that is the root of the surface memory is positioned in the depths of the vortex. Watch the light penetrate the vortex, travelling right down to the lowest point, completely encasing all aspects of the vortex and then vaporising the core memory and all attached memories including the surface memory.

9. As you see this occurring, repeat aloud the following statement three times,

Eat Cake

> *'I clean, clear and transmute this core memory and all attached memories, across all time, space, dimensions, and realities'*

10. Now make the intention to replace the vaporised memories with new and powerful ones. You may already know what empowered memory you wish to use, and in which case, simply visualise the new memory (it may be useful to give it a shape, colour, texture, and any other element) connecting and absorbing into the area of the body that was once storing the old negative memories. Alternatively you may wish to ask the Universe, 'What would it take for me to feel completely and utterly…(the opposite to how you felt in the past. For example you may now wish to feel abundant, supported, loved, accepted, free, etc)?' and wait for a positive response. When you receive one, visualise it moving into the area of your body where the old memories were once stored. If you do not receive a positive response in that moment then be open to the fact that it will come to you whether by a thought, a feeling, a knowing or even a synchronistic event in the near future.

11. Breathe deeply to centre yourself and visualise the white light coming back to your heart centre now. Back from the outer Universe, back into the room you are in, back into your body and back to your heart. Realise that although the light is stored in your heart centre you can expand it anytime you wish to connect to the Universe. After all, you are never *really* disconnected.

12. When you are ready, you may open your eyes.

13. Now reflect on the original surface memory and ask yourself, 'On a scale of 1 – 10, how connected to that belief/memory am I now?' (1 = Not connected at all so it is not affecting you, 10 = severely connected so it is severely affecting you). Compare the number to the original one you had chosen at the beginning of this activity. Chances are, it will be closer to '1'. Repeat activity if you feel it is needed.

Chapter 15 – What if Your Desires Do Not Manifest?

Peace comes when you can be in love with the duality of this world.

I am not naïve in thinking that this is the only manifestation book written on Earth. In fact I have no doubt there are hundreds of different versions which all aim to assist people to create a life they want in their own unique way. What I have found however is that there is one huge elephant in the room that is rarely (if at all) written about when it comes to effectively manifesting, and I have decided that now is the best time to write about it.

Most people, more often than not, consciously go through the manifestation process because they have identified something in their life that is lacking; lack of money, lack of love, lack of happiness, lack of safety and security, lack of purpose…the list goes on. From this particular space of *feeling* the scarcity in an area of their life, there can come a sense of desperation that something needs to change. And it is through this desperation where most people actively and consciously manifest what they want. But what happens if what they want does not actually manifest? Undoubtedly you have heard about the importance of positive thoughts because when you think positively and maintain a positive attitude, more positive things will come to you. But it is certainly difficult to maintain a positive outlook to your life when what you want is not manifesting no matter how much old memory cleaning and clearing you have done, how often you have visualised the outcome of your desire or referenced your vision board, or how often you have repeated affirmations and manifestation-related mantras. When you

What if Your Desires Do Not Manifest?

have applied yourself to the manifestation process and yet still nothing happens, you are highly unlikely to stay positive. If anything, all this would create is negative thinking and then BAM! There goes your dream life! Interestingly however, the negative thinking only stems from the belief that in order for your life to be *good* you must have *more* of something. And with that comes the desperation and the obsessiveness over your dreams manifesting. So many of us place heavy duty pressure on our desires manifesting because we truly believe that what we want is the *only* thing that will make us happy or it is the *only* way we can become happy. There have been countless times I have heard others say, 'When I have *that* then I'll be happy', such as 'When I have more money, when I am living in a bigger house, when the new car is my driveway, when the pool is installed in the backyard, and the credit card is paid outright, then I'll be happy'. This is a key reason why some people's desires do not manifest because they have placed far too much emphasis on their ability to be happy through the creation of their desire. And it is not only happiness that is at stake here. It is also love and safety. Even though these three things; happiness, love and safety, are more often than not part of the outcome to our manifestation journey, it does not mean that our feelings of happiness, love and safety should be *dependent* on the outcome of our desires manifesting. In actual fact, we should be *feeling* these things with or without material possessions *now*.

We live in a world of duality; good and bad, hot and cold, yes and no. It is the contrast of this world that we live in that makes our lives so exciting. And ironically it is the contrast that allows us to create and manifest whatever we want. We have all come to Earth to create so it stands to reason that we should not love *just* one aspect of this world of duality but instead love both; the good and the bad. Our mission is to appreciate every single experience as an opportunity to be happy, to love, and to feel safe and supported. It is the proverbial phrase; the glass is half full.

Wanting material things is perfectly fine but not if it is the sole thing that makes you feel happy, loved or safe. These feelings must be rooted in the heart of your soul instead of in the attainment of material things. So how do you have complete and utter faith that you will be perfectly okay no matter what happens? How do you stay in the frequency of love and happiness when everything else around you falls away?

In my search to find the answer I turned to my 5 year old son. Naturally I spoke to him in a way I knew he would respond to by talking about 'farts'. Our conversation went a little like this;

> Me: 'Say someone let out a huge fart and it blew away everything; our house, the cars, your toys, *everything*. This fart was so huge that there was nothing left but you. How do you stay feeling happy when everything around you has blown away?
>
> My son: 'I would laugh at the fart'.

And he actually started laughing at this. I love my son's response because he is essentially saying he would laugh at the very thing that had completely vaporised all material things that we so often look to to feel happy, loved and safe. He did not go into panic mode and question me about whether we would get our house back (including his toys) nor did he question me as to who was to blame, or why the fart was aimed at our house in particular. Children have such a connection to the truth; it is such a shame that we as adults damage that over time.

What if Your Desires Do Not Manifest?

From my son's answer, I have concluded that happiness is in the present moment, never is it in the future. And although it is wonderful to have a plan for the future, it should not be the *only* thing that promises happiness. Happiness can only be truly felt right here and now.

There have been times when I have struggled maintaining a sense of happiness and security particularly during times that were personally challenging or when I watched the news on the rare occasion and heard devastating stories about the world in which we live in. As such I had found it difficult to believe I would remain happy and safe even if I lost all the material things in my life. So when I was guided to write this chapter, I experienced writer's block. How could I write about something that I too needed help and guidance on? The best thing to do in situations such as this, where I am completely lost as to how to move forward, is to turn to my Spiritual Support Team. So I connected to Benoit and we had a wonderful and enlightening conversation about this particular topic. Here is Benoit's take on how we can have complete faith that we will be okay even if our heart's desires do not manifest.

> *"In order for you to create a sense of harmony in your life despite the lack of material possessions, you must have faith in something that is not only outside of you but also within you. We say there must be a connection between yourself and something else that builds strength and courage in the face of anything that comes into your life or anything that does not. When there is separateness and disconnect, we call this the hindrance effect. It is a state of obstruction from the truth. For you all to live your lives successfully as a human and create your desires, you have come to believe that you are separate because it helps you to make choices for yourself; it abides by the universal law of free will. But what we see happening here is that the law of free will has created, in some, a state of separation and disconnect. The lower mind has evolved to a*

point where the truth is further from the truth. It has created a 'me versus them', 'me, myself and I', 'all for me, none for all' way of living. This is so backward in nature is it not? To believe that Earthling life can only be enjoyed through the eyes of division from source? We say there cannot be separateness if you and ourselves are all one and the same. If there is an absolute certainty in the time space continuum (which means you have a connection to source at all times) then you can never be not okay. You will always be okay even in the face of danger. Existence is not confined to Earth—it is infinite. When you take the foot off the brake a little and let life roll, then your faith in your own power as a co-creator to your life will strengthen. The Universe does not focus on the negative because that is where the lower mind lies. The Universe wishes only to focus on your positivity. It will not abandon you nor will it single you out and punish you. In fact, there has never been a time of abandonment. And if there is a sensation of this, then the assumption of this has only been created by the lower mind—it is not the truth.

We believe there is great benefit to the material world but we also believe some material aspects of the world seem to only to distract you from yourselves. They seem to create false pretenses about who you should be and how you should live your lives. If you own a red convertible sports car then are you automatically successful? No. Everyone is successful in their own right; you made it to Earth and are living a life there—that is success to us! With the objects around you, we encourage you to use them as a way of expanding yourselves and your creativity. Begin to look at each object as a method to express your generous spirit. Objects that only serve to create a false sense of power and prestige are not worth your time. It is all false and the Universe knows that that is not who you are.

In terms of happiness, we say happiness is not a fixed state of emotion. It will ebb and flow with each experience. Sometimes you will feel elated

What if Your Desires Do Not Manifest?

and overjoyed while other times you will experience pain and hardship. But even during those times of hardship, you can still master happiness by the way in which you react to the experience. There is always a choice to how you respond to each and every experience. And you knew this; the world you are in is a double coin—two sides to the spectrum of human life. When there is positive, there is also negative. And there is no way of avoiding the negative throughout your life. But you knew this before coming to Earth and you agreed upon these teachings before entering the third dimensional plane. What we wish to say is that there is always good even in the bad. If you can see the bad as a way of redefining who you are, if you can see the bad as an opportunity to know what to do next time, and if you can see the bad as a way of learning about this dual world, then you are coming from a state of positivity that generates happiness. Always.

In your world, you are all thought leaders—you lead with your thoughts and sometimes the thoughts tell you, 'This is wrong. You should get angry about this. You should start seeking revenge, or you should start feeling like a victim here because what has just happened to you is not fair'. That's a thought. You could also look at it and respond with, 'Well that was interesting. That was an experience I will never forget. I'm glad I had that so I know now what not to do. Perhaps I can teach other people about that so they don't have to go through it either'. Sometimes the bad is about sacrifice for the greater good. Sometimes your own spirit must feel the sensation of lack and hurt to know what is actually right and then follow it through. If you can see the opportunity that comes with the bad, then you can never really 'feel' bad, you can only feel happy for the opportunity.

Now in terms of love and possessing that emotion through times of hardship, well, we say, love is you. Love is just that. When you realise you are love and there is nothing you need to do to activate or attract it into your life, then you will love with or without objects. You cannot lose love or fall out of love or be unloved because love is forever. We understand it is easy for us to say this as we do not contain ourselves in a physical body so our form of love is somewhat differently expressed to yours. But perhaps it is beneficial to understand how your love can be expressed because when you express love, you are essentially expressing your spirit; your soul. Love is your ability to be creative, generous, thoughtful, kind, purposeful and appreciative. Love is when you can laugh at yourself instead of taking yourself so seriously. Love is knowing that you have flaws and they are wonderful because they give you opportunities to embrace, accept and heal. Love is power—the most powerful energy there is. Nothing can penetrate it or eradicate it. You simply cannot lose something that makes up your entire essence. If you do, then you do not exist and that is impossible.

It is okay to want material things but not to the extent that you believe the only way you can love life is by having those things in your life. That is when you know you have lost your way. And if you do find that you have lost your way and your life has become dependent on material things to feel happiness and love, then give some material things that you currently have to others who would benefit from them—that would create pure non-material love; do it for the love of generosity. Instead of expecting things from the future to come into your present, simply just 'be' in the moment and love that moment. Then when the next moment comes, love that too. And the next and so on. We would love for you to realise that all you have is now. That is all. There is one dot in the Universe and that is you; that is your location. That is where your awareness lies as a human and a spirit. So do not waste the opportunity to love in every moment. It is futile to place expectation on loving your future when in reality it will never come.

With deep love and happiness, Benoit.

What if Your Desires Do Not Manifest?

So it is within your willingness to accept the connection you have to the Universe where love, happiness and safety are forever there. After all that is the makeup of the Universe. So how do you reconnect to those aspects of yourself? Perhaps consider answering these questions; when did you stop dancing? When did you stop singing? When did you stop laughing? When did you do anything for yourself just because you wanted to without there being a benefit to others? Doing those things will reignite the love for life that your spirit is yearning for.

The fact is, this is your journey, your path and your choice. This is a unique opportunity that we all have as spirits living primarily a third dimensional experience. If the Universe did not want us here then we would not be here. So it has our back. Our lives are creation in motion. And our role as spirits on Earth is to see every opportunity on this planet as a way to close the gap of separation and to trust that the Universe loves us all. So much so that it knows you can handle this. It knows that even if your heart's desires did not manifest, you would still be absolutely fine. It knows that if your heart's desires do not manifest then it is only because there is an opportunity to move closer to the sensation of connectedness instead of separation. It also knows that with each 'negative' outcome we are faced with, we can use it to grow as a loving entity. Every single opportunity is for your highest good, *always*. There is no exception. You are so divine and so loved that even in the midst of supposed chaos, there is always an opportunity to cultivate happiness, safety and love. It is easy to do when it is already within you.

Your life purpose is to close the gap of separation and grow as a loving entity

Eat Cake

When you realise this, or at least become willing to absorb this information into your heart centre, then you will eventually become comfortable with the knowingness that you will be fine even if your heart's desires do not manifest. And when you breathe a sigh of relief knowing that all is well and that all things that have happened are opportunities to close the gap of separation, then you will find it easy to release the reins off the importance of your desires becoming reality. With those loose reins you can actually enjoy the process. Interestingly, as you place trust in the Universe as it does in you and you fill your well up with joy and love for the life you have, then your heart's desires will come to you full force.

Chapter 16 – Thank You, Thank You, Thank You

Be content with what you have; rejoice in the way things are. When you realise there is nothing lacking, the whole world belongs to you. — Lao Tzu

Benoit had spoken about the importance of being in the present and appreciating moment to moment since that is all we have. When our spirit is well and truly in our body and we are using all our bodily senses to absorb the world around us in that very moment, we become an extremely powerful magnet for our desires to manifest. I know it might seem a little strange since when we are thinking about manifesting and what we want in life, then we are essentially taking ourselves away from living in the moment. Yet our future emanates *from* the present. And so it is important that we all engage in the present moment because what is happening presently is what our future will become.

Our present is an oracle to our future.

If we desire happiness, then it means we are not in a happy state *presently*. And so the future will also be fuelled by this unhappiness that you may be experiencing right *now*. Your heart's desires cannot come to you if you are not aligning your frequency to what you want. If you want love in your life, then you must love the present. If you want money in your life, then you must focus on the abundance that is all around you right now. If you want a relationship or a meaningful career, then you must find a way in the present moment to feel the same way you would feel if you were in a loving relationship or working in a meaningful job.

Eat Cake

To manifest what you want, you must be present

I believe the best and most effect way to stay in the here and now and create the good vibes that will encourage a great future is to practice gratitude. Gratitude is also known as being thankful. Gratitude allows us to celebrate the present and in doing so we start to, and continue to, appreciate the value of something or someone. The importance of this is enormous in terms of manifestation. Essentially we are thanking the Universe for providing us with something that supports our existence and growth. Knowing that by expressing sincere gratitude for all the things you desire in your life and for all the things that are already in your life, you move closer to manifesting your dreams into reality. How? Well, positive thoughts attract more positive thoughts which eventually turn into positive opportunities in your life. Remember that you need to build momentum with positive energy—once the momentum is there, the manifestation process will become a lot easier.

Naturally the mind must be deliberately trained to 'think' more positively. A major problem with manifesting is that we identify what we want because we are currently lacking and suffering. For instance, if you were not feeling the pain of financial difficulty, then it is likely you would not desire more wealth. It is easy to remain trapped in a suffering mindset where we feel as though the world is against us. We may even say to ourselves, 'Why me? Why does this horrible thing keep happening to me? What did I do to deserve this?' But the reality is that somewhere in our consciousness we have accepted suffering to be a part of our existence. In fact the suffering becomes a habit. Many times the suffering originates from childhood experiences where our mind acted like a sponge—

Thank You, Thank You, Thank You

collecting information about our world and about ourselves even if that information is horribly damaging. Realise that suffering is simply an old memory which can be easily shifted by following the activities throughout this book.

However it is not always easy to simply start thinking more positively because it has taken you years to shape your beliefs about yourself, what you deserve, and whether your dreams are even possible. But in order to manifest your goals and therefore turn your desires into reality, you will need to refocus your thoughts on the more positive things in your life no matter how small those positive things may be. Being grateful does not necessarily mean your entire life is perfect but it does allow you to recognise your blessings. And as you have just learned, recognising your blessings means creating positive thoughts, feelings and beliefs, which is exactly what you will attract in future.

I have written a chapter about keeping a manifestation journal (Chapter 25—*Putting it all into Action*, page 341) which includes information about being grateful every day. Essentially the journal will help you reprogram your mind so the art of gratitude will become an easy and welcomed habit. You will definitely want to look at starting your own manifestation journal when you come across that part of this book. However if writing in a journal is not really your 'thing' then you may like to practice the art of gratitude through meditation. I have included a very simple gratitude meditation in the next activity that you can easily do each morning before you begin your day and each evening before you go to bed. This is a great way to instantly place your vibration into a state of love and joy for all that you are and all that you have. Alternatively, if you like to engage in creative drawing and writing, you may like to start a Gratitude Jar as described in Activity #19: *How to Create a Gratitude Jar* (page 250).

Activity #18: The Gratitude Meditation

1. Sit in a comfortable and relaxed position.

2. Close your eyes and place your awareness on your breath without forcing it. Continue to do this for a few minutes; simply watching the breath moving into your body through your nose or mouth and out of your body through your nose or mouth.

3. Now move your awareness to your heart. You may like to place your hand on your heart centre to connect with this awareness.

4. Ask yourself the simple question of, 'What am I grateful for?' Allow any impressions, images, sensations, feelings and thoughts to come to you without judgement or resistance.

5. Stay in this moment for a few minutes and experience all the sensations that come with the gratitude you have.

6. If there is anytime you become distracted by noises or thoughts unrelated to what you are grateful for then simply bring yourself back to the question of, 'What am I grateful for?'

7. Now affirm to yourself, 'Today I judge nothing that happens'. Repeat this affirmation as many times as you wish.

8. Take a deep breath in and let go any residual resistance as you breathe out.

Thank You, Thank You, Thank You

9. Open your eyes and enjoy the rest of your day with gratitude.

If you have practiced this meditation *before* starting your day, then remind yourself throughout the day to not judge yourself or others. I like to keep a hair tie around my wrist so each time I find myself judging I will flick it to disconnect my attachment to the judgmental thought (I also like to use the hair tie flick anytime I have other disempowering thoughts). The presence of the hair tie around my wrist also reminds me to ask the question of, 'What am I grateful for?' in that moment. It instantly opens my heart to all the goodness in my life. Try it for yourself!

Eat Cake

Activity #19: How to Create a Gratitude Jar

I believe the biggest mistake we can make as humans is to think we need to make huge changes in our lives to get results. But this is not the case at all! It is in those tiny changes we do day by day that lead us to our biggest wins. Practicing gratitude is one of those 'tiny' things and using a gratitude jar is the perfect way to place ourselves into the flow of positivity and abundance.

All you need to do is to set aside a few minutes each day and reflect on what magical things are already in your life—because no matter who you are and what you are going through, there is *always* something to be grateful for!

1. Choose a sacred jar; be it any jar that you feel drawn to. Mine is a mason jar because I love the vintage look, the feel of it, and it is larger than other jars so I can fit more magical notes in it!

2. Decorate your jar (if you wish). You may like to place stickers on it, wrap ribbon around it, or use glitter pen for example. Your imagination is only your limitation so get creative.

3. Cut up some paper into pieces that are large enough to write a quick note about what you are grateful for. Scrap paper that would normally end up in the rubbish bin would be perfect. Keep the paper and a pen near the jar for quick 'gratitude' access.

4. Consider your life and think about what you are thankful for. What made you smile today? What did you accomplish

today that brought you happiness? Who are you grateful for? What is something beautiful you saw today? What do you like about where you live? Is the sun shining today? Did something unexpected happen that made you feel wonderful? Simply focus on the very things that make you feel appreciative and happy.

5. Write your grateful moment on one of the pieces of paper. Aim to write at least one each day but if you want to write more than that than that is great too. After writing it down, fold the slip of paper and place it in the jar. You may wish to share this experience with someone else so there is a heightened sense of gratitude.

6. Keep your jar in a place you can see it to remind yourself to practice gratitude. I also like to look at my jar and see the abundance of folded pieces of paper already in it which tells me just how wondrous life is!

7. At the end of the year, pour all the entries into a bowl and re-read them either to yourself or with someone else. You could even organise a gratitude party for those who have also taken part in keeping a gratitude jar and share those special moments together. After all, life should be celebrated!

Intuitive Action

There is a voice that doesn't use words. Listen
– Rumi

Chapter 17 – Tune the Radio

Your intuition is your only true guide in life.

I am sure you are aware by now that the manifestation of your dreams can not just appear out of thin air. Besides becoming clear of your heart's desires and working through the old memories that would likely, if ignored, sabotage your manifestation success, there may also be a requirement for you to take action. So how do you know what action to take? Sure Mary Smith followed X,Y and Z to fulfil her dreams but does that mean your dreams, that may be fairly similar to Mary's, will manifest if you too follow the same path? Perhaps or perhaps not. Would it not be comforting to be connected to some kind of superpower that can steer you in the right direction; some kind of frequency that you could easily tap into anytime you needed guidance on the next step of your manifestation journey? Well lucky for us there is such a thing and it is called; intuition or sixth sense.

Your intuition is your inner knowing or inner teacher. It is your natural being, your protection, your sage, your inner compass, the voice of your Higher Self. Your intuition can lead you to meet the right people, the right places, and the right moments in time that can help you create the reality of your dreams. It is the very thing that paves the way for you to cease imagining what your dream life may look like and instead actually *live* it. Sometimes what we want can seem so farfetched on a logical level that we simply cannot even imagine how it will happen. Our intuition on the other hand is able to connect you to possibilities, and if you follow it, you can be led to the fulfilment of your desires. This is called intuitively inspired action. But before you can take intuitively inspired action, you must first reconnect to the sixth sense.

My Story to Help with Yours:

I had dabbled with developing my sixth sense on and off throughout my childhood and adolescent years. When I was twelve years old I decided to fully commit to my sixth sense; this was my heart's desire at the time. Naturally the Universe responded to my request by providing me with an opportunity to learn the art of tarot. I was nervous and excited at the same time. Personally the thrill of learning tarot was not to look into the future but rather to use it as a tool to help me unlock my sixth sense. As it happened however my lessons in tarot were short lived after a school friend's mother approached me warning me that tarot is the work of the Devil and I would be punished by God if I continued down that path. Even though I did not have a connection to the particular God she was referring to, there was still an element of fear and doubt associated with working with tarot. 'Maybe opening up to my intuition is something to be scared of' I thought. Since I was worrying about the potential dangers of using tarot cards, I decided it was best to close shop on my sixth sense altogether. As I reflect on the experience, I feel a pang of disappointment. It was such a good opportunity, in fact I can only marvel at the Universe's way of fulfilling my heart's desire to learn tarot particularly at the age of twelve! I believe that had I listened and trusted my intuition, there is no doubt I would have continued with the tarot lessons. Ironically though, I needed to be in tune with my intuition to know which path was the best for me. Who is to say the decision I made to avoid learning tarot at that time was the best decision for me? That is something I will never know.

Tune the Radio

Six years later the Universe gave me another shot at fulfilling my heart's desire. I became very close to my cousin Nikki who is a natural born intuitive. I say 'natural born' as she had the connection right from the beginning of her life. Nikki had suggested that despite us *all* having an intuitive connection, it is mostly our family that greatly influence how good of a connection it is for us when we are children. Some families are associated to certain faiths that disapprove of any kind of spiritual connection so most of the time the children do not learn to embrace their natural intuitive abilities. Some families base their own childhood experience on whether spiritual connection is safe to do (or not) and therefore pass their own experience onto their own children. Some families are open to embracing the sixth sense but are unsure how to do it so are unable to nurture the sixth sense of their children. Whatever the case may be does not matter. No matter your age, you can still gain a connection to your sixth sense because it is the voice of your spirit. How can that be seen as a bad thing?

Nikki was my ticket to re-establishing the connection to my sixth sense. We began by talking about intuition. The more we spoke, the more I found myself opening up to the idea that I too have more than just five senses. No longer did I look at intuitive healers, psychics and mediums as the 'special' or 'chosen' people. I began to adjust my viewpoint to one of possibilities and openness. This was the beginning of fine tuning the signal; accepting that connecting to my intuition is my natural state of being. Once the 'intuitive gate' began to open, I felt more connected to the outer world. My body became an antenna of information since it is the body that is intuitive not your spirit. When you decide to embrace your sixth sense and acknowledge that it *is* your natural state of being, you too will likely notice unusual things happen. It is possible you will become more sensitive to your outer world as your body becomes accustomed to picking up energetic signals. For example you may walk into a room and sense the energy of the room is low. Perhaps an altercation just broke out or people are feeling extra negative that day. You may see things that are not physically there such as other spirits or brightly coloured orbs, or you may hear something that no one else heard. You might even receive random images in your mind that make no sense to you at the time but later turn out to be premonitions. You may physically feel something touch you when there is no one around or a cold draught even though the doors and windows are closed. Everyone experiences their intuition in a variety of ways; we may feel it, see it, hear it, or simply know it. Some people can smell it or even taste it.

I began feeling things (for example tingles, shivers, and gut feelings) and seeing things either physically (seeing spirits) or in my mind's eye (premonitions). Of course this opened up Pandora's box of questions for Nikki. I wanted to know everything; 'What does this mean?, I saw this so what was it?, I felt uneasy today, was that my intuition?, how do I strengthen this connection?, am I doing it right?, will I get hurt doing this kind of thing?, should I be afraid?.....' I was like a Chihuahua nipping at the heels of a person with Cynophobia (fear of dogs). At first Nikki was accepting of my curiosity and tried to help me as often as she could but after a while she became less available to me. Unfortunately this only made me more desperate to get answers. I would often email her and log into online chat rooms to get in touch with her. I no longer wanted answers, I *needed* answers. Like a dog with a bone, I had become obsessive. Although I was receiving intuitive hits as I like to call them, they were very few and far between. It seemed the harder I tried to be guided by my intuition, the less guided I felt. Eventually I felt nothing; just a void of emptiness. I wanted to feel connected to my intuition again so badly but through my obsessive wanting came nothing.

Through all the constant questions and the doubts and fears I shared with Nikki, she finally told me what I needed to hear; 'Erin' she said with great conviction, 'Just give it a bloody rest!' Her comment took me by surprise. I had not realised how obsessive I had become. Picture a Cheetah with a thousand legs sniffing catnip and that may help you visualise the extent of my franticness! Needless to say my logical mind began questioning my motives; do you really need to put yourself through this? Should it really be this hard? You're getting nowhere—it's best to stop now'.

So I gave it a rest. I decided that pursuing the art of connecting to my intuition was all too hard and because of that I threw in the proverbial towel. Naturally it was my ego that wanted to blame someone or something for this so I directed my anger toward the Universe for not helping me become the intuitive person I thought I could be, 'I get it now. Only special people are given the gift of intuition and clearly I'm not one of them. So you know what Universe? Screw you!' I felt abandoned and stupid. There were so many questions running through my mind; why won't the Universe help me? Why is it that every time I try something new, I fail at it? What is so wrong with me that the Universe doesn't believe I'm good enough or entitled enough to be intuitive? Undoubtedly you are reading this and thinking to yourself, 'Wowser! That's a lot of negative self talk Erin! You have got some serious old memories to work on!' and you would be right. That is what the ego (old memories) does; it loves to create drama and play the victimhood game. It loves to be in the limelight and sabotage our lives in a variety of ways. The important thing here is to realise that it is okay to have outbursts from time to time. In fact I believe it can be a great opportunity to witness the old memories expressing themselves. The difference in terms of allowing an outburst to occur is in the time you spend entertaining the ego because;

the longer you spend choosing to listen and acting upon the ego's demands, the less time you have towards hearing and acting upon the whispers of your soul.

In a parallel Universe somewhere I would have dusted myself off and attempted it again; after all, pursuing the art of connecting to my intuition brought me so much joy despite some hurdles along the way. But it is so easy to play the 'coulda shoulda woulda' game. The hardest thing is to accept the past for what it is, learn from it with equanimity, gratitude and grace, and move on with openness to receive your heart's desires. Unfortunately I was not in the parallel Universe. I was in the Universe where the old memories were interrupting the voice of my higher spirit; my intuition. It was time to 'build a bridge and get over it' in more ways than one.

The parallel Universe of dusting myself off eventually caught up to me as I decided in my mid twenties that I was in fact *not* done with my pursuit to reconnecting to my sixth sense. No sooner had I decided to give it another go than an advertisement for a psychic development workshop landed in my inbox. Yet another demonstration of how the Universe will provide you with an opportunity that matches your desires! I felt excited and certain that this would be it; finally I would become fully attuned to the intuitive frequency I was searching for.

Tune the Radio

Right at the beginning of the workshop the workshop leader, a renowned psychic medium, said to the group of us, 'Not everyone is psychic. Some people will work at it, but they may never get there...' She then proceeded to draw something on the whiteboard but I cannot recall exactly what she was talking about because my mind was focused so intently on the bombshell that had just been delivered—'What do you mean we are not all psychic?!'

> Gentle Note: The terms psychic and intuitive are often interchangeable. Intuition (sixth sense) is our inner compass that steers us toward living an authentic and meaningful life. It is the little voice in our mind, the gut feeling in our stomach, or the tightness in our throat that warns us of danger or relays information that is beyond logical reasoning. Psychic ability is not different to intuition. It is simply an aspect of our intuitive faculty that has been developed over time; that is, it is an ability that can be consciously and deliberately used which is probably why it is sometimes seen as a supernatural phenomenon since not everyone chooses to consciously refine it.

For the rest of the day I found myself going back and forth with the idea that we are not all psychic; we are not all born with the sixth sense. I swirled this information around in my mind as if I was tasting a new herbal blend of tea. I had driven two and a quarter hours only to be told by a popular psychic-medium that she too believed in the very same thing I had surmised for so long. The synchronistic event of this was uncanny. Of all the psychic development workshops I enrolled in, I had chosen the one where the teacher begins the lesson by telling me that I may not be psychic or have the ability to tune in. This is such a wonderful example of how the Universe will only provide you with experiences that match your thoughts, feelings, values and beliefs.

Eat Cake

Not surprisingly the statement made by the workshop leader further concreted my past experience with intuition. 'That's it!' I thought to myself. 'I give up!' I completely surrendered to the idea of being intuitive and just sat on the grass holding my cheese sandwich with barely a thought about my past or future. I was there in the moment, simply witnessing my surroundings instead of being in my head. I noticed the brown and green leaves placed randomly on the grass, the warm sun kissing my face, the whirring sound of the cars driving on a nearby busy road. I noticed the unusual architecture of the Church to my right, the gentle swishing sound of the Eucalyptus leaves dancing together in the breeze and the smell of the Earth after the recent rained. And like the clouds parting after a heavy storm and the sun shining its rays on the landscape, a new thought popped into my mind. Only this time there was delicateness about it with an element of power and certainty. It said,

> *'This is your sixth sense. This is it'*

Instantly I jumped to the thought of, 'Wait. What was that? Where did that come from?' but then I notice how differently I felt; uplifted, hopeful…connected. It was true! This was it. This was my intuition. I had heard and felt it, and it only needed me to be in the moment to sense it! Finally I understood what Nikki had meant when she told me to give it a rest.

> *We are all born with the sixth sense.*
> *It is the most natural thing in the world.*
> *And because it is so natural,*
> *we do not need to work at it,*
> *we need to work with it.*

Tune the Radio

I had been working against it that entire time. I had been *trying* too hard. I had been creating expectation on what I thought intuition was and how it should show up in my life. I had questioned every thought that came to mind, every tingle in my body, and every hair raised on my arms as to whether or not it was an intuitive sign. I had consistently employed the logical mind to try to decipher the so called 'intuitive codes'. I consistently looked to the outer world for proof that I am intuitive because I did not truly believe it was something I could naturally possess.

You are intuitive.
It is not something you need to gain from the outside,
it is something you already have.

And once you believe with absolute certainty that you have the sixth sense, then you will start to open the intuitive doors and receive inspiration from your Higher Self and the Universe.

Because the Universe is *always* trying to help us on our manifestation path; it is always trying to give us clues and nudges, but with so many noises and distractions on this planet, it can be incredibly difficult to sense the support and guidance we are all being given. This is why I was having so much trouble connecting. My mind was so occupied on wading through all the thoughts, worries and fears that it was practically impossible to sense anything else.

You have always been intuitive.
You may just need to recalibrate the frequency
to sense again.

Eat Cake

Think of it like tuning into a radio. If you rely heavily on your logical mind and remain non-committal to developing your sixth sense then you will likely receive static. That is, the intuitive based information is there but you just need to fine tune your own signal to pick it up. Or you may receive all the information from the Universe but the volume is turned right down so you cannot hear it. Alternatively you may be moving through the channels so quickly that you miss the Universal signal completely. And when you expect to receive some inspiration but all you get is white noise then you may even assume the radio is broken. But the truth is it is not the radio that is the issue, it is the way in which you are using it.

So perhaps your intuitive channel is a little on the 'white noise' side of things right now. This of course it going to make it difficult to receive manifestation inspiration from the Universe! How are you going to know what the next step is to take to move you forward if you are not connected to the divine energy of your spirit? Why choose to live a life of restriction when you can choose to live a life of freedom?

When you are completely tuned into the same frequency the Universe is broadcast on, then you will be open to the nudges, the tingles in the body, the simple knowingness of the right path, the words of wisdom, the flashes of images in your mind's eye, and the synchronistic events that the Universe loves to surprise us with. Nothing makes the Universe happier than to see amazement in our eyes when something magical and unexpected happens. It leaves us with that pure sensation of joy and love in our hearts and it is then that we know we have come home.

Activity #20: Intuition – Are You Tuned In?

The first step to receiving intuitively inspired information about your heart's desires is to tune in. The number one cause of blocking intuitive guidance stems from old memories. These have been created either from this lifetime or past lifetimes, and like most old memories, if left unhealed they will likely sabotage your ability to finely tune your intuitive connection.

In this simple activity, you will be practising the chosen Self Muscle Test from Activity #11: *Discovering Whether You Truly Believe Your Desires will Manifest* (page 154) to find out if you are holding onto any old memories relating to your ability to tune in to your intuition. Then you will be making a conscious effort to heal the old memories and replace them with new and empowering ones that will open up your intuitive channel.

1. Prepare yourself to practice the Self Muscle Test (instructions on how to do this can be found on page 154)

2. Read through each of the following Old Memory Statements (these are surface memories) whilst practicing the chosen Self Muscle Test to uncover if your subconscious mind is holding onto the particular limitation. Make a note of which one/s are affecting you right now (if any).

    - It is unsafe and dangerous to be intuitive
    - It is wrong to know the next step
    - I will be punished by others if I allow my intuition to lead me
    - Being intuitive is hard work

- I do not have the gift of intuition
- It is impossible to learn how to be intuitive
- I will never be intuitive
- Being intuitive is against God's will
- Intuition is nothing but coincidence, luck or chance
- I am uncomfortable connecting to my intuition
- Connecting to my intuition will take too long and I do not have enough time
- Learning to connect to my intuition is too hard
- There is too much responsibility associated with being intuitive
- I don't need my intuition
- Intuition is for the insane people
- I'm scared of what I will see, hear, or feel if I allow my intuition to lead
- People will call me crazy if I tap into my intuition
- I'm scared of the power that comes with being intuitive

I have only listed the more common of old memories you may be holding onto in relation to tapping into your intuition. If you sense there are others that I have not included then simply write them down and continue with this activity.

If you found you are completely free from these old memories then you have successfully completed this activity and can move on.

3. Now it is time to uncover the core memory associated with each surface memory. Refer to Activity# 14: *Isolate Old*

Memories (page 187) to reach the core memory. Remember that when you uncover and heal the core memory then all subsequent memories linked to the core are automatically healed too.

I have included two real life examples to demonstrate how asking digging questions can easily locate the core memory.

Example #1
Surface Memory: I will never be intuitive

- ❖ **Surface Memory:** I will never be intuitive.
- ❖ **Digging Question:** *Why* won't you ever be intuitive?
- ❖ **Old Memory:** Because being intuitive is only for the special and gifted people and I'm not special or gifted.
- ❖ **Digging Question:** *Who* told you that you're not special or gifted?
- ❖ **Old Memory:** I don't know if someone has actually told me that, I think it's more just a sense I get. If I compare myself to others, I just see myself as average – I'm nothing special.
- ❖ **Digging Question:** *How* does that make you feel when you say you are average and nothing special?
- ❖ **Old Memory:** I feel ashamed, embarrassed and pathetic.
- ❖ **Digging Question:** *What* is the worst thing about feeling ashamed, embarrassed and pathetic?
- ❖ **Old Memory:** I'll never be able to be seen as anything but those things, I'll always be seen as a loser.
- ❖ **Digging Question:** If it were true that people saw you as a loser, *what* is the worst thing about that?
- ❖ **Old Memory:** My life would be pointless.

- ❖ **Digging Question:** *What* is the worst thing about living a pointless life?
- ❖ **Old Memory:** Then I'm just wasting my life without anyone to share it with – I'd be alone and unloved.
- ❖ **Digging Question:** *What* is the worst thing about being alone and unloved?
- ❖ **Core memory:** Nothing is worse than being alone and unloved. I would prefer to not exist at all if I had to choose between those options.

So the core memory linked to the surface memory of, 'I will never be intuitive' is the fear of being alone and unloved. Once you have uncovered the core memory, you can move onto Step 4 of this activity.

Here is another real life example of a client struggling to tune into their intuitive abilities.

Example #2
Surface Memory: Learning to be intuitive is too hard

- **Surface Memory:** Learning to be intuitive is too hard.
- **Digging Question:** *Why* is learning to be intuitive too hard?
- **Old Memory:** Because there's a lot to do and I don't know if I have the time.
- **Digging Question:** *How* do you know there's a lot to do?
- **Old Memory:** I assume there is a fair bit to work on when I see other people so connected. I feel very distant from ever being able to do that.
- **Digging Question:** So you feel distant from where they are compared to where you are, *how* does that affect you?
- **Old Memory:** I feel quite disconnected from being very intuitive.
- **Digging Question:** *What* does that say about you?
- **Old Memory:** It instantly makes me feel that I'm not good enough to be intuitive.
- **Digging Question:** *What* is the worst thing about not feeling good enough to be intuitive?
- **Old Memory:** Well since being intuitive is supposed to be our natural ability and yet I'm struggling to obtain that ability then I have to wonder why I find it so hard yet other people find it easy.
- **Digging Question:** *What* are you saying about yourself then?
- **Old Memory:** That I must be stupid.
- **Digging Question:** *Who* told you that you are stupid?

- ❖ **Old Memory**: I don't recall ever being told directly, but there have been times when I have felt stupid compared to other people.
- ❖ **Digging Question**: *What* is your earliest memory of feeling 'stupid'?
- ❖ **Old Memory**: I was about 5 years old and was given a school book to read at home. I had so much trouble reading and it didn't matter how hard I tried, it seemed impossible. At one point my Dad yelled at me because I couldn't read a particular word.
- ❖ **Digging Question**: *How* did that affect you and your relationship with your Dad?
- ❖ **Old Memory**: I felt that he saw me as a lost cause. If my own Dad couldn't be patient with me while I tried to read, then what hope do I have for other people to be patient!
- ❖ **Digging Question**: *What* is the worst thing about your dad seeing you as a lost cause?
- ❖ **Old Memory**: The worst thing is that I've let him down. I didn't meet his expectation and so at the time I felt I wasn't good enough in his eyes.
- ❖ **Digging Question**: If that were true, that you are not good enough in his eyes, *what* is the worst thing about that?
- ❖ **Old Memory**: I'd forever be a disappointment and likely rejected from the family.
- ❖ **Digging Question**: *What* is the worst thing about being rejected from the family?
- ❖ **Old Memory**: Well for the rest of my life I would carry the knowledge that my family didn't want me. I would live out my days knowing that the reason for the abandonment is because I am stupid.
- ❖ **Digging Question**: *What* is the worst thing about being abandoned?

- **Old Memory**: I would end up alone and feel that I was not worthy of any kind of love.
- **Digging Question**: *What* is the worst thing about being alone and unworthy of love.
- **Core Memory**: There isn't anything worse than that.

So the core memory linked to the surface memory of, 'Learning to be intuitive is hard work is the fear of being alone and unworthy of love. That is the *real* issue.

4. Now that you have uncovered the core memory, you can move onto clearing it and all associated memories from your energetic system and replace it with something far more powerful and enlightening. To remove the core memory and associated memories, you can:

- practice the Ho'oponopono prayer (Activity #2: *Releasing the Old Memories*, page 62) or,

- employ the help of your Spiritual Support Team (Activity #16: *Healing Old Memories with Divine Energy*, page 215) or,

- connect deeply to the energy of your body whilst incorporating the light of the Universe (Activity #17: *Working with the Light*, page 232).

Chapter 18 – Come Back into Your Body

Trust your vibes because your body never lies.

Once you understand what your intuition is, what it does, and how it does it, then you can easily recalibrate yourself to connect to it. This is not about communicating with the dead but rather about communicating with your Higher Self; the absolute truth of who you are. And it is this truth that wants to help you create miracles, so you may as well listen for it! Quite possibly the number one question I receive about intuition is, 'How do I know when it is my intuition or something else?'

The easiest way to answer this is to get back into your body because it is not *you* that is intuitive, it is your body. Clairvoyance (clear seeing), Claircognizance (clear knowing), Clairsentience (clear feeling), Clairaudience (clear hearing), Clairalience (clear smelling), and Clairgustance (clear tasting) can only be possible with the body. And if we are indeed a spirit living a human existence, then it stands to reason that when we take good care of the body, we can then easily receive intuitive inspiration to help us navigate the path we seek.

> *For us to seek enlightment,*
> *we must first seek embodiment*

Hence if the body is treated badly, for example, consuming too much alcohol, smoking, taking recreational drugs, not exercising, overeating fatty and sugary foods, or not drinking enough water, then the ability to receive intuitive insights will diminish. Similar to the radio analogy I wrote about earlier; the signal is there but the radio cannot pick it up properly. The only way to realign to the inspiration from your Higher Self is to get back into your healthy body because it is the only thing assisting you on this human journey. Without it you would not be on the Earth plane at all. So perhaps today is the day to change the not so favourable eating habits and sedentary lifestyle and embrace a new and healthier style of living; one that makes you feel truly good.

The next part of 'knowing' when you have received intuitive inspiration is to determine *where* in the body the inspiration shows up. Do you feel it? Do you know it? Do you see it? Do you hear it? Do you smell it? Do you sense a combination of these things? We all have one primary intuitive sense, but we can also have more than one to amplify the primary form of communication. Knowing your primary sense can help you pick up intuitive 'hits' for not only manifestation purposes, but for all life purposes.

Eat Cake

Activity #21: Discovering Your Primary Intuitive Sense

When you become aware of your primary intuitive sense, it can make your manifestation journey a *lot* easier because you will be intuitively guided to reach your goals. The best way to discover your primary sense is to reflect on how you interact with the world.

To discover your primary intuitive sense, answer each of the following questions (only choose one response for each):

1. When in conversation with a friend, do you find yourself regularly responding with:
    A. 'I see what you're saying'
    B. 'I feel what you're saying'
    C. 'I hear what you're saying'
    D. 'I know what you're saying'

2. When learning something new, would you prefer to:
    A. Watch a documentary about the topic
    B. Build something new with your hands
    C. Attend a lecture
    D. Engage in problem solving activities

3. What agitates you the most?
    A. Trying to find an important item in the dark
    B. Sitting in a draughty cold room unable to get warm
    C. Repetitive loud noises
    D. A thumping headache

4. Choose a movie you truly loved watching. When you reflect on the movie, what comes to mind first?

A. The scenery, the costumes the actors and actresses were wearing, or the look of the props
B. The way the movie made you laugh, cry, cheer or moved you in some other way
C. The music or the sounds of the actors' and actresses' voices
D. The elaborate plot, the life lesson you learnt, or the overall storyline

5. You decide to spend the day exploring your creative side. What do you most prefer to do?
   A. Experiment with different paint colours on canvas
   B. Create a sculpture with clay
   C. Compose a song on a piano, guitar or other instrument
   D. Build a complex paddle pop stick (or popsicle stick) house

6. Think of a happy childhood memory. What part of the memory stands out the most?
   A. The vibrant colours of the toys, the look of your friends face as you play together, the appearance of the playground or something else you witnessed
   B. The excitement, joy, freedom, peace or any other feeling associated with this memory
   C. The laughter, music, the chatter of friends or family together or any other sound
   D. The imaginative games, the puzzles, the Battle Ship challenges or any kind of thinking-oriented game

7. When you are meeting someone for the first time, what is the first thing you notice?

Eat Cake

> A. The way the person looks, their clothing, hair, shoes, smile, or general appearance
> B. How you feel around the person such as feeling comfortable, safe, amused, carefree, and so on
> C. The sound of the person's voice or laughter
> D. Whether you find the person interesting, easy to talk to, or believe they may be able to help you in some way

RESULTS:

Take notice of which letter of your answers occurred the most. This is your primary intuitive sense.

Mostly A's signifies CLAIRVOYANCE: This is the ability to 'see' either physically or through your mind's eye (third eye). It is quite possible you refer to yourself as a 'visual person' whereby you process information about your world through what you see. Knowing you are clairvoyant, in terms of manifesting your heart's desires, means you can pick up on the subtle images in your mind. When you receive an intuitive hit, the image (or short-length type movie) will generally appear without warning or without any active participation on your behalf. And just as quickly as the image or short-length movie appears in your mind, it is likely it will just as quickly disappear to. This is why it is important to strengthen your clairvoyant ability so you can decipher between when it is your imagination and when it is your intuition. You can do this by, for example:

> 1. Visualising your dream life in as much detail as you can as often as you can. Make a point of doing this every morning just before you start the day and before you go to bed in the

evening. The more you practice, the stronger your clairvoyance will become.

2. Stimulating your third eye (the area between your eyebrows) with Lapis Lazuli, Clear Quartz or any other crystal you are intuitively drawn to with intention to clean and clear the third eye area. For people with clairvoyance ability, it is the third eye that receives intuitive inspiration. You can place the crystal on your forehead, under your pillow at night, or keep it in your pocket to align your body to the frequency of the crystal.

3. Keeping a dream journal. People with strong clairvoyant abilities tend to have vivid dreams. Dreams are a way the Universe can communicate to us without our ego mind interrupting. It is so much easier to freely accept guidance this way which is why keeping a dream journal is important so as you do not forget the messages later in the day.

As a clairvoyant you will also likely receive signs from the Universe in the form of repeating numbers, finding coins, seeing feathers, noticing butterflies and anything else that is meaningful to you. Think of it as your own personal language that your Higher Self and Universe can respond to.

Mostly B's signifies CLAIRSENTIENCE: This is the ability to 'feel' so you generally interact with the world through your physical and emotional senses. When you receive an intuitive hit it is mostly picked up as a gut feeling, butterflies in your stomach, shivers, goose bumps, tingles, tickling, pressure, heat or coldness. This is the way your Higher Self and Universe are able to communicate with you. As you continue on the manifestation path, you may feel excited or uplifted which generally means you are on the right track. If you feel dread, sick or anxious then it may be a warning for you to pause and re-evaluate your decisions. As a clairsentient, you may also find it easy to pick up on other people's emotions and even physical issues such as headaches and backache. This is known as empathy and in my opinion it can be a blessing and a curse at the same time! I could write a whole other book about Empaths but for the sake of keeping this book relevant to manifesting, simply realise that by building upon your empathic gift, you are also building upon your clairsentient ability. You can do this by, for example:

1. Asking permission of someone you know if you can tune into their energy, which is to say, connect to how they are feeling emotionally and physically. Then when you have connected, simply tell them what you sensed. You will be surprised just how much information you can pick up! And if you find you are wrong then continue to practice. Practice does not always make perfect (because what is 'perfect' really?), but it certainly helps.

2. Focusing on your solar plexus chakra (just above your naval and below your sternum). This chakra is responsible for processing intuitive insights through feelings and emotions. Now imagine a bright yellow light infusing this area of your body; cleaning, cleansing and opening up like a Morning Glory flower opening it's petals to the rays of the sun. Stay with this feeling for as long as you want to.

3. Keeping with you a Tigers Eye, Citrine or any other crystal you resonate with that is specifically aimed at restoring and balancing your Solar Plexus chakra. Simply place the crystal on your Solar Plexus area for as long as you feel it is needed.

As you do so, try to tune into how the crystals' energy feels on your body; perhaps you feel tingling in that area or somewhere else on the body or maybe you feel energised and confident. Simply use this time to *be* with your body and notice any obvious and subtle changes. Ironically you will be using your body's intuitive capabilities to know when it is the right time to cease using the crystals.

Mostly C's signifies CLAIRAUDIENCE: This is the ability to 'hear' using your physical ears or through your mind. When you receive an intuitive hit it may come through as ringing in the ears or even as simple words that are spoken in the mind that are not your own words even though it will likely sound like your own voice. Just to be clear, anything that is spoken in the mind that comes from your Higher Self and the Universe is always from a place of love. Never will there be messages that encourage self-mutilation, self criticism, judgment, ridicule or any other character diminishing advice. You may also hear certain music playing on the radio that is meaningful to where you are on your manifestation journey. In fact there have been many times I have asked a question relating to my path and it be answered by a certain song playing on the radio or over the supermarket speakers. Recently I was in the car thinking about my chosen career path. I put it to the Universe, 'Okay, this is my intention; write books, host workshops, and help as many people as I possibly can. Can I really do that?' And sure enough the radio played the song; Bloody Well Right by Supertramp, a song I had not heard before but the chorus completely spoke to me as if it had been written just for me – 'Right (right) you're bloody well right...' It instantly put a smile on my face because I knew that I was 'bloody well right' on the path.

As with all intuitive senses, it is important to practice various techniques to continue to strengthen your clairaudient abilities. You can do this by:

1. Practicing the art of listening. During bedtime, when you will be less distracted, practice listening for the subtle sounds around you. Perhaps you may hear a car driving in the distance, an owl hooting from the trees, or the wind whooshing through leaves of the trees. Try to tune into as many sounds as you can and determine which ones are loud and which ones are subtle. The more you focus on the subtle noises, the more your clairaudient abilities will strengthen.

2. Making the intention to your Higher Self, Universe, angels, spirit guides and higher beings of love and light, that you are ready and open to hearing their guidance. You can say this out loud so you can hear your voice and the words of intention.

3. Visualising a radio in your mind whereby you can turn the dial to tune into the radio channel of your Higher Self and Universe. Mentally ask a question and listen for a response. If the signal sounds fuzzy, visualise yourself playing with the dial of the radio to find the right channel. You may then receive a clear voice replying to your question, or you may hear nothing at all. Continue to practice. It is very common to hear nothing on the first attempt so do not give up because persistence is the key to hearing your intuition clearly.

Mostly D's signifies CLAIRCOGNIZANCE: This is the ability of simply knowing certain things without being told. This is quite possibly the hardest intuitive sense to explain because there is no proof to any of the claims made. As a claircognizant, you are likely saying in conversations, 'I don't know *how* I know, I just know' despite having absolutely no logical proof. This knowingness generally comes through your thinking mind as a thought or an idea. It is because of this that you tend to be quite analytical and good at problem solving. I believe the biggest issue with being claircognizant is knowing the difference between a thought and intuitive guidance. When you receive intuitive guidance, it will just come to you out of nowhere and often has nothing to do with what you were thinking about. And because your Higher Self and the Universe want the best for you, the information sent will transcend any kind of fear your ego would normally indulge in. Another point to realise is that your own thoughts will usually not ask you to take a leap of faith (because that would likely be too scary), yet your own Higher Self and the Universe may. The key is to become aware of and strengthen your claircognizant abilities. You can do this by:

1. Reflecting on the times when you *knew* something would happen and it did. For instance, if you hear yourself saying, 'Oh I knew that was going to happen!', then consider when and how you received that information about the particular event in the first place. Focus on how it came to you whether by words in your mind or images as well as how it made you feel.

2. Practicing automatic writing. This is my personal favourite method of communicating with my Spiritual Support Team. All you need is a piece of paper and a pen. On the top of the page simply write a question you would like answered that

relates to your heart's desires or anything else for that matter. Then simply make the intention either out loud or in your mind that you wish to connect with your Spiritual Support Team to help you answer your question. Next, write down anything that comes to mind in response to your question. Do not judge what you are writing or worry if it is making any sense, just continue to write. Eventually the chatter will subside and the divine messages will come through. When I first did this exercise I had a few pages of gobbledegook before my Claircognizance was able to come through. The trick is to surrender to your thoughts and just let your hand do the writing (or typing if you choose to use a computer instead).

3. Practicing mindfulness. Since your claircognizant abilities rest solely on using the mind to receive the intuitive insights, it stands to reason that the mind must be fairly calm and centred. A frenzied mind is less likely to pick up intuitive hits because the focus is placed on distractions. To be mindful is to simply be in the moment such as focusing on a drinking a cup of tea; taking in the colour of the tea, the scent, the warmth, and taste. This instantly removes any overpowering emotions and allows your mind to be in the here and the now. This will instantly power up your Claircognizance as your mind declutters itself from ego-based thoughts.

When your body is healthy and maintaining homeostasis then it is far easier to pick up the intuitive signals. And now that you know which of the intuitive senses is your primary sense, you can then start to build and strengthen the connection for guidance on manifesting your heart's desires.

If there is ever a time you feel blocked from receiving intuitive inspiration, then I highly recommend freestyle dancing. Dancing is such a wonderful way to reconnect to your body and allow your spirit to move your body instead of your ego taking over. This is not about specialised choreographed steps such as dancing the foxtrot or doing a pirouette, this is simple free-form dancing. However you want to move your body, do so. If you want to shake your hips, do it. If you want to fist pump the air, do that too. If you feel like doing high kicks then by all means, go for it! It does not matter how good or terrible you dance, just move. When you become fully present in your body and you place yourself in the moment without engaging in mindless chatter, then you will find it far easier to connect to your intuition because it is your body that is intuitive.

Chapter 19 – Expect Guidance

What you expect will show up one way or another. Intuition is no different. Expect it to provide you with answers, and it will.

Earlier in this book I wrote about how important it is to expect your desires to manifest into reality. Because when you expect something to happen, it will. The same goes with intuition. If you expect to *receive* intuitive guidance then that is exactly what you will get. There will come a time when you will be able to ask a question and receive an intuitive response as easy as if you were ringing up to order a takeaway pizza. Of course this may take practice in terms of strengthening your primary intuitive sense, but with practice comes a greater connection.

'I expect it to happen, therefore it will'

So how do you *expect* intuitive guidance? Well put it this way. Your intuition is the most natural part of you. So too is the air we breathe. I can honestly say I have not once started the day wondering if there will be enough oxygen for me to breathe or whether I will remember to breathe at all. It has become so ingrained into my human existence that I simply assume that there will be an abundance of oxygen for me to inhale and that my body will know when the right time to breathe and exhale is. I expect to breathe, therefore I do. Intuition is no different. I expect my intuition to guide me because my intuition is *me*. And that is the key; it is *always* there for you. There is nothing you need to do to call it in nor do you need to go through any kind of initiation to become 'intuitive'. It is not a gift; it is your natural state. It has and always will be there because it is *you* as a pure loving spirit connected to universal

Expect Guidance

support at *all* times. If you can realise that your intuition is right there with you in this very moment as you read this book, then you will come to realise a powerful secret; when it comes to loving guidance and support, you are never (and never will be) alone in this lifetime or any other lifetime whether it be on this planet or in another dimension. It is impossible to be spiritually alone when you are connected to the Universe. And once you realise this, then you will understand how easy it is to live an intuitively guided and inspired life.

But if you place worry around the idea that your intuition will not come to you then you will likely miss the intuitive hits. Your mind will be so focused on the inadequacies of your intuition that it can make it fairly impossible to hear the gentle whispers of your soul. Of course there may be an old memory lurking in the background that is stopping you from expecting your intuition to work so ensure you practice the Self Muscle Test (page 154) and if it turns out you do not expect your intuition to work then continue with Activity #14: *Isolate Old Memories* (page 187) to reach the core memory, and then Activity #2: Releasing the Old Memories (page 62), Activity #16: *Healing Old Memories with Divine Energy* (page 215), or Activity #17: *Working with the Light* (page 232) to remove the core memory and subsequent memories before replacing them with the actual truth of who you are.

Don't just expect your intuition to work, rely on it

I believe the biggest reason why it can be difficult to expect intuitive guidance to work is because many people do not trust it, or more to the point, they do not trust themselves (their own counsel). For many people, decisions are made solely on facts, statistics, and past events. This is where the logical mind and ego thrive. And because the left side of the brain is on high alert and making a lot of mental noise as it constantly thinks and calculates, the intuitive aspect of ourselves (the non-linear guidance that bypasses the logical mind) cannot be heard. All those intuitive based messages that serve to guide you on the path of least resistance go to waste because of the incessant chatter! Imagine trying to have a nice romantic dinner with your partner whilst rap music is being played so blaringly loudly that your ears hurt. If you simply turned the volume down then the music could still play in the background whilst you enjoy your partners company. This is not about resigning the logical mind completely but simply changing the roles around.

> *The logical mind was never created to be the dominant force of decision making, it was always meant to be the servant to our intuition.*

So the key is to listen, feel and trust your intuition *first* and then use your logical mind to take action. When you do this, both will be in harmony with one another.

For example, Lucy has decided to leave her office job and run her own business as a natural therapist. She has handed in her resignation but is now unsure what the next step is for her. She decides to ask her intuition for guidance. Her intuition tells her to register a booth at her local health expo to showcase her work as well as sign up to do a talk on stage during the expo. Upon receiving this information, Lucy begins to feel nervous and starts thinking about how she has only just started as a natural therapist. She wonders what she would offer at the expo and what she would talk about on stage. Then she starts to question why anyone would seek her out at all if she has only just started in the industry with very little experience. She realises that the expo would be full of well seasoned natural therapists and she would simply not belong. After a few minutes of negative self talk, Lucy decides it is not 'logical' to continue down this path so she ignores the advice made by her intuition.

Unfortunately it was not logic (or intuition) that was telling Lucy to avoid the expo. It was her underlying fears and old memories sabotaging her ability to move forward. What her logic was *actually* telling her was:

- Research the needs and wants of the expo attendees and offer a natural therapy service to help them with their biggest problem.
- Consider which natural therapy technique has been useful to Lucy and talk about her own experience on stage to empower others.
- Create a way to follow up with expo attendees so she can help them even when the expo event is over.

Fear is not your intuition (read the next chapter about this because it is such an important topic), but it can be useful as a feedback mechanism. It is not an indicator of where you will be in the future but rather it a sign of where you currently are. In Lucy's case, she has some old memories attached to the belief that she is not good enough, smart enough or experienced enough. She also has old memories around the fear of speaking her truth, shining her light and being successful. If Lucy were a client of mine, we would be doing some old memory clearing!

Eat Cake

So you see, your intuition and logical mind work together in harmony to provide you with a clear and whole picture of your potential and how to reach it. This is so important as you move toward your dream life because it is my belief that deep down what we all truly desires is wholeness. This wholeness may look different on a physical level but on an emotional and spiritual level it is the same for all of us. But we cannot all experience wholeness, or even have the wholeness of an experience, if we remove either logic or intuition. The two must work together.

So if intuition comes first, then how do you receive intuitive guidance? Easy! Ask for it. You do not need to create a sacred space, beat a drum, or dance an elaborate number before 'connecting' unless you really want to of course. All you need to do is *ask* for guidance and then importantly, listen with your body using whichever primary intuitive sense you discovered earlier in this book.

Activity #22: Connecting to Your Intuition for Divine Answers

Since your intuition is the voice of your Higher Self (and sometimes your Spiritual Support Team), and since your Higher Self is always there by your side, then you can easily ask questions to help you move forward and create your dream life. The key to establishing a good connection to your intuition is to get back into the body and be in the moment. Here is a wonderful and simple exercise to help you receive intuitive guidance.

1. Think about an area of your life you would like guidance, clarity or perspective on and create a question around it. Try to keep it clear and succinct as this will help you receive the clearest answer. For example:

    - *What do I need to know about _____?*
    - *What is really going on with _____?*
    - *How can I improve this situation?*
    - *What is the best course of action to take regarding _____?*
    - *Why do I feel stuck / confused / blocked?*
    - *Is there something I am missing or not seeing? And if so, what is it?*

2. Keeping in mind the question you have just formulated, invite your logical mind to step forward to provide you with guidance. There are two additional questions to ask your logical mind following your original question:

    *'What does my **mind** say?'*
    *'What does my **fear** say?'*

For example.

- How can I improve the relationship with my partner so that we feel the passion again? What does my mind say? What does my fear say?
- I want to get excited about our family getaway but I'm not. Is there a good reason for this? And if so, what is it? What does my mind say? What does my fear say?
- Why am I struggling to attract more money into my life? What does my mind say? What does my fear say?

It may be helpful to write down your mind's response. Continue to repeat these two questions until you have 'brain dumped' all the possible answers from your mind. Interestingly enough, the more spiritual work you do, the less fear-based answers you will receive.

3. Now that you have given your logical mind a voice, it is time to invite your intuition to provide you with the guidance you seek. Close your eyes, and take a few slow deep breaths to bring yourself back into your body and back into present time.

4. Focus your mind on your breath as the air moves in, either through your nose or through your mouth, and out again. Simply watch the breath and become aware of any sensations the breath creates in your body. As you breathe in, you may notice the sensation of the breath moving in through your nose, the expansion of your chest and abdomen, or the way your body seems to relax as it is

nourished by life force energy. And as you breathe out, imagine any tension easily leaving the body.

5. Continue to do this until you feel calm, relaxed and centered.

6. Now ask your intuition the original question you had formulated at the beginning of this activity and follow it by saying,

> *'What does my **spirit** say?'*

(You may like to place your hand on your heart to become completely connected to your spirit)

For example:
- 'Why do I feel like I have hit a roadblock when trying to reach my weight loss goals? What does my spirit say?'
- 'What is the best course of action to take regarding my relationship with my brother? What does my spirit say?'
- 'When is the right time to ask for a promotion? What does my spirit say?'

7. Be open to any impressions or answers you receive and try to avoid employing your logical mind by 'thinking' into it. Since it is your body that is intuitive, notice how it feels, any physical sensations, as well as thoughts, images and auditory cues that may arise. This is a perfect time to tune into your primary intuitive sense.

8. Take notes during this time. Do not sensor your thoughts or process them with your logical mind, just keep writing. Sometimes intuitive guidance may seem to make no sense or the answers will seem incomplete but write it all down anyway. If you do not receive an answer then try sitting with the question in silence and stillness. Do not try to push an answer; just wait for it to come.

9. If you feel called to, you can continue to ask one question at a time and write down the response but ensure you employ your logical mind first and then your intuition so the two have an equal say on the matter.

10. When you have finished, read over all that you have written from the perspective of your logical mind and intuition (spirit). You may surprise yourself just how much wisdom has come through that will help you move forward in life.

Chapter 20 – Live an Intuitively Guided Life

She was ready to surrender. Since following her ego was only leading her to a dead end, she decided to follow her vibes instead. It was the best decision she had made.

Depending on the situation, your intuition (and the Universe) will not always wait for you to consciously ask a question before it provides an answer. This is quite possibly the trickiest aspect of deciphering intuitive nudges since you are not intentionally focused on receiving guidance. We all receive intuition through our body and you have already uncovered your primary intuitive sense which will make it easier for you to tune in, so now it is simply a matter of remembering some key points to live an intuitively guided life. When you incorporate the naturalness of your intuitive sense, it will make the art of manifestation easy and in most cases, incredibly fun!

Know your primary intuitive sense and be open to the fact that you may have more than one. When you are aware of the area of your body that picks up the intuitive frequencies, then you can be aware of the subtle changes of that particular part of the body caused by an intuitive nudge. So practice *being* in your body and sense it's energy. When you feel, see, hear, smell or taste something that does not seem to relate to your current surroundings or situation, then stop and tune in because your intuition is likely telling you something important.

Name and claim your intuition. From now on, honour your intuition by acknowledging when it has provided you with guidance. For example you might like to say, 'My gut feeling tells me…', 'My vibes are saying...', 'My spirit is encouraging me to...', 'I have a hunch about...', or 'The goose bumps on my body are telling me...' Make your intuition part of your language so it becomes a part of you even in conversation. When you name and claim your intuition, you open the door to creativity and authentic self-expression; two highly potent aspects of yourself that when embraced will provide the wholeness you are searching for.

Be aware that intuitive guidance can appear subtly and quickly so it is important to pick up on the signs early. Unfortunately when intuitive guidance is received the logical mind can be fairly quick to react. Often times it will ask questions such as, 'What was that? or, 'Where did that information come from?' and when it comes to taking action, the logical mind may jump to asking, 'Where is the proof that it will work?' or, 'Show me this has been done before!' It simply cannot help it! The truth is your intuition cannot always provide proof. Sometimes the intuitive guidance is beyond logic and reason. In fact often times the guidance received will make no sense at all in that very moment and since the logical mind loves proof before making a decision, it will likely dismiss the guidance and move on. It is only a week, a month or even a year later that you discover your intuition was right all along. So the trick is to notice the subtle messages the body picks up and then see how quickly the rational mind will jump in and question the truth and validity. Then it is a matter of rewinding the logic-based thoughts like a movie until you get back to the moment you initially received intuitive guidance. You may like to ask yourself, 'What message did I receive before my logical mind took over?', 'What was it that I was feeling before my body started reacting to my logical mind?', 'What did I see in my mind's eye before other images came to mind?' and then breathe and wait. It will come to you.

Live an Intuitively Guided Life

> **The Case of the Missing Bra.** It was only this morning that my intuition helped me greatly. Today was an important family event and naturally I was running late. Frustratingly, somewhere in the vortex of unfolded clothing, socks and underwear, I had lost my bra. I looked everywhere; in the drawer, under the clothes sprawled on the bed, under the bed, in the bathroom, in the wash basket, on the couch, and even on the dining room chairs, but it was nowhere to be seen. It is the second most comfortable bra I own so I was really counting on wearing it today! Through the inner loud noise my mind was making about how I really need to start putting my clothes away properly and how I should really start getting ready earlier, a little and subtle voice said, 'Check the drawer again'. "I already have!" I thought with a bit of annoyance that I was being guided to do something I had already done, but the voice repeated, 'Check the drawer again'. So I did, and there it was, my second most comfortable bra sitting right there in plain view. I must have overlooked it in my haste to find it!
>
> Now although this is not a 'blow your socks off' kind of example, I invite you to realise that your intuition is not always going to provide firework worthy outcomes nor is it going to scream at you to get your attention. For the most part intuition is the little voice or the little nudge, and when you know what to look for it will become incredibly easy to notice. Also realise that your intuition will help you in subtle ways that seem small and insignificant but really, when you stop and think about it, the guidance truly does make a big difference to your life. Even finding a lost bra is a big deal. In fact, every intuitive hit is a big deal that should be celebrated with gratitude and love.

Trust your intuition. To help you gain trust in your intuition, I encourage you to keep an Intuitive Journal and write down every intuitive insight you receive even if you are unsure whether it was indeed intuitive based. This is such a powerful way of honouring your natural sixth sense because:

1. You are recording all possible intuitive messages which means you will never forget them and therefore can act upon them even if the logical mind has already tried to interfere.

2. You are giving your intuition a voice which means deep down you hold a belief in its power and are therefore open to receiving more guidance (this is so important when it comes to manifesting and knowing which path to take!).

3. You are accumulating evidence that your intuition is to be trusted. When you act upon the guidance given and it changes your life in powerful and positive ways, then you can stop wondering if your intuition should be trusted, and start believing it as *your* truth.

Come to understand that your intuition is the most natural part of you and quite frankly *essential* to living the life of your dreams. When you understand this you will become comfortable confiding in it and trusting the guidance you receive. And when you do receive guidance, try not to interpret it as a 'weird' or 'freaky' thing. For example, instead of say, 'Oh my gosh! The freakiest thing happened! I felt drawn to go into an antique shop yesterday, and when I did I found an old blanket box I've wanted for months! What are the odds of finding it?!', why not celebrate the naturalness of your sixth sense and own it by saying, 'Oh my gosh, I followed my gut feeling yesterday which told me to go into an antique shop, and I found the blanket box I knew in my heart I would eventually get. I'm so grateful for trusting and following my intuition!'

Know the difference between intuition and fear. The first thing to realise is that intuition will not diminish your soul in any way. It knows what is best for you and it will encourage you to take inspired action but it will never force you to do anything, insult you, or judge you. Your intuition is not emotional, it is simply neutral, therefore when your receive an intuitive nudge, it will feel, look or sound neutral.

I was in the car with my husband and I caught an image in my mind of a left wheel coming loose from what I thought was the car we were travelling in at the time. There was no emotional attachment to this image; I was simply observing it in my mind's eye. I relayed what I had seen to my husband who checked each of the car tyres just to be sure. Everything seemed to be fine. It was the next day that my husband rang me and told me that he was driving the truck at work and discovered that the truck's left front wheel had come loose. This is a classic example of the neutralness of intuitive nudges; there was no emotional attachment or charge, just a vision that disappeared just as quickly as it appeared.

Some people often mistake the feeling of excitement as an indicator of being on the right track, or the feeling of dread as being on the wrong track, but these emotions are secondary to the intuitive nudge. The emotion we feel is the reaction we have to the intuitive nudge. Normally it is fear that creates drama around the intuitive guidance. Fear will feel anxious, stressful, and negative. It will build upon itself to a point where you talk yourself out of whatever it was your intuition had originally encouraged you to do. On the other hand, intuition will bring about a sense of knowingness with an affirming tone.

Eat Cake

The best way to tell the difference between intuition and fear is to get a gauge on your emotions. Ask yourself, Where does fear, or worry, or anxiety show up in my body? And what does it feel like? Because you simply cannot receive intuitive inspiration and fear at the same time; they are entirely different frequencies. So if you receive a nudge and then you feel fear or any other highly emotional state, or you feel a negative physical reaction such as a headache or stomach ache, then I encourage you to stop and acknowledge what your fear is telling you. Anytime you feel fear, it is simply an old memory coming to the surface of your existence. It is your opportunity to break the pattern because when fear enters the mind, it can become like a runaway freight train; very difficult to stop. So challenge the old memory. Simply realise that, 'Okay, I'm telling myself a lie right now. What is this lie and how can I move past this?' and then use your intuition to connect to an answer by practicing Activity #22 – *Connecting to Your Intuition for Divine Answers* (page 287). The idea behind this is to give your fear a voice because fear is not our enemy but rather an old memory of what we have either experienced in the past or what we have been told from, for example, family, friends, news reporters and social media.

Fear has no way of knowing the true magic of the Universe nor does it understand the higher plan the Universe has for you. It wants to protect you from the unknown but the unknown is where the greatest of creations come from. And since you are constantly creating through manifesting a life of your dreams, then your fear will need to learn to take a back seat and let the intuition be the driver. Of course sometimes your intuition may warn you of upcoming challenges which can create feelings of anxiety, worry and stress. But remember that your intuition is neutral and unemotional. So if you feel fearful of the information you have received, then ask your intuition; 'Was that my fear speaking?' If the answer is, 'Yes', then you know there are some old memories that are ready to be cleaned and cleared. If the answer is 'No', then take appropriate action to follow through on your intuitive vibes.

At the end of the day, if your intuitive nudge inspires you toward something that would make you feel passionate, elated, and happy, then it is good advice. If it pleases you, interests you, and thrills you, then it is good advice. If it sparks enthusiasm and creativity that serves others in wonderful ways that will also bring wholeness to your life, then it is good advice. But if it is a heart's desire-challenging belief, then it has no place in your world. Always do what your *intuition* tells you to do. It knows the path that fear does not.

*When I follow my sixth sense,
I am led on a road of creativity, wonderment and wholeness. There is nothing greater or more powerful than that.*

Additional Manifestation Tools

Message from your future self: 'Psssst…you will be okay. Life is wonderful. I'm proof of that.'

Chapter 21 – Manifesting with the Energy of the Moon

She realised that want she wants will not manifest until she consciously aligns with it.

Cast your mind back to when you first got a mobile phone. I remember mine as clear as day. It was a Nokia 5110—a big bulky phone with large rubber buttons and a bright green cover. I thought I was so cool walking around with this phone; taking it out of my bag (it would not fit in my pocket) to play with the buttons, navigate the menu and touch the outer casing. And the Snakes game! Oh my gosh! Do not even get me started on the loveable Snakes game! But a few weeks later the new and fancy mobile phone began to feel familiar. I had scrolled through all the options, tested all the ringtones, and played the Snakes game until I could no longer beat my own score. It did not feel as exciting anymore. It was just another device that became a part of my everyday experience; just another thing in my life I would take for granted. Sound familiar? Even if you have never owned a mobile phone in your life, which by the way good on you as they are distracting as heck, then think about the other times you were excited about shiny new objects only to find that the novelty eventually wore off.

What about this book? If this is your first time reading this book then you are currently in the honeymoon phase. This is the 'novelty' part of the shiny new object. Looking at the cover of this book is a new experience, reading each page is a new experience, and practicing the techniques may be new for you too. It is all refreshingly new and exciting. But what happens when you finish this book and pop it in your bookcase? Will the FEPMIA method continue to be your best friend? Will you continue to participate in the activities? Will the gratitude for the life you have and the abundance that is already on its way to you continue to be at the forefront of your mind? Likely no. I will just be honest here and say that the new, shiny, and sparkly aspects of this book *will* eventually wear off. And I can honestly say that I am the least happiest about it because it means that even though you will create excellent momentum to fulfilling your dreams, it is likely you will fall short if you become victim to Shiny Object Syndrome. So in light of that, I encourage you to do something extremely important.

Replace 'novelty' with 'commitment to the cause'

Firstly, I ask you to embrace the fact that the novelty *will* disappear. This book and the techniques in it will not always give you the a hit of Dopamine and Norepinephrine (the feel good neurotransmitters of the brain), so when this happens you will need to choose from two options. You can either disregard all the techniques in this book and do something else (but remember that any new thing you try will eventually lead to the novelty wearing off, ultimately placing your life in a habitual shiny new object cycle), *or* you can see the novelty wearing off as an opportunity to deepen your roots and commit to the importance of releasing yourself of the old memories, loving your true self again, and turning your desires that you have uncovered into reality. Perhaps it may be useful to relook at Activity #3: *Discovering Your True Desires* (page 76) where you explored how fulfilling your true desires benefits you and others. Your answers are part of the *cause* and it is your responsibility to commit to the cause and make magic happen. The Universe can only do so much. It will bring the right people and experiences for you to find the perfect career. It will provide you with numerous opportunities to find love. It will create what seems like chaotic situations to help you decide what you *do not* want in life. It is limitless in power but it cannot force you to do *anything*. You have the power of free will. You choose whether you are prepared to commit to turning your life around or not. No one can change your life for you. But there are resources that can help and a primary resource that has been invaluable for me during my manifestation journey (and continues to be) is the moon, specifically moon rituals.

Moon rituals are a beautiful way to connect to your true self, your Spiritual Support Team, and the Universe. It is a simple way of removing yourself from the daily grind and honouring the importance of yourself and the manifestation of your dreams. This is especially crucial when the honeymoon phase of this book is over and the novelty of manifesting has worn off. So if you feel a little blasé about putting in the effort to create your dream life, then I encourage you to practice the moon ritual so you can fully commit to your cause; recharge and recalibrate your energy, make new intentions of where you want your life to be, and release anything that no longer serves you. Another positive aspect of a moon ritual is that every one of them will turn out differently. I can honestly say that not one of the rituals I have done have been the same as another. They have all brought about new information and insights into my life, and importantly, they have all played a big part in my manifestation and spiritual journey. I do not see a moon ritual as homework but rather an absolute necessity for my wellbeing.

So why conduct a ritual during particular moon phases? Personally I enjoy the cyclic nature of the moon. There are times I have become completely engrossed in life that is occurring all around me that I forget to check in with myself to evaluate what my spirit wants in order to grow and flourish. Ironically, when I put my own needs on hold, I become less useful to others because I am so physically, emotionally and spiritually drained. The part of me that wants to help others eventually becomes affected which is certainly not what I want! So the moon is my naturally occurring calendar. In fact, not only am I able to commit to my manifestation-cause regularly, as guided by the moon, but the phases of the moon can also determine the kind of ritual I am going to do. For instance, during the full moon, it is the perfect time to do some shadow work (page 140); uncover, cleanse, and release old memories. During the new moon, which occurs on average 14.75 days *after* the full moon, it is an opportunity to focus and plan on new beginnings. So when it comes to manifestation, your intentions to work with the new moon should revolve around attracting, building and growing because that is what the new moon represents. If it is about releasing an old memory then you will need to focus on what you will *gain* when you release it (complete Activity #15: *Making Peace with the Core Memory*, page 204, and Activity #16: *Healing Old Memories with Divine Energy*, page 215 during the full moon to release an old memory).

Make moon rituals a naturally occurring habit to release the old memories and embrace the new ones

The internet has all the information you need on the yearly lunar cycles and when the full moon and new moon will occur. In fact I recommend you make a note at the beginning of the new year of when the different moon cycles are occurring for the upcoming year and then you will be all set to manifest to your heart's content all year round.

Activity #23: Moon Ritual – Manifesting with the Moon

There is no right or wrong way of practicing a moon ritual; it is entirely up to your own preference and what speaks directly to your heart and spirit. The ritual I have included here is the one I use. This is to give you an idea of what a ritual may look and function like. You can follow it step by step or you may like to take various aspects of it and create your own unique practice.

Preparation:

- **Gather your manifesting tools**: Use tools that make you feel inspired and connected to your Higher Self, Spiritual Support Team and the Universe.

    Essential Tools:
    - This book (for guidance)
    - Blank paged journal (try to use a journal that contains no lines so you can freely write and draw, but if you can only find a lined journal that is okay too)
    - Pen to write and draw with
    - Two pieces of paper*
    - Candle and matches*
    - Crystal or rock
    - Incense or white sage to burn*
    - One bowl with salt water (add salt to water)
    - One empty fire-proof bowl*
    - Hand towel

    Optional tools:
    - Coloured pencils

Eat Cake

- o Oracle cards
- o Crystal pendulum
- o Flowers
- o Cup of green tea or other comforting beverage to place you in a relaxed state which is the perfect vibration for consciously creating your own reality.

*Fire Safety Note: During the moon ritual you will be using an exposed flame. Ensure you are fully versed in fire safety and have fire safety equipment close by before taking part in the ritual.

- **Create a sacred manifesting space**: This is simply a personal space indoors or outdoors that you wish to dedicate to the practice of manifesting. It can be for instance, an altar, your kitchen table, an area of grass in your backyard, or your bedside table. Just choose a space that provides you with some privacy and comfort as you do this work. When you have chosen the space, make it beautiful. Keep candles, flowers, incense, crystals, a journal to write in and other symbolic items that create a deep feeling of spiritual connection and inspiration.

- **Clear your sacred space**: Every item no matter how big or small stores psychic energy (including you). If the psychic energy consists of a negative vibration, it will likely interfere with the manifestation practice. Think of it like eating a piece of rotting fruit. The nutrients from a rotting fruit are not as prevalent as they are when the fruit is ripe. The same goes for yourself and your sacred space. A negative low vibrational space is not ideal when working on attracting your high vibrational desires. So before you commit to the ritual, it is important to clear yourself and your sacred space by, for example, burning white sage (smudging), clapping, or ringing a bell. Whatever method you choose ensure you make a small invocation *before* you clear the space such as;

'Dearest Universe. With this tool (e.g. smudging, clapping, ringing a bell etc), I make the intention to clean and clear myself and this sacred space so that the power of this ritual is magnified and amplified with the energy of the moon, the Sun, the Earth, and the higher beings of love and light. Thank you. And so it is'

Once you have gathered your manifesting tools, created a sacred space, and cleared the sacred space and yourself of negative psychic energy, then you are ready to take part in the moon ritual.

Moon Ritual

1. **Connect with the four elements of the Earth:** Our deepest want in life is to go home; reconnect with the divine and remember our inner most truth. This can be quite spiritual work and because of this, much emphasis tends to be placed on doing 'spiritual things' such as balancing the Chakras, drawing oracle cards or praying. Unfortunately for some people who have dedicated their lives to follow a spiritual path, they fail to connect to the other part of their spirit which is their connection to Mother Earth; the organism that nurtures and supports both our spiritual selves and human selves. Without Mother Earth we would be living in an entirely different dimension and so we would not have the physical opportunities we have right now. This is why I like to connect with the four elements of the Earth as a way to honour her and to recognise the love I have for my own human self. The way I do this is by bringing in

different items into the sacred space to represent the four elements of Earth:

- **Earth:** Hold your chosen crystal or rock to connect to the Earth for a few minutes and then place it near you
- **Fire:** Light your candle
- **Air:** Light your incense or white sage
- **Water:** Fill a small bowl with water and add some sea salt to represent the Earth's oceans

2. **Open the space and centre yourself:** Take a few deep breaths in and out to centre yourself as you connect to the four elements of Earth.

When you are ready you can make an intention of the purpose of the ritual, whether it be to explore your shadow self and release the old memories (this would be done during a full moon), or to explore your heart's desires and bring them into your awareness for manifestation (this would be done during a new moon). If you feel inspired to do shadow work and manifestation work at the same time, then do that instead. You may like to call upon your Spiritual Support Team for protection and guidance during this ritual. You can do this in any way that resonates with your spirit. Here is a simple invocation I like to do to bring in the energies of the Higher Beings of Love and Light into my sacred space before I continue with the rest of the ritual:

'Dearest Universe, Angels, Spirit Guides, my Higher Self and other Higher Beings of Love and Light. I am so deeply grateful for your presence and protection. I honour your willingness to speak into my

heart; helping me to call forward my heart's desires with ease. I thank you for guiding and supporting me to move my desires into creation. I open my heart to your powerful and loving energy and I am ready and honoured to receive all that is in alignment with my highest good. Thank you for reminding me of the power I possess, the grace I hold in my heart, and the knowingness that I deserve to receive simply because I infinitely exist. With love and light. And so it is.'

Words made with love and intention create powerful frequencies that radiate out to the Universe which are then reciprocated back to you (what goes around comes around). This is such a wonderful way to begin your ritual because you are placing yourself into a state of love and light; both are essential vibrations for effective shadow and manifestation work.

3. **Reflection Time –** ***Honour the Past Moon Ritual:*** Each moon ritual is an opportunity for growth so before you do any kind of shadow self work or invite new desires to consciously come forth for manifestation, I encourage you to honour the previous moon ritual with gratitude and reflection. Doing so will help you understand what came to be, what fell away, and what lessons were learned that can assist you in moving forward during *this* ritual.

So use this time to journal what comes to heart. I have also included some questions below that you may like to explore during reflection time:

- What intentions (if any) did you accomplish since the last moon ritual?

- What was the biggest challenge since the last moon ritual?
- What (if any) would you have done differently? Is this something you are willing and ready to do this month (if required)?
- What positive lessons did you learn about your spirit during this challenge?
- What positive lessons did you learn overall from the previous moon ritual?

Follow the reflection time with a prayer of gratitude and forgiveness even if the goals you intended to fulfil did not meet your expectations.

I will be honest with you; there were times I felt disappointed or frustrated when I reflected on the goals I had made from previous moon rituals, only to realise that they had not been met. When this happened I would allow myself to play the victim role and blame my circumstances on the Universe to try to make myself feel better, but of course that was completely counterproductive. It meant I was closed off from learning valuable spiritual lessons that are there to help me evolve as a spirit and reconnect me to the divine. I have since realised that even if my goals have not been met within the timeframe I expected, that it is still a great opportunity to re-evaluate them, redirect them, or replace them with new ones that meet my higher purpose.

Our lives are not lived in a linear fashion. When we make a decision to do something differently with our lives, it can ultimately change the entire course of our future. And when change occurs, so too do our goals and desires. So if you ever feel disappointed by the lack of speed in which your goals are being met, or you feel confused or frustrated by old memories surfacing whilst you try to fulfil the creation of your desires, then use this time to be kind to yourself. There is no need to judge yourself. Instead use this time to forgive yourself and others for resisting the flow of life. Also use this time as an opportunity for new insights, new awareness, and new desires to be born. Even during the times that are seemingly difficult, have gratitude for what lessons are waiting to be learned. Nothing happens to you, everything happens *for* you. Every moment is an opportunity to raise your vibration to a state of love and joy, and gratitude is the fastest and easiest way to do it. When you show gratitude for all that you have, you open the doors to abundance. And when you show forgiveness for all that has happened, you reconnect with your divine spirit and the infinite power of creativity which means your ability to manifest is limitless in nature.

Here is a simple prayer of gratitude, however you may wish to create your own from the heart.

Dearest Universe and all connected higher beings
of love and light.
I thank you from the centre of my heart for your unconditional
love, support and guidance.
I thank you for all the experiences I have had and yet to have
no matter how challenging and confronting they may be because
I know they help me recognise the miracles of life.
I thank you for this opportunity to grow as a spirit, to learn
my true power, and to express myself through joy and love.

Eat Cake

> *I thank you for helping me open my heart and allowing the energy of forgiveness to dissolve any resistance, anger and judgement I may be holding onto.*
> *And I thank you dearest Universe, for blessing me with your wisdom and for helping me meet all my spiritual, emotional and material needs effortlessly and with grace.*
> *With love and light, and so it is.*

4. **Release the Old (you may wish to do this during a full moon):** Use the power of the moon and your connection to the divine to dissolve any old memories inhibiting your ability to move forward in life.

    - On the top of a piece of paper, write, 'I am ready to release…' then write down all that you wish to release from your life. What old memories are you ready to be free of that no longer serve you?

    - Once you are done, sign and date the piece of paper.

    - Breathe in deeply and read over your list aloud then declare with an open heart, *'I am ready to be free of this and I willingly and lovingly let this go now. And so it is.'*

    - Place a corner of the paper over the open flame so the paper can ignite*, then place it in the empty bowl as it burns—watch the flames engulf the old memories; burning away any negativity while the smoke takes your intentions to the Universe.

        *Note: If the paper does not ignite or it seems to struggle to burn, then consider whether you are truly ready to let the particular old memory go. It is only when you are *truly* ready will the paper burn completely. In fact, the faster the flame, the more willing you are to surrender and release.

- Now dip your hands in the bowl of salt water to signify the cleansing of the old and embracing the new.

- Remove your hands from the water and dry them using a hand towel.

- Use the next few minutes to journal any inspiration you received during this part of the ritual. You may like to draw some oracle cards from your deck for further insights.

5. **Embrace the New (you may wish to do this during a new moon):** Now it is time to uncover what it is you specifically desire and start the exciting journey of creation.

    - On the top of a piece of paper write, 'I am ready to receive...' then write a list of all your wishes and desires. You may like to revisit page 89 where you wrote your heart's desires, and choose one (or more) that you feel closely aligned with right now, or alternatively you may wish to complete the following statements:
        - I am ready to release...
        - I am ready to nurture...
        - I am ready to heal...
        - I am ready to create...
        - I am ready to start...

- I am ready to finish…
- I am ready to offer…
- I am ready to learn…

  - Read over your list and check in with your body; can you sense any doubt, fear, frustration, guilt, shame or any other old memory that may sabotage your ability to create the life you wish? If you do, simply breathe into the sensation with an open heart. Realise that these are just old memories that are ready to be released if you are ready to actively release them.

  - Next, pass the paper through the incense smoke or white sage with the intention to clear away seen and unseen old memories that relate to the fulfilment of your heart's desires. You may like to say out loud as you do this, *'With this smoke, I release the old memories that no longer serve my highest good'*. Continue to pass the paper through the smoke until you feel cleansed and clear of any negative energy.

  - Now read over your desires and wishes once more, only this time read it out loud so the Universe can hear you and pick up on your vibration. Feel how your body responds to the desires. You may feel a sensation of excitement, joy and passion, or even a feeling of electricity pulsing through your body. Simply allow yourself to stay in this state of pleasure. You may even like to watch your desires take shape in your mind as if it is already in your life. When you are ready, breathe in deeply and say out loud, *'I am ready to receive. And so it is'*.

- Next, you may like to burn the list of desires, bury it, or place it somewhere that is sacred to you. Use your intuition to tap into whatever you feel is right for you.

- Now sit in silence for a while and open your heart to receive any inspiration and guidance from the divine. This is also a perfect time to journal freely; bringing forth inspiration from your Higher Self and the Universe. You may also like to draw some oracle cards from your deck, or use a crystal pendulum for further insights.

- Once you have finished the ritual you may like to close your sacred space with your favourite mantra or a prayer as you sense the energy of the ritual gently closing. During this time you can thank yourself for being present, thank the Earth, sun, moon, and the Universe for their presence. Another thing you may like to do on closing is to speak a few words about what you are most grateful for in that moment whether it be for the ritual, releasing old memories, embracing love, or anything else that inspires you. As you know by now, gratitude is the most powerful force of manifestation and so sealing the ritual with the vibration of gratitude places a great force behind your desires.

Conclusion

A Moon Ritual is your opportunity to honour the importance of yourself and the manifestation journey. It will always be a unique experience no matter how many times you do it. Just remember that this ritual is an example; a recipe of what I have found to work for me. But as with any recipe, you can add or remove ingredients for your own personal taste. This will come with confidence and experience.

Chapter 22 – In Case of an Emergency

The unexpected usually brings a gift of
unexpected delightfulness.

By now you realise that belief in the manifestation of your dreams is important and so too is being grateful for all the things currently in your life. You also realise that with positive thoughts, feelings, values and beliefs, positive experiences will follow. Hence a negative belief can truly impact the manifestation of the goals you have set yourself, particularly the ones you want to manifest quickly such as those you wish to manifest in less than thirty days.

As life would have it, sometimes we are thrown unexpected curve balls which may require our immediate attention. When this happens you may find your desires changing. You may suddenly go from desiring a holiday beach house to simply needing a house that does not have a serious Termite problem! When the unexpected happens, it can be hard to stay positive and energised. In fact you may find yourself feeling desperate and creatively stuck as to what action is needed to build the momentum around manifesting a solution to this unexpected curve ball (remember that even the bad situations are a gift in itself).

This is why the 'Letter to the Universe' method is useful for emergencies such as these. This method can help you vent to the Universe all your concerns about the impending challenge. Doing so will move the negative energy built up in your body and transfer it through pen and paper. Acknowledging the worry and stress you may feel about a particular situation is far more beneficial than holding on to such emotions. Remember that manifestation is simply a mirror of your own thoughts, feelings, values and beliefs.

Eat Cake

Writing all your concerns down will clear your mind and body of the associated negative beliefs and feelings, and put you in a much better state of being so that you can tackle whatever requires your attention right now in a positive frame of mind.

Give up your worries to the Universe
to make room for divinely guided solutions

Activity #24: Emergency Letter to the Universe

1. Sit or lie down where you will not be distracted.

2. Close your eyes and breathe deeply in through your nose and out through pursed lips. Repeat until you feel completely relaxed and then return to normal breathing.

3. Spend the next minute clearly visualising in your mind's eye the very thing you want to manifest. Try to create the exact experience of your dream by sensing how it feels to have it in your life right now. Try hearing how it would sound, see how it would look, and even taste and smell how it would taste and smell (if applicable).

4. As you focus on the visualisation before you, ask yourself, 'Do I have any fears or doubts relating to this particular thing I want to manifest?' With this question, watch how your visualisation changes. Do you see your visualisation changing to reflect fear and doubt? Do you feel fearful or doubtful that the situation will not be solved? Allow the visualisation to occur because it is simply showing you what you truly believe about the situation. The sooner you allow the doubts and fears to surface, the sooner you can overcome them. Remember to breathe calmly throughout this process. Once you have visualised what you *really* sense will happen, say out loud, *'Clear, cancel and delete that'*. Making such a command is telling yourself that you do not accept that visualisation as being the truth for you and that you can easily choose, by firstly clearing, cancelling and deleting your initial view of the situation to make way for a far more positive alternative.

5. Now open your eyes. The initial part of the activity may well be enough for you to get back into a positive state of mind to receive inspiration and guidance from the Universe as to what to do next, however, if you still feel an element of resistance and fear as to whether your desire will truly manifest then move on to the rest of the activity.

6. Get a piece of paper and a pen and begin writing a letter to the Universe. The letter will help you to become very clear on the dream you will manifest whilst also bringing all your doubts and fears out from the dark shadows of your subconscious mind and into the light where they can be released. Include the following in the letter:

   a. Today's date.

   b. 'Dear Universe' (or any name you associate with the energy that hears your inner feelings and thoughts).

   c. Describe where you are currently placed in life right this very moment (for example, *I am currently living in a house that is extremely unstable. I have been recently told there is a Termite infestation and the damage is extensive. Apparently it will take at least four months to fix so I need to move to another house during that time*). Essentially you are letting the Universe know that there is definite room for improvement regarding your situation right now.

   d. Describe the fears and doubts that came up for you when you did the visualisation earlier; for example, '*I'm afraid I won't find a house in time that is close to work or within*

In Case of an Emergency

my budget. Leasing a house is so expensive right now and I'm so scared I won't be able to afford it. I can't think of anyone I could live with either. This is such a disaster. How am I going to get through this—paying for not only the lease of a house but also paying for the Termite damage? I don't know if I can—what if I go bankrupt? Who can I turn to for help? I can't see a way out of this'. This helps bring the fears and doubts (old memories) to the surface. Issues such as these are far easier to deal with when you are honest about their existence. So list all the fears and doubts you have that relate to the particular thing you want to manifest.

e. Describe to the Universe what you want (your desire) in present tense using only positive words. Use the vision of your ultimate dream that you had in your mind's eye earlier to write this portion of the letter. Ensure you incorporate how it feels, looks, sounds, tastes and smells. Start the paragraph by writing, *'Thank you for taking care of all those fears and doubts I had earlier. I realise that any fears and doubts I had did not negatively affect the outcome of my desire because I have... [insert what it will be like when your desire has manifested—ensure you write in the present tense].'* You may also like to consider what the upside of this issue is; what positive lesson is it trying to teach you about yourself and your world?

For example, *'Thank you for taking care of all those fears and doubts I had earlier. I realise that any fears and doubts I had did not negatively affect the outcome of my desire because I am renting the most beautiful home that is within 20 minutes of my work. I am easily able to pay for the lease as well as the Termite damage without sacrificing my other needs which is such a relief! The entire process was very easy and stress-free—in fact, I'm unsure what I was worried about as I know you (the Universe) always has my back. Thank you for delivering me the most perfect outcome. I am so grateful! If it weren't for this experience then I wouldn't have learnt how supported I truly am or how flexible and adaptable I am in situations I cannot predict. Thank you, thank you, thank you!'* Here you can see that not only is the letter written as if the desire has already manifested, but it also includes how you would feel if certain things about the manifestation occurred; for example, 'It is such a relief!' or 'I'm really grateful.' This generates more positive energy because it is reminding you of how you will feel as a result of your desire becoming reality. This sense of feeling is far more powerful than the fears and doubts you may have been experiencing earlier.

f. Thank the Universe for doing such a wonderful job in helping you overcome the recent curve ball you were faced with at the beginning of this activity. Being grateful expands that positive energy even more. It also shows that you have full faith in the ability of the Universe to truly help you manifest a solution to the recent challenge.

g. Sign the letter with your sign-off name as you would for any letter you write.

In Case of an Emergency

    h. Fold the piece of paper, place it in an envelope and address it to: The Universe.

    i. Keep the envelope in a box that is especially for 'Letters to the Universe' until your dream of solving the challenge has manifested. From here, you do not need to worry any further about your dream becoming reality. You have already demonstrated that you have an expectation to the Universe that your dream of solving the challenge will come true whilst also letting go of any fears and doubts revolving around that particular dream.

Now all that is left is for you to be open to the inspiration and opportunities that come your way that will help to solve the situation you are faced with. You can also use the goal-setting activity (Activity #4: *Your Desires are Your Goals*, page 93) and the journal activity found in this book (Activity #27: *Keeping a Manifestation Journal*, page 342) to build momentum around fulfilling a desire that requires a more immediate manifestation response. Remember that once the opportunities present themselves, it is up to you to take action!

Chapter 23 – Declutter Your Life

When you make room for more, you receive more.

How do you feel when you enter a shop that is overstocked with 'stuff' coupled with hundreds of other people trying to sift through all the items? Do you generally feel calm and happy or does it create a sense of overwhelm and agitation? There is one particular shop I like to visit occasionally however it is full to the brim of unusual and random things which can make it difficult to see everything; it truly is a giftware store on steroids! In order to browse, I generally need to walk sideways so as to not bump anything off the shelves or bump into other shoppers. There are thousands of items hanging from the ceiling so I also have to be aware of when to duck down to avoid getting hit in the head by a random dream catcher or sun catcher. So I have a bit of a love-hate relationship with the shop. I love the huge number of objects stocked within such a confined space because it gives it character. I almost feel as though I am on a treasure hunt, and when I find something that I want to take home with me (or to gift to someone special) I get a rush of excitement as though I have won the lottery. But if I am already feeling irritated then I know to stay away from the places that can cause further irritation; this shop included! Some shops are simply meant to stock a large number of items in confined spaces but, like me, if you are already feeling a irritated, you may find the whole experience a little overwhelming; especially if you need to duck and weave throughout the store like a shopping ninja!

When you step into the vibration of overwhelm and agitation, you immediately step out of the vibration of openly receiving and experiencing peace.

So why am I telling you about this particular shop? Because when we surround ourselves with an abundance of objects that take up every single nook and cranny of our lives, we can eventually feel as though we have no control. Suddenly objects are no longer seen as pleasurable things but rather nuisances that are difficult to shift. And considering your heart's desires are a result of how you want to feel, and how you want to feel revolves around feeling 'good' in some way, then anything that takes up residence in your life that does not serve you in a good way is affecting your ability to manifest what you want. The 'things' in your life that impact your feel good vibes are referred to as clutter.

Clutter is stuck and stagnant energy that can prevent you from creating the life you choose, desire, and deserve. Throughout this book you have learned the importance of healing old memories particularly the core old memories. This is a form of emotional, spiritual and mental clutter. In terms of physical clutter, you may for instance, feel that there is not enough time to sort through the mail so the pile of mail gets bigger and bigger, or you may feel that there is not enough space in the home or office to file away important documents so the documents become randomly scattered. You may even place emotional baggage onto physical items so it can make it difficult to part with them even though you know deep down that holding onto those items is not healthy for you. Strength comes in choice, therefore if you wish to free yourself of old energy that is not serving your spirit, then you must choose to let it go.

This is why it is vitally important that you 'declutter' your life; meaning you remove all the things in your life that are not supporting your highest good. When you declutter your life, you are basically clearing the unneeded energy and making space for new and uplifting energy. Remember energy loves movement so you may as well make room for positive energy to fill the space instead of inviting negative energy into your life!

Everything I choose to have in my life is in harmony with my highest good. All my desires flow to me effortlessly because I have an abundance of space to invite them in.

Activity #25: Declutter Your Life

If you wish to invite more goodness into your life and remove the stagnant old energy that is no longer serving your highest good, then you must declutter your life.

I truly believe that if you declutter your environment, relationships, money and health, then you are well on your way to receiving abundance. The big take away from decluttering is to only surround yourself around people and things that you love. It truly is that simple!

1. **Declutter Your Environment:** Your home or office should be a sanctuary for your spirit. It should invoke feelings of calm, elation and peace instead of feeling overwhelmed and restless.

    a. Make six signs for sorting: Keep, Donate, Sell, Trash, Recycle and Can't Decide. Then place these signs in different areas of the room or house, or you can place them on individual boxes depending on how large the boxes are.

    b. Choose an area of your home or office you wish to start with, even if it is a small corner—just start somewhere!

    c. Start sorting with the intention of clearing the space to make way for the new.

        i. **Keep:** Choose items that light your spirit up with joy and love, or have great importance to your life, but ensure you are very selective. If something is sentimental, then consider if taking a photo of it would suffice in bringing forth those fond memories.

ii. **Donate:** Choose items that you no longer need or want that would be suitable for others to use. And when you are done, donate those items to your favourite charity or to someone who would benefit from receiving those things (donating to others in need generates wonderful vibes).

iii. **Sell:** Choose items that are worth your time to sell and of which other people would pay you money for.

iv. **Trash:** Choose the items that can be tossed away because they are unsalvageable, stained or damaged.

v. **Recycle:** Choose items that you no longer want or need which can be recycled into new products (it is such a wonderful feeling knowing you are doing your bit for the environment).

vi. **Can't Decide:** If you cannot decide what to do with a certain item, just pop it into the, 'Can't decide' area instead of interrupting the declutter flow. When you have finished decluttering, place these items in a labelled box and put it in storage for six months. In six months time review the box and repeat the sorting process. More often than not, you will realise just how much you do not need certain things you thought you did six months ago! In fact, if you have not needed the item during the past six months then it is likely you do not need the item at all.

2. **Declutter Your Relationships:** You are the company you keep. If you surround yourself around people who like to, for example, play the victim card, or take great pleasure in judging others or judging themselves, then you are essentially aligning your own energy to the negative beliefs that others hold. Now is the time to reconsider the relationships you keep in your life and determine whether they are helping you shine your own light and lift your spirit up, or if they are diming your light and pulling your spirit down so that it cannot flourish and attract all the goodness in this world. Although this activity may seem a little harsh, it can be quite an eye-opener as to who is enriching your life and who is not.

   a. **Uncover your main relationships:** Make a list of all the people you have regular contact with (e.g. family, friends, co-workers, boss etc).

   b. **Determine if the relationships are worth keeping:** Focus on each name and assign each a number from a scale of 1 – 10. Number one on the scale represents a person who *does not* support and encourage you. They judge you, criticise your choices, make you feel unhappy, lie to you, do not seem to care about you, embarrass you and enjoy belittling you. Number ten on the scale represents a person who fully supports and encourages you, raises you up when you are feeling low, makes you feel happy, lets you be yourself, listens to you, and is truthful and loyal—in fact, you cannot imagine your life without this person. When in doubt, tap into your intuition to sense if a certain person is genuine or not.

c. **Take the required action to declutter your relationships:** For those who have been assigned a number of six to ten, you can be sure that they genuinely and selflessly want to be a part of your life. Yet for those who received a number five or less, you may wish to reconsider your relationship with them and whether it is worth keeping them in your life. Ending a relationship with someone can be difficult but keep in mind that you deserve to do what is best for you. This is about practicing self care and compassion which is vitally important to receiving your heart's desires. If you surround yourself around people who emit toxic energy (including those who like to feed off your energy) then your own vibration will become affected. It is not an environment that you would wish to stay in if it does not nurture and support your highest good. For those who you are unable to remove completely from your life then you may like to practice the Ho'oponopono prayer (Activity #2: *Releasing the Old Memories,* page 62) to forgive those who have hurt you and to put closure on the past with certain relationships. You may even find that when you practice forgiveness, the person just naturally drifts out of your life.

d. **Surround yourself around positive people that you enjoy being around:** Continue this same decluttering exercise as you make new relationships. Only surround yourself around those who light your spirit up as you do for others.

3. **Declutter Your Money:** If it is more money your heart desires, then you may want to focus on the state of your wallet or purse because that is where your financial power lies. Your wallet or purse is the very thing that signifies your wealth yet if you do not respect this item, then it cannot respect you (remember, like attracts like). What you are aiming for in life is to fill it with love since that is who are after all. All energy wants to receive is love; even money does because money is just energy. So if your wallet or purse is full of old receipts and expired gift cards and coupons, or it is completely disorganised with coins from different countries and notes that are just stuffed in various compartments, then the energy around this sacred item is one of chaos and neglect. Money wants to be loved and respected. So here is how to declutter your money:

   a. Remove all expired gift cards, coupons and old receipts from your wallet, purse or bag. They are stagnate energy which is not conducive to receiving abundance. Doing this is sending a clear message to the Universe that you are ready to receive more.

   b. Look through your coins and determine if there are any that are of foreign currency. Put them in a jar elsewhere for safe keeping while placing your other coins in a safe place within your wallet or purse.

c. Unfold money notes and place them in a 'note allocated' compartment.

d. Inspect your wallet or purse and consider if holding it and looking at it evokes the feelings of love and happiness. If you are not in love with the look and feel of your wallet or purse then consider getting another one. Also ensure there are no rips and tears that would allow items stored within the wallet or purse to escape as this could signify abundance drainage.

e. Organise your wallet or purse so the placement of cards, notes and coins make sense.

f. If there is an old photo that you no longer like, remove it and replace it with something that brings a smile to your face. You may even like to cut out a heart from cardboard and write on it, 'I love money and money loves me', or 'Thank you Universe for unlimited abundance' and place it in your wallet or purse to see every time you open it. Then you will always be filled with gratitude for the abundance in your life.

g. Make a conscious effort to declutter your money once a week.

4. **Declutter Your Health:** Where would you be if it were not for your healthy body? Not on Earth that is for sure! Our wonderful bodies are our vessel to co-create a life we desire but it cannot do this effectively if we do not take

good care of it both physically and emotionally. Throughout this book you have explored and mastered how to look after your emotional self, so we will concentrate on how to declutter your health on a physical level.

  a. **Eat a healthy diet:** Each time you reach for the sugary or salty snacks consider whether it is the healthiest option for you. Instead, choose foods that will support your body such as fruits and vegetables. When in doubt, consult a healthcare professional or dietician who can guide you on which foods are suitable for your body and metabolism.

  b. **Sort out your refrigerator and pantry:** This is such a liberating experience as you can remove all the foods that only serve to add toxins to your body, including the sugary and salty foods. Removing these items will also stop temptation during those times when you crave unhealthy foods.

  c. **Stay hydrated:** On average our bodies are made up of 57-60% of water which means trillions of our cells need water to survive. It is vital that you drink plenty of water to stay hydrated to support your body and each and every cell. I take a water bottle everywhere I go—it has become a healthy habit! There are so many beautiful and unique water bottles available so you may like to purchase one that invokes feel-good vibes. There are also water bottles that have inspirational quotes on them which can also add to the good vibes in your life.

d. **Move that body:** Let your body move you in any way it wants. Moving your body instantly moves the energy within which is exactly what you want when manifesting. You may go from feeling cranky and irritated to feeling powerful and energised (remember, like attracts like). So turn on some music and dance even if you believe you are a terrible dancer, it truly does not matter. Go for a walk outside for 30 minutes a day to clear the mind and body. Enrol in a new fitness class you have wanted to participate in but just could not justify it (until now!). Whatever you do, choose something that you enjoy doing. It is pointless signing up for a particular exercise regime when you are not in love with the process. If you truly dislike a certain regime then you will likely give it up within a week anyway.

If you make a conscious effort to declutter these aspects of your life and other aspects if you feel called to, then you place your vibration into such a wonderful state to receive all the abundance and prosperity you desire and deserve.

Chapter 24 – You Are a Work in Progress

Today is the beginning of the rest of your life.

We are always going to want to create a life of our dreams yet when we get there, it is not final; life is never complete. There will always be more to do and more to learn. Everything in your life in this very moment is a result of the thoughts, feelings, values and beliefs you held the day before.

> *And so tomorrows manifestations are simply a result of today's thoughts, feelings, values and beliefs you focused and held onto today.*

This is potent information for you as you travel on this manifestation journey.

But of course life is not always smooth sailing. There will always be bumps in the road to overcome because that is just what life is at times. These bumps may appear for instance as a feeling of guilt, fear, disgust, frustration, disappointment or sadness. But these feelings are okay too. Since we live in a world of duality (good and bad) we must not disregard these valid feelings. They have just as much place in your life as does happiness, peace and love. There is very little point pretending that life is ponies and rainbows when in reality you are storing feelings that are causing you pain. Because if you store away the *bad* feelings then you are essentially amplifying them. This means you will still receive more experiences to fuel those feelings since it is the vibration you are *truly* emitting. You simply cannot lie to the Universe, and importantly, you cannot lie to yourself. So during those times when you are challenged with an

Eat Cake

apparent setback, the best thing you can do is to face it, feel it, and understand the gift it brings.

Whenever there is a roadblock in your life, you can choose to go over it, under it, around it, or through it. Either way, there is always a way.

Activity #26: Overcoming the Funk

When you are feeling low or in a bad mood, then it may be useful to look through these suggestions to help you move through it with ease and grace.

1. **Invite the negative feelings into your consciousness:** I know you do not want to *feel* negative in any way but you will. We all do at various times in our life. But instead of dismissing them as irrelevant, I invite you to welcome them into your consciousness. This may seem a little scary as most of us are taught that feeling 'bad' *is* bad. But I encourage you to instead see this as an opportunity to understand where or why it has come into your life. Sometimes the greatest gift comes from feeling the lows.

   Take some time away from distractions and announce to yourself how you are feeling by welcoming it into your consciousness. You may like to say, *'I acknowledge and welcome this feeling of..........'* And simply allow the feeling to come to the surface. You may find the feeling increases in intensity but that is okay. It may make you want to cry and shake, and that is okay too. You will be okay. This feeling cannot harm you; it is simply there as a messenger to tell you that something is unbalanced within your energetic system. It is a gift.

   I acknowledge and welcome this feeling of...

2. **Locate the feeling in your body:** Now that you have acknowledged the existence of this negative feeling, it is time to locate it in the body. The feeling may be felt for instance in the stomach area, chest, throat, or head. You may even find it is stored in multiple areas of the body.

Where is this feeling in my body?

3. **Feel into the feeling:** Now that you are aware of where in the body the feeling resides, you can simply *be* with it. This means you are not judging, blaming, or attaching the feeling to *anything*. You are simply *allowing* and witnessing. Let this feeling have its own moment—if it wants to intensify then allow it but do not act upon it. All you are required to do in this moment is to hold the space for it and *accept* it for what it is; a feeling. If the feeling is fairly intense, continue to remind yourself that you are okay. As my Gran loves to say, 'This too shall pass'. You may even receive flashes of images in your mind's eye as to where this feeling originated from. That is okay too. Simply remain detached to the 'where' and 'why' and just allow this feeling to exist.

I am holding this space for this feeling to be truly felt. I feel you and I see you.

4. **Give the feeling a voice:** Some would say it is the external world that makes us feel negative emotions. I believe however that external events and people cannot *make* us feel a certain way. It is my belief (as you have read throughout this book) that we have old memories within our energetic system coupled with expectation of how things *should* be. It is these things that create our feelings. Therefore the cause

of our feelings is *us*; it is a choice we have made. Our negative feelings are not caused by other people. They simply act as mirrors as to how we already feel or believe about ourselves and our world. To understand why the feeling is present within the body, it is necessary to give it a voice.

I am open to receive the gift of this feeling

To do this, I encourage you to invite your Higher Self into this space so that you can learn what special gift this feeling is giving you.

a. Place your hands on the area of the body you are feeling the feeling.

b. Breathe deeply with the intention to connect to your Higher Self (you are always connected to your Higher Self since your Higher Self *is* you) as the feeling can communicate through your Higher Self rather than your ego.

c. Ask the feeling self-exploration questions (or statements) such as,

- 'What are you teaching me about myself?'
- 'What is the gift you are giving me right now?'
- 'What is something I can do so I can let you go?'
- 'This feeling of…is teaching me to…'

- 'This feeling of...is helping me understand...'
- 'This feeling of...is protecting me from...'

You may receive divine insight into these questions or statements through your thoughts, images in your mind, or as a sense of knowingness. You may even *feel* another feeling. This would be a good time to journal the insights you receive. Simply trust that whatever it is that comes to you is exactly what is meant to in that moment. All that is needed is to keep an open channel of communication so that you can truly heal and grow.

5. **Release the feeling:** Now that the feeling has had a chance to pass on its gift, it is time to release it from your energetic system since it is no longer needed.

    a. With your hands placed on the area of your body where the feeling is felt, simply thank it for it's presence and assure it that you will integrate it's divinely inspired advice into your life. For example you may like to say:

    'Thank you for leading and guiding me. Thank you for helping me realise what is best for my highest good. I gladly and openly integrate your teachings into my life now.'

    b. Now ask the feeling to come with you to your heart centre (if it is not there already). Move your hands to your heart centre with the intention of moving the feeling into this space as well.

c. In the heart centre, simply bath the feeling with all the love, compassion and gratitude you have. You may like to envisage a soft green or pink light circling your heart and gently absorbing into the feeling; slowly allowing it to dissolve. Ultimately, you are showering this feeling with so much love that it no longer needs to stay.

6. **Integrate the teachings:** Now that you have uncovered the valuable lesson/s from this experience, it is time to integrate the lesson into your life. If the feeling asked that you practice more compassion, self love, strength, and bravery then consider how you can show up in every moment with those qualities. If you are unsure how to do it, then let the information settle for a while. The *how* will be revealed to you when you are ready. Just be open to inspiration and guidance from the Universe.

7. **If a negative feeling arises again:** Repeat this activity. Ensure you allow yourself the time to *feel* the feeling. Sometimes the feeling is a 'once off', so it is still just as valid to acknowledge, accept, release and act upon the guidance you receive from your Higher Self. If you feel guided to cry, then cry. If you need to scream into a pillow, then scream. If you need to go for a run to 'sweat it out', then do that too. That may be all that is needed. The key is to not hold onto it for too long. But if it is a feeling that continues to surface off and on, then the steps in this activity can help.

The fact is, you cannot block negative feelings from your life completely, so instead welcome them, acknowledge them, and thank them for gifting you with valuable lessons. It is only then that you

Eat Cake

can let the feelings go. This is about learning to appreciate this world of duality and seeing that all experiences, good and bad, are a gift in some way. Once you step into this realisation, then manifestation will be a piece of cake.

Chapter 25 – Putting it all into Action

Don't sit and wonder if taking a little step will bring you closer to your dreams. Get up and find out!

My absolute favourite tool for manifesting my heart's desires is writing in a manifestation journal; one that contains specific questions that help me stay on track to reaching my ultimate goals. In my opinion, keeping a journal that has meaningful purpose is the most potent and powerful practice you can do, especially if you make it a habit. This is why I recommend you commit to this next exercise for at least thirty days. Writing in your journal every day for thirty days may sound like a lot of work, particularly in this day and age when we have so many distractions! Unfortunately distractions only serve to keep us hostage from the limitless possibilities that serve to create a life we have always wanted. So to overcome this predicament, I invite you to select a set period of the day when those distractions are at their most minimal and when you know you can dedicate a bit of time reflecting and writing in the journal. If possible, I recommend you write in your journal first thing in the morning to start the day off with positive energy that will continue to flow throughout the day.

Your sacred journal is your way of keeping your thoughts, feelings, beliefs and values in check. These are the very things that determine what tomorrow brings. Your journal is also your way of connecting to your Spiritual Support Team on a daily basis which is absolutely essential if you want to live an intuitively guided life. If you do not believe me, start a journal anyway. After all, you have nothing to lose but oh so much to gain!

Activity #27: Keeping a Manifestation Journal

There are a number of sections to the manifestation journal I use which I have included here. This is not the *only* kind of manifestation journal. There are many and varied ones out in the cosmos so please feel into it and see if it is something you resonate with. You can of course select the parts of the journal you like and leave out the rest. It is entirely up to you.

1. **Choose a journal:** Some will say select a blank-paged journal while others will suggest a lined journal is best. Ultimately it comes down to personal taste. If you like to express yourself by way of drawing, then I recommend finding a blank paged journal. Whatever you decide upon, just make sure it is a good size (not too big and bulky but not too small where it does not allow for much writing space) and it feels good to hold. You may even like to decorate the cover if you feel inspired to. Simply make it as personal as you wish; this is yours after all and no one needs to see it unless you want them to.

2. **Write your intention for the journal:** On the first page of your journal you may like to write an intention; what is it that you hope to get from keeping a journal in your life? Who do you hope to connect with? Here is an example however I encourage you to feel into your own intention so the journal becomes more personal.

    'I call upon my Spiritual Support Team and the energy of divine white light to bless this journal. May this journal be the gateway for manifesting all that my heart desires and all that is for my highest good. May this journal help me to grow and develop from every experience.

May it show me gratitude and appreciation for all that is in my life and all that is coming. May the Universe weave its magic in and around my life; supporting me, guiding me and co-creating with me with love.'

3. **Write in your journal each day:** You may like to freely write in your journal about what it is you are excited and grateful for (whether present or future), or you may like to follow a more structured sequence. There is no right or wrong way. For me personally I like to go with a more structured approach as a way of keeping me on track. Then as I go about the day I consciously refer back to the journal to remind me of my intention for that day. This is truly powerful as it means I remain (as best as I possibly can) in the flow of abundance since my thoughts, feelings, values and beliefs match my heart's desires and my highest good.

At the end of this chapter you will find the one page journal I use. If you resonate with it you can easily follow the same pattern for your own personal needs. There are six parts to the journal which ties in beautifully with the topics covered in this book; be grateful, lead your life by how you feel, make time for love, release the old, embrace the new, and connect to higher wisdom.

a. **Be grateful.** *Today I am grateful for...*

In this part of the journal you will writing about what you appreciate in your life that has made you feel what you *want* to feel (e.g. happy, elated, peaceful, calm, inspired, motivated etc). You may be grateful for worldly things (material and earth-related) such as food, the house, car, trees, and the air you breathe. Perhaps show gratitude for the things you have witnessed such as the sun shining through the green leaves outside your bedroom window. You may like to write about a recent experience you have had or are going to have, or what you love about yourself such as your sense of humour or smile. You can write about your gratitude towards the people in your life, even if they are in your life briefly; for example you may be grateful for the person who helped you carry a heavy box to your car.

As you write in this section, I encourage you to also reflect on what you are grateful for in the future but write it in present tense since the present tense is all you have and that is the vibration the Universe responds to. For example, if your heart's desire is to travel first class to an exotic location of your choice, then you may like to write, 'I am so excited and happy to be travelling to [*insert exotic location*] flying first class during the month of [*insert month and year*]. Thank you Universe!' Be specific!

b. **Lead your life by how you want to feel.** *How does my soul want to feel today? What is one or more thing/s I can do today to feel that?*

Since every experience is based on a feeling, it stands to reason that for your heart's desires to manifest, your vibration must match the *feeling* of what those desires will create for you when they appear in the physical. The best way to do this is to declare how you want to feel and then do something during the day that generates that same feeling. When you raise your vibration to that particular feeling then you automatically step into the flow of receiving more of the same emotion.

For example, if you desire to be highly successful, then consider what it would feel like to be successful. Would you feel love, freedom, or creativity? Perhaps you may feel relaxed, excited or grateful. The trick is to get to the core feeling of what you want and then mirror that feeling into your everyday life. If you discover the core feeling of becoming highly successful is freedom, then consider what you could do today that generates that sensation of freedom. Perhaps it is a walk barefoot outside. Maybe it is painting to freely express yourself. Or maybe it is practicing the powerful 'F' word; forgiveness. Decide on what actions you can take to create the core feelings you desire.

c. **Make time for love.** *What is one thing I will do today that I love to do?*

Benoit had spoken that love is the most powerful universal energy or emotion (energy in motion) and since love is the source from which we are created then it is only fitting (and completely necessary) that we honour that and do something each day that intensifies that love. This does not mean you have to stand on the rooftop and declare your undying love to yourself or others, but rather, do something big or small that you truly enjoy doing.

You may love a special clothing item that has been hanging in the cupboard for years. Perhaps now is a good time to wear it even if it is around the house. You may love surrounding yourself around flowers, so perhaps go to your local park, plant nursery or even wander around your own garden. You may love sitting in silence for a while, so dedicate time today to simply 'be'. It does not have to be an exercise that takes up your entire day. It can be a simple activity that has no purpose other than to make you feel *extremely* good. After all, is that not what we all want to feel?

d. **Release the old.** *Today I am ready to let go of...*

What emotion, habit or circumstance are you ready to let go of that causes you to feel bad, disempowered or disheartened in some way?

Consider yesterday, last week, last month, or last year and reflect on whether there were times you did not feel good. Once you have identified a time then focus on what it was that you were doing that made you feel that way. Perhaps you found that you were constantly judging yourself. Maybe you found yourself blaming other people for the situation you found yourself in, or perhaps you were blaming yourself. Maybe you had been in an argument with a friend in the past but you are still feeling hurt by it or you are still replaying it in your mind over and over. Perhaps you found yourself becoming more impatient with your children, or with the long shopping queue. Maybe you are unable to forgive your past; hoping that by holding onto it that it will somehow magically change. So consider as you focus on this part of your journal, what is it that you are ready to let go of in your life? What is something you know is not improving your life that you are ready to release?

Once you have identified what it is, then make the intention that you are ready to let it go by writing it down. Even bringing awareness to the circumstance, feeling or habit will start the releasing process. You can also check in with your Spiritual Support Team and ask for their help in guiding you to resolve this. You may find that as you go about your day, synchronistic opportunities arise that will help you move forward. You can also refer to the mindset tools in this book to let go of what you no longer wish to hold onto.

e. **Embrace the new.** *Today I am ready to embrace...*

What is something about you that you wish to embrace and appreciate that you may have forgotten or ignored in the past? For example; your beautiful body, your sense of humour, your patience, your empathy, your optimism, your smile, your determination...(I could go on and on!) To make this even more empowering, consider the parts of yourself (particularly your body) that you may not like and give it gratitude and love. Our supposed flaws can be our greatest gifts.

You can also use this section of the journal to reflect on what are you ready to bring into your life e.g. a simpler minimalistic life, healthier eating, more exercise, crystal therapy, aromatherapy, read more fictional novels, a new career etc.

After you have written down what you are ready to embrace, then you can start to consciously choose habits, thoughts and actions that complement this new intention you have made.

f. **Connect for higher wisdom.** *The message my Spiritual Support Team has for me today is…*

The last part of the journal is where you will be connecting with your Spiritual Support Team. Sometimes the best messages are those that do not answer anything specific that you want answered but rather act as daily insights into your own life.

Often my Spiritual Support Team provides me with reminders of what I may have forgotten such as 'breathe' or 'slow down'. Then if I find the day is becoming fairly busy or overwhelming, I will reflect on the guidance I was given and do what they say, breathe deeply to ground and collect myself or take some time out to slow down from getting too caught up in the hustle and bustle of life. Your Spiritual Support Team may also provide you with information about upcoming events to be aware of particularly ones that relate to the manifestation of your heart's desires.

You have already uncovered your primary sixth sense but you can also use divination tools such as oracle cards as a way to strengthen the channel. You may like to write in your journal, *'Today I drew the oracle card… My interpretation of this is…'* Just let your intuition guide you toward a method that is best suited for you.

Putting it all into Action

I also like to include quotes in my journal from people I admire (I have included some quotes on page 351 to get you started), or affirmations and mantras if I feel inspired to.

The key to realise is that this is *your* sacred manifestation journal. The point of this is to help you raise your vibration to meet what your heart desires. But if I am honest, this is so much more than a manifestation journal. This will be a journal that encourages you to live the fullest life you can. It is a self-exploration journal that helps you master your own life on your own terms. So do not put this activity in the, 'I'll do it later' pile. Do it now!

Example of my Manifestation Journal

The Universe will deliver to you what you think, feel, believe and value.

1. **Be grateful.** Today I am grateful for…

2. **Lead your life by how you want to feel.** How does my soul want to *feel* today? What is one or more thing/s I can do to feel that today?

3. **Make time for love.** What is one thing I will do today that I love to do?

4. **Release the old.** Today I am ready to let go of…

5. **Embrace the new.** Today I am ready to embrace…

6. **Connect for higher wisdom.** The message my Spiritual Support Team has for me today is…

Putting it all into Action

Inspirational Quotes

Progress always involves risks; you can't steal second base and keep your foot on first.' Frederick B. Wilcox

Do not be afraid to take a big step if one is indicated. You can't cross a chasm in two small jumps. David Lloyd George

... life never calms down long enough for us to wait until tomorrow to start living the lives we deserve. Sarah Ban Breathnach

Life is like riding a bicycle. To keep your balance you must keep moving. Albert Einstein

Everything is habit-forming, so make sure what you do is what you want to be doing. Wilt Chamberlain

The more you praise and celebrate your life; the more there is in life to celebrate Oprah Winfrey

Every choice moves us closer to or farther away from something. Where are your choices taking your life? Eric Allenbaugh

Life is either a daring adventure, or nothing. To keep our faces toward change and behave like free spirits in the presence of fate is strength undefeatable. Helen Keller

Courage: the most important of all the virtues because without courage, you can't practise any other virtue consistently. Maya Angelou

There came a time when the risk to remain tight in the bud was more painful than the risk it took to blossom. Anaïs Nin

Eat Cake

Let me fall. Let me climb. There's a moment where fear and dream must collide. Lyrics from *Let Me Fall*—collaboration between Josh Groban and Cirque du Soleil

The future belongs to those who believe in the beauty of their dreams. Eleanor Roosevelt

Without leaps of imagination, or dreaming, we lose the excitement of possibilities. Dreaming, after all, is a form of planning. Gloria Steinem

Nothing is impossible... the word itself says 'I'm possible'! Audrey Hepburn

If your dreams don't scare you, they aren't big enough. Lowell Lundstrum

Life is not measured by the number of breaths we take, but by the number of moments that take our breath away. Anonymous

Courage is not the absence of fear, but rather the judgement that something else is more important than fear. Ambrose Redmoon

Only one thing has to change for us to know happiness in our lives: where we focus our attention. Greg Anderson

The secret of genius is to carry the spirit of the child into old age, which means never losing your enthusiasm. Aldous Huxley

I think of life itself now as a wonderful play that I have written for myself, and so my purpose is to have the utmost fun playing my part. Shirley MacLaine

It takes as much energy to wish as it does to plan. Eleanor Roosevelt

Life begins at the end of your comfort zone. Neale Donald Walsch

When you are stuck in a spiral, to change all aspects of the spin you only need to change one thing. Christina Baldwin

Putting it all into Action

Happiness is when what you think, what you say, and what you do are in harmony. Mahatma Gandhi

Happiness is having a sense of self—not a feeling of being perfect but of being good enough and knowing that you are in the process of growth, of being, of achieving levels of joy. Leo Buscaglia

A strong passion for any object will ensure success, for the desire of the end will point out the means. Henry Hazlitt

You only lose energy when life becomes dull in your mind…Get interested in something! … The more you lose yourself in something bigger than yourself, the more energy you will have. Norman Vincent Peale

Don't ask yourself what the world needs. Ask yourself what makes you come alive, and then go do that. Because what the world needs is people who have come alive. Harold Thurman Whitman

If we did all the things we are capable of doing, we would literally astound ourselves. Thomas A. Edison

Whenever there's a roadblock in your life, you must go over it, under it, around it, or through it. Either way, there's always a way. Erin Furner

Chapter 26 – Where to From Here?

Don't follow the path. Blaze the trail. – Jordan Belfort

Manifestation is not a destination; it is an ongoing and exciting life-long process. It is your chance to co-create with the Universe and work together in harmony. I guess you could say it is the ultimate relationship!

Some days you will feel as though you are completely in the flow of abundance; everything will seem to work seamlessly like a well oiled machine. Other days it will feel as though everything is working against you despite trying to rectify the issues. When these days crop up it is not a sign you are being punished, but rather it is an opportunity to place your faith in the bigger plan; knowing that whatever the issue, it is a chance for you to learn an empowering truth about yourself and others. Perhaps the issue will make you re-evaluate what you want from life instead of settling for a below average existence. Perhaps it is there to teach you compassion, empathy, forgiveness and gratitude. Maybe it has surfaced to provide you with an opportunity to realise who your true friends are and to no longer be treated like a doormat. Perhaps it is teaching you to be courageous, brave and strong. Whatever the case may be, it is an opportunity for you to be in love with the good *and* the bad. To be honest, I am still learning how to do it. Sometimes I feel as though the Universe could throw anything at me and I would approach it from a completely loving perspective; my positive vibes would extinguish any negativity. Other days I feel like curling up into the foetal position with a box of Aloe Vera tissues and triple chocolate mud cake in the hope the issue would just magically disappear. All you can do is approach each day as best you can and try to see that even a bad day is a hidden gift; it is up to you to uncover what it may be. Realise that life ebbs and flows—there will always be good and bad days. That is the nature of this dual world! When you become completely content with duality, then you will have nothing to fear and nothing to worry about. You will become the ultimate spirit living a human existence! *And* you will stay in the frequency of receiving what you want.

You will remember that the Universe does not listen to your words but rather your frequency (vibration) which is a combination of your feelings, thoughts, values and beliefs. So if you can live 80% of your day in a state of positivity then you are doing a wonderful job maintaining the frequency to get what you want. I say 80% because I do not believe it is possible nor fair to expect that we remain positive 100% of the time. Perhaps that time will come but I am certainly not there yet!

So how will you maintain a state of positivity at least 80% of the time? Keep working on those old memories. Anytime an old memory surfaces (you will know when an old memory has appeared because you will feel blocked, fearful, or doubtful in some way) then take action to clear it by following the techniques in this book. This may seem like a never-ending task but it is completely necessary. The one thing I want to stress however is that by doing 'shadow work' (exploring your old memories and actively clearing them) you may start to feel as though the task is pulling you down into a state of never-ending misery. If you start to feel this then this is a big warning sign! When I decided to do my own shadow work, I had not realised how exhaustive it could be and how much I would come to dislike doing it simply because there never seemed to be a break; there was always an old memory that needed clearing. I began to feel saddened by how much psychic baggage I had accumulated over time. It was very hard to see the light at the end of the tunnel when the old memories continued to surface one after the other. Ding, ding, ding! These were warning signs that told me I was working too hard on myself. It does not have to be this way. You can still do the shadow work but just make sure there is a balance between that and doing what you love; bring more joy and fun into your life so you do not feel completely consumed by all the negative beliefs and limitations. Of course shadow work is a vital ingredient to manifesting your desires, but if it starts to take its toll on your life and you are really beginning to hate the process then back away. Take some time out and refocus your mind on other things that bring you happiness. Because if you start feeling burnt out then that will affect your vibration which could potentially halt the manifestation of your heart's desires until you are back in a positive state of mind, body and spirit. Unfortunately some people are never able to get themselves out of the vicious burnt out cycle so the rest of their lives are spent wallowing in their own self pity. That is not a good place to be!

Shadow work is not the only thing you will be working on to change your vibration. You will also be decluttering your life; physically, emotionally and spiritually. Clean up your house, get organised, consider the people in your life and whether they raise your vibration or bring you down, clean up your finances to make room for more financial abundance, practice forgiveness toward the people and situations that have impacted you in some way, show gratitude for what you have in your life, and shower yourself with love and affection. Honour the importance of you and your own needs. When you become your own cheerleader and promote the importance of self love, then you become an advocate for others to do the same. That is powerful!

You can also focus on strengthening your primary intuitive sense so you can access the limitless support and guidance your Higher Self, Spiritual Support Team and the Universe have for you. This is especially useful if you are wondering what the next step is on your manifestation journey.

At the end of the day, the manifestation journey is a two-way street. You are not doing this alone; you are co-creating with the big U (the Universe). It is your job to do the actionable things—become crystal clear on what you want, keep a positive mindset, do what you love and live an intuitively guided life. Suddenly the idea of manifestation does not seem like an element of life, it is a way of life. And just like cake, you can create anything you heart's desires.

In finishing this book, I will leave you with a manifestation cake recipe to tickle your taste buds. And remember, be all that you can be for yourself and for others in this lifetime—make this one really count!

The Manifestation Cake

Ingredients

4 tablespoons of belief in miracles
1 cup of clarity of what you want
100 milliliters of expectation and hope
3 sticks of flexibility
250 milliliters of fun and laughter
¼ cup of shadow work
1½ cups of higher self connection
1½ cups of spiritual support team connection
150 grams of love
2 cups of a belief in something bigger (e.g. the Universe)

The Power of Your Desires

170 grams of gratitude
1 pinch of forgiveness
1 teaspoon of dancing like no one is watching
An infinite amount of love and support from the Universe

Method

1. Preheat oven to moderate temperature (180°C). Prepare two 22-centimetre cake pans by buttering and lightly flouring with the belief in miracles.

2. Sift the clarity of what you want into a large bowl to remove procrastination and uncertainty.

3. Add expectation and hope, flexibility, and fun and laughter Whisk through to combine, ensuring there are no lumps of seriousness, rigidity, and doubt. Set aside.

4. Melt the shadow work in a heatproof bowl set over a pan of barely simmering water. Stir occasionally to evaporate the core old memories. Once new and empowered layers have been created, remove bowl off heat. Cool slightly.

5. Carefully add the newly created shadow work mixture to the rest of the cake batter, stirring until well combined.

6. Slowly add higher self connection, spiritual support team connection, love, and a belief in something bigger. Combine until the batter turns into a bright white light.

7. Finally, make a well in the centre of the cake batter and add gratitude, forgiveness and dancing like no one is watching,

Where to From Here?

and fold gently until well combined. You may hear angelic music whilst doing this.

8. Distribute cake batter evenly between the two prepared cake pans. Bake for 30 minutes to keep the momentum going or until a skewer inserted in the centre of the cakes come out clean. Throughout the time in the oven, you will notice the cake batter bubbling and rising. This is a good sign the ingredients are harmoniously integrating with one another.

9. Remove from oven and allow to cool for 10 minutes before inverting onto a rack to cool completely. Try to be patient.

10. **To Make the Frosting:** Using an infinite amount of love and support from the Universe, spread evenly on the top of one of the cakes before marrying them together. Next, spread more infinite love and support around the entire cake as thickly as you wish (the thicker the layer, the better).

11. **When to Eat:** Cut up the cake into 30 pieces and eat one piece per day to build the essential manifestation momentum. You may also like to serve it warm and share it with another close soul.

12. Enjoy!

Acknowledgements

To Benoit and the Higher Beings of Love and Light. Thank you for your endless guidance and support. There is nothing quite like tuning into your energy and feeling such an immense amount of love. I am so grateful for you all; for all that you have done and all that you are doing.

And to all those committed to creating a life of their own design. You may not feel that by living a life of joy that you are impacting other people in such profound and positive ways, but you really are. When you commit to healing your life and raising your own vibration to a state of positivity, you are indirectly helping others to do the same. Thank you for putting yourself first, having the courage to receive what you truly deserve, and helping others realise that they too can be free of limitation to create whatever their heart's desires. If everyone allowed themselves to be loved and purposely create a life from their Spirit's perspective then we would all be savouring every mouthful of our favourite cake with big smiles on our faces.

About the Author

In Gaelic, one of the meanings of the name Erin is, 'Peace' and that sums up Erin's mission completely. Her introverted and empathic nature has helped Erin sense the world around her with a heightened understanding of why we are here and how we can all overcome our own limitations that get in the way of living a life of peace, love and purpose.

Erin's peacemaking mission became profoundly apparent when she worked as a medical scientist at Gosford and Wyong Hospital, Australia. Erin continually found herself acting as a sounding board for very ill patients—listening to them talk of their fears about their future and their life regrets. It was heartbreaking to know that they felt they had not lived and loved as fully as they had wanted to. The most common message Erin received from such ill patients was, 'Don't make the same mistakes I did' and it was through truly hearing and sensing the urgency behind the message that Erin realised her true life's purpose—to help, inspire and support thousands of people to realise and experience their limitless potential. Her way of doing this is by showing them how to tap into the power of creativity and intuition that is such an integral part of being a spirit and a human being.

To support her mission, Erin became certified as a Counsellor, Meridian Psychotherapist and Neuro-Linguistic Programming Practitioner. With her interest around healing old memories and attracting more of the good things in life, she also became a practitioner in the areas of Law of Attraction, Reiki, Ho'oponopono Therapy, and Life Coaching. Yet it is mostly Erin's life experience

Eat Cake

and intuitive connection to her Spiritual Support Team which have really helped her to fulfil her mission to this day.

Erin completely loves and adores her family and cherishes spending time with them. She also loves adventure, sharing fabulous food with friends and family, and dancing as if no one is watching. Her favourite way to ground her spirit is by digging her feet into the sand at the beach and listening to the waves roll in and out. When she is not immersed in family life or work, you will find her experimenting with new songs on the piano or sitting on the couch indulging in a hot cup of tea with a slice of frosted carrot cake (or chocolate cake depending on the mood of the day).

For more information about Erin and her products and services, visit:

www.ErinFurner.com

www.ingramcontent.com/pod-product-compliance
Lightning Source LLC
Chambersburg PA
CBHW070529010526
44118CB00012B/1079